JOSIE'S JOURNEY

Shaun Russell

For Josie who is my reason for living,
and for Lin and Megan
who will never die in our hearts.

This book accompanies the BBC documentary,
Josie's Journey, broadcast in 2000.
Producer: Maurice Melzak
Assistant producer: Laura Fairrie
Executive producer: Edwina Varley

Published by BBC Worldwide Ltd,
80 Wood Lane, London W12 0TT

First published in 2000
Copyright © Shaun Russell 2000

ISBN 0 563 53714 0

Commissioning editor: Sally Potter
Project editor: Sarah Lavelle
Copy editor: Georgia Litherland
Designers: John Calvert and Isobel Gillan
Picture researcher: Miriam Hyman

Set in Sabon
Printed and bound in Great Britain by Butler and Tanner Ltd, Frome and London
Jacket printed by Lawrence Allen Ltd, Weston-super-Mare
Colour separations by Radstock Reproductions, Midsomer Norton

Contents

Acknowledgements

For help in writing this book I am indebted to the copy editor Georgia Litherland, whose combined technical skill and emotional sensitivity have contributed greatly to the finished account. For their cajoling and forbearance I must thank Sally Potter, Sarah Lavelle and Miriam Hyman at the BBC, without whom the book would never have seen the light of day. However, I alone can be held accountable for any errors or omissions that have found their way into the text. My gratitude also goes to TV producer Maurice Melzak, who has remained steadfast in his belief in this 'project' and who has always been a dedicated friend to Josie and me.

So many people have contributed to the story through influencing mine and my family's lives, that sadly there is not space here for me to thank them all. Of those who can be mentioned, the most important are Lin's parents, Irene and Peter, who have endured so much and who suffer still, but whose love keeps Josie and me strong. My mother Margery and my sister Jeannie have ignored their own pain to care and be there for us always. Lin's best friends Primmy and Liz have honoured Lin's memory by helping Josie and I through our darkest times, and Primmy's daughter Jessie has been an unfailing friend to Josie through all her hardships.

Josie and I owe an enormous debt to all the professionals who have been involved in Josie's recovery, particularly the staff at Kings College Hospital, London, and Manchester Children's Hospital. Dave Stevens, Pauline Smith and Ed Tingley not only carried out their difficult police jobs with sympathy and sensitivity, but were also kind and constant friends at a time when we most needed support. My solicitors Sarah

Harman and Mark Stephens have been far more than legal aides. Without their sage judgement and committed friendship, Josie and I could not have weathered the storm.

The teachers at Goodnestone School, particularly Lynda Roberts and Darryl Peek, did so much to ease Josie back into a semblance of normality. And Susan Owen, Siân Thomas and the other staff at Ysgol Baladeulyn continued with this loving work to prepare Josie for her teenage years. Catherine Williams and other staff at Ysgol Dyffryn Nantlle carry on this task, and Josie's friends and their parents are also now indispensable to our well-being. To these and all the many others in our present and past lives, thank you so much for your commitment and care for us.

Shaun Russell

Picture Credits

Foreword

Josie's return to the country of her birth, South Africa, in the summer of 2000 was only the most recent step in a much longer journey.

Four years earlier, she had survived an appalling and tragic attack in which her mother and sister were killed. Who could forget that day in the summer of 1996 when the lives of Shaun Russell and his daughter Josie were changed forever – a day when the idyllic peace of the countryside took on a face of fear?

Was Lin too trusting? No – surely trust is a quality that makes us human? She loved this earth, this planet, and as ecologists, she and Shaun shared the same passionate commitment to its preservation.

In this unique and compelling account, Shaun voices all the feelings of a man who not only lost his wife and child, but gained at the same time unexpected worldwide attention. We learn how he coped: the anger, frustration – even guilt – at the constant attention of the press towards Josie; the emotional rollercoaster of ups and downs; how his elation turned to pity at the trial . . .

Life and laughter return in some semblance to these two remarkable survivors – but only because of extraordinary courage and a bonding between them forged through adversity.

The Duchess of Kent

Introduction

On 10 July 1996, people listening to the radio or watching daytime television in Britain started to receive newsflashes about a multiple murder committed the night before in the south-eastern English county of Kent. As details of the killings started to emerge, shock and fear spread among the inhabitants of the countryside near to the murder scene, and ripples of horror and disbelief began to extend across the nation. The victims of the crime were a mother and her two daughters and their pet dog. They had been walking home from the girls' primary school on a sunny summer's afternoon and, before they could reach their home a mile away, all but one of them had been beaten to death by an assailant wielding a hammer. The surviving child had had her skull crushed during the brutal attack, but was clinging to life in the intensive care unit of a London hospital, under police guard for her own safety. Her name was Josie Russell and she was my daughter.

In the preceding weeks, Britain had been rocked by a spate of unconnected and senseless attacks on innocent, vulnerable children. In March the country had been stunned by the massacre of school-children at Dunblane, while within the space of only three days in July, nine-year-old Jade Matthews was murdered on Merseyside, teenager Nicola Parsons was raped and killed in Plymouth, and nursery nurse Lisa Potts fought to protect the children in her care from a crazed machete attacker at St Luke's School in Wolverhampton.

The media reflected the mood of the nation as, on the morning of 11 July 1996, millions of people awoke to front-page headlines that rang with dismay and despair. In a blood-red banner, the *Daily Mirror* screamed 'IS ANYWHERE SAFE?', while the *Daily Telegraph* proclaimed, 'ANOTHER KILLER STRIKES'. The *Daily Mail* shouted, 'NIGHTMARE – even more horror for Britain', and the later editions of the *Sun* carried pictures of my two daughters under the headline, 'VICTIMS OF A MONSTER'. Why was this happening? Was this latest outrage yet another symptom of a deepening malaise in our society, an accelerating descent into violence and chaos? At the time, such academic questions could not have been further from my thoughts, as the events of the previous thirty-six hours had focused my mind and my actions on one thing and one thing alone: the survival of the only remaining member of my family.

And out in the wider world something similar was happening; thousands of people were focusing their thoughts too on the injured child, and many began to pray for her recovery. I know because I began to receive hundreds of sympathetic and supportive letters from well-wishers. But the senders of many of these condolences seemed dazed and bewildered. Of course people wanted Josie to pull through for her own sake, but they were also desperate for answers to the perplexing question of why this tragedy had happened at all. Some wished for Josie to recover quickly so that she might help identify the killer, thereby hastening retribution as though this would somehow mitigate the pain of this latest atrocity. And there were others who yearned for Josie's survival to prove that something positive could come from bad, that good would always triumph over evil. The burden of notoriety and the expectations of others were already starting to press heavily upon us.

Through no fault of her own, and in the most tragic circumstances imaginable, the name of Josie Russell came to be known throughout the land; it came to elicit sorrow and sympathy on the one hand, and to evoke bravery and courage on the other. Josie's story is one of desperation and despair, overcome by her strength and spirit. But it is also one of weakness and doubt in other quarters. It involves the great and the good, the famous and the infamous, celebrities and unknowns. Politicians and royalty, clerics, convicts and cranks all feature in the narrative, but always Josie's will and fortitude shine through, enough to make even a hardened cynic like her father start to believe in the 'power of miracles'.

This book is a retelling of the events of the 'The Russell Murders' from the point of view of those most closely involved. It describes the aftermath of the killings, and the ways in which a daughter and her father have coped with the repercussions of a tragedy that touched the hearts of millions. Part of that coping has involved a degree of denial and much shutting out of memories, especially as the pressures of survival in the wake of such a catastrophic event leave little time for mourning or introspection. Instead there is a legacy of guilt, that because I have camouflaged my grief, my daughter may think less of the love that I held for her mother and sister. It is this aspect that contributed to my decision, four years on from the murders, to take Josie with me on a personal pilgrimage to the land of her birth – South Africa.

Twenty years earlier, Josie's mother Lin and I were career-orientated scientists, rapidly ascending the ladder of academic success in South Africa. We were well heeled, childless and egocentric thirty-somethings, keen to indulge our taste for ever-wider experience, adventure and world travel. In 1980 I spent eight months doing ecological research on one of the sub-Antarctic islands, before leaving with Lin for a further six months' sabbatical in Australia. Looking for ever more exotic destinations, we travelled on to Fiji and then back to Indonesia before returning to South Africa. However, in Asia and the Pacific we found more than we had bargained for. We realized that our British middle-class upbringing had shielded Lin and me from the harsh realities of subsistence in environments of rapidly dwindling natural resources. And in South Africa residential segregation and the closeted atmosphere of life in a rural university had insulated us from many of the cruel truths of existence in the apartheid state.

Our Asia/Pacific experience left a lasting impression on Lin and myself, and we returned to South Africa with a determination to do more to help solve the problems of poverty and environmental destruction both there and in the world at large. Back in South Africa we moved house to a very beautiful area of the Eastern Cape known as the 'Hogsback'. But there we found ourselves living side-by-side with families who were in deep poverty and who lacked almost all rights and privileges. Our outlook on life and work began to change, and with it grew a desire to settle down and start a family of our own.

Our first child, Josie, was born in 1987 and she spent the first two years of her life at our beautiful Hogsback home. So when, in the year

2000, the opportunity came to visit one of my research students working in South Africa, I resolved to take Josie back with me to the place of her birth – the land of which she had heard her parents speak so often. For my animal-loving daughter, the greatest anticipation would be the wildlife that she had heard me talking so much about. For me, I hoped that the journey might bring back memories of one of the happiest times of my life with Lin, and that in this environment I could convey to Josie some sense of the empathy that existed between Lin and me. I wanted to explain to Josie something of the hopes, dreams, beliefs and love of nature that Lin and I shared, while memories of her mother were still relatively fresh in her mind.

On one level, therefore, *Josie's Journey* is a story of a physical journey, a pilgrimage to the place where her mother and father enjoyed a special kind of happiness as they worked and played and nurtured their first child. But it is mainly a story of one girl's journey through an as yet short and scarred life that has been filled with more than enough pain and suffering to last any normal lifespan. Josie's story *is* one of searing horror and tragedy, and of her own indomitable resolve and shining spirit. But beyond the public perceptions lies another, simpler story of twenty-first-century family life: the fraught teenager–parent relationship, the balance between school, home and external influences, the difficulties of life as an only child with a single, working parent. It is a story about a girl whose life and character have been influenced by the sometimes extraordinary people and events around her. But it is also a glimpse into the realities and normalities of a daily life that is neither unique nor exceptional, whatever the legacies of injury and bereavement, and the distortions born of notoriety.

Josie and I have been the objects of an outpouring of love on a colossal scale, and it is this that has helped to banish the dark aftermath of tragedy from our daily lives, and to anaesthetize the pain of the loss of our loved ones. It has not been easy, and through it all the legacy of Lin's strength has helped to sustain us. For me I hoped that South Africa would be a place to seek solace in beautiful memories, and that the trip would give Josie and me a chance for a deeper mutual understanding as she enters her teenage years. One day she will embark on a life of her own, when her father will of necessity slip into the background as she starts to make her own way. But, to help her remember where she came from, this is the story of Josie's Journey.

Life Before Josie

Lin Wilcox was the beautiful, fashionable, scary new technician that every young man in the department wanted to date but few had the nerve to ask. I clearly hadn't a chance. And to be honest the thought never crossed my mind – or if it did I filed it quickly under 'pie in the sky; pigs might fly'. In 1973 I was wrapped up in my third year of a degree in botany, zoology and geology at Plymouth Polytechnic, absorbed in studying the moors and coastlines of Devon and Cornwall and enjoying the licence to devote myself to knowing better the landscape and plants that had attracted me since I was a child. In my spare time, I was in popular demand as a DJ running 'discos' at parties, where I played to the crowd with the Motown, R&B and Soul I'd grown up on, and added a trendy 'dangerous edge' with music from the psychedelic underground. I hadn't much time for girls, I liked to think; and I was terrified! I remember my mousy long hair, duffle coat and shyness, but Lin always said she remembered me as the tall, dark, interesting one lurking in the background.

By my final year, however, things were looking up. I had learned to drive, got myself a gun-metal blue Triumph Herald Estate and was sharing a house with lecturers rather than students. And it was these trivial distinctions that made all the difference when Lin Wilcox needed new accommodation fast. Lin had been suffering harassment from male neighbours and on hearing that our household was equipped with cars and a semblance of maturity, she came to look at the spare room. She liked it immediately, and after she had left, I was subjected to all kinds of laughing and pointing as my friends saw how excited I was about our new housemate. The very first evening that Lin moved in, the two of us took a walk down to Looe harbour. We stayed up late, watching the lights come on over the fishing boats. That was where we first kissed and set the seal on a love affair that endures to this day, even though Lin is now with me in spirit alone.

Over the next two years we grew together, supporting each other and making compromises in order that each of us could realize more of our potential through our studies, our shared scientific and aesthetic passion for the natural world, our various career plans and always, always travel. Early joint trips to the Isle of Skye eased into longer, more adventurous trips. With friends, we took a van across Morocco and encountered the desert for the first time, paying for the trip by collecting and selling on plant specimens (we were always resourceful!).

Having moved with me for my Masters degree, Lin then went to train as a teacher. She gained a distinction but developed an aversion to children that lasted right up to the birth of her own! Meanwhile, I had decided that botany should be my career. I applied for a PhD research degree, but was unable to get funding for my research. Lin, then, was highly qualified to do something she loathed and I was unable to progress with something I loved. So you can imagine our excitement when, acting on a tip from a former lecturer of mine, I got an interview for a job teaching botany in South Africa. It was based at the famous University of Fort Hare in the Eastern Cape province, where Nelson Mandela, Sir Seretse Khama, Robert Mugabe and many other African leaders had studied. This could be my 'big break'; for it was possible then to secure overseas jobs that would not have been open in the UK – I could never have lectured in science in a British university without a PhD.

Lin and I were thrilled. Great vistas of possibility opened up for us. These were still the days of significant British emigration to Australia and South Africa, and a contract overseas was seen as a passport to adventure and prosperity. But there was the interview to get through first. I had my hair cut for the first time in five years, purchased a jacket and tie especially for the occasion and presented myself at the South African Embassy's Science Liaison Office in London. I was asked whether I was a Jehovah's Witness or a communist and 'whether I would mind having a black man as my boss'; to which I could answer honestly and firmly 'No'. The interviewer was very positive, but precipitated a big piece of bureaucracy in our lives when he made it clear that Lin, if she came with me as an unmarried partner and without a job of her own, would only be granted a six-week tourist visa.

And so it was that after two years of living together happily, Lin and I were married on 19 April 1975 at Exeter Registry Office, accompanied by our parents, my sister and three close friends from college. Lin's mother Irene pressed a silver good-luck horseshoe into my hand and I felt her emotion as she entreated me to care for her only child. It was a time of mixed emotions for all our parents, as they felt the happiness of our marriage but tried to cope with their knowledge that soon we would be off to the other side of the world. Just one month later our parents Peter and Irene, Pat and Margery waved us off from the dockside at Southampton as we sailed away in the *Windsor Castle* steamship. Lin and I watched their figures disappear into the distance and felt pangs of guilt as we bore on our shoulders the weight of their love and anxiety, their sorrow, and their hopes and expectations for us. Yet, even more, we were charged with excitement and anticipation as we looked ahead to what lay in store for us in Africa.

Reflecting on our family histories, it comes as no surprise that Lin and I were both eager for adventure, preferably outdoors and even more preferably in foreign parts. Our parents were all of the war generation that had adventure and travel thrust upon them however reluctant they were, and each of us grew up with stories and pictures of exotic places and cultures. Lin's father Peter had been in Burma and India during the war and his photographs fascinated Lin as a child. Her mother Irene was in the WAAF, and the only one of the four not to have worked abroad. Both my parents spent time away from their home: my mother Margery with the WRNS, training in the USA then working in the Orkneys and Mull of Kintyre; and my father Pat trained as a pilot in Canada, before flying many missions over Germany and, to his greater pride, over Holland to drop food for the occupied Dutch at the end of the war. Pat too had many photographs, taken with an illegal miniature camera. As histories were written, more writers and film-makers sought out his collection, and so I learned more about his involvement in a war that at first he hated to speak of. Indeed, both Peter and Pat had that reserved silence about their wartime experiences so common to men of their generation, who have seen things no one should have to see. I believe it is from my father I inherit the stiff-upper-lip tendencies that have helped me so much in the last few years. And then there was Uncle Edmund! Uncle Edmund was a legend in his own lifetime, a larger-than-life hero and inspiration to me in my boyhood. A dashing Polish army captain who had swept my mother's sister off her feet, Uncle Edmund had been awarded the Iron Cross by the German government during the war, while all the time he was working as a double agent! His stories of hunting lynx in Eastern Europe, his underground activities and traveller's tales fired my lust for adventure and gave me a sense of the wideness of the world.

On the thirteenth day of the voyage to South Africa, Lin and I rose early and went on deck to the cool, fresh air of the southern winter and an awe-inspiring view of Table Mountain. As we first set foot on South African soil, we had no idea that southern Africa was to be our home for the next eighteen years. We knew something of the politics of the land and so we were calmed by our initial realization that no baton-wielding security officer would come and break up our conversations with friends on the streets. We concerned ourselves with building our careers, continuing our studies and enjoying salaries at last after so many years as students. It was in South Africa that we first bought a tumbledown house to renovate and make our own – an act that was to recur and recur in our lives together. It was here too that Lin at last had the space to keep the menagerie she had always wanted. Her love affair with horses went back a long way and now she bought and trained Trixie, a tough local horse well used to survival in the scrubby South African *thornveld*.

Lin sent newsy and exuberant letters home to our parents to keep them informed of all our escapades. We had our brushes with the security forces, who saw Fort Hare University as a hotbed of anti-government plotting and insurrection – and were suspicious of my long hair! We had a few burglaries too, but they were never serious and we did not begrudge the local teenagers a bit of food and clothing. We never felt seriously threatened. We were young and adventurous and we had no responsibilities to family or children. No great tragedy had ever befallen our wider families or come close enough to dent our optimism and sense of immortality.

Five years down the line we were both doing well, and the opportunity arose for me to study in Antarctica, working for a government programme. Lin knew how I loved wild, wet and windy places (nurtured by holidays on Dartmoor and in North Wales) and she told me to go for it. It would mean spending over eight months apart, but our relationship was deeply rooted by now and we promised ourselves that we would travel to Australia together once I returned. To spend time with killer whales, elephant seals, king penguins and wandering albatrosses is a rare privilege, even for a biologist; and I was stunningly lucky to see an unexpected volcanic eruption on Marion Island, where I was stationed.

Only once during the eight months did I find myself slipping into *bombaltsch*, the team's name for the debilitating attacks of apathy and indolence that got to us all at one time or another during our stay on the island. I found it increasingly difficult to get out of bed in the mornings and was less interested in my scientific work. I wondered for a time if I was coming down with 'The Nadgers', as my father had called the depression that dogged him in middle age, but it turned out to be no more than a few days of feeling low, and I was very relieved. What I had not truly prepared for, and perhaps the source of this misery, was how much I missed Lin. I found myself looking forward more and more to our weekly radio calls and felt the separation keenly. The calls were often interrupted by technical difficulties and poor reception, and I would slink off to my room in tears, frustrated and heartbroken that our conversation had been cut short.

Lin, on the other hand, was in fine fettle and could not understand what I was getting so sentimental about! But perhaps it is always easier to stay busy when surrounded by people, than when in isolation. By the time the supply vessel came to collect us, there was only one thing on the mind of every team member, and that was to get home as soon as possible. We all had our reasons, and mine was simply to get back to Lin as fast as the ship would carry me.

Our reunion on Cape Town dock made up for all those months of separation as Lin ran suntanned and laughing towards me. I looked pale, weatherbeaten and rather unkempt – and Lin said she was reminded of when we first met! And we experienced again the excitement of new love as we rediscovered each other after so long a separation.

Within weeks we set off for six months in Australia, where we revelled in the ecology and helped each other out with our studies. It was through a colleague in Queensland that we were given a contact at the University of the South Pacific in Fiji, and decided to fly there for our last two weeks. The trip to Fiji turned out to be much more than an exotic holiday, however, as within an hour of our arrival we had bumped into a friendly local islander who invited us to share the New Year celebrations with him at his family home on one of the smaller offshore islands. For five days we lived a fascinating traditional Pacific islander lifestyle. However, during this time we became aware that this culture was perched on the brink of irrevocable change. The island had no proper harbour, no roads, no cars, no tourist accommodation and only one small post office and radio telephone station. The houses were mainly built of wood and grass. But there was corrugated iron creeping in everywhere, and most people aspired to live in a house built of concrete blocks. 'Shops' generally comprised a tin shack in each village with a few packets of things like boot polish, sugar, cigarettes and matches for sale.

We had noticed other signs of external influence creeping in, with global proprietary brands on tins and bottles in the kitchens, and electronic consumer goods that relied on expensive battery power appearing in all the huts. There were plentiful signs of conversion of the island's interior forests, to groves of citrus, chillies, cassava, taro and bananas, and the marine resources that the villagers relied so heavily upon for protein were also dwindling.

One day we accompanied the young men of the village in canoes, out to the lagoon to fish. Despite their best efforts, only one sizeable fish was caught all day, and the villagers complained that the fishing had become consistently disappointing in recent years. They explained that their fathers only ever caught fish for their own consumption, but now the fishing was done for commercial gain and most of what was caught was taken to the markets on the main island. There, it was sold in order to get money to buy the branded goods, cigarettes, alcohol and electronics we had seen. The strapping young Melanesian islanders who might go on to play the national sport of rugby were being replaced by a generation of sickly, undernourished children, who were no longer seeing the fruits of the lagoon in the abundance that their parents had been used to.

The old men at the New Year's ceremony had also complained to us of a lack of commitment to the island's development among the younger members of the community, many of whom left the island and never came back. The islanders we met were happy and generous, but many of the villagers could see what was happening to their environment and were concerned about what the future would hold for their children.

We felt that we were truly experiencing a tropical paradise in the South Seas. Yet our experience in Fiji convinced Lin and myself that we should try to learn more about natural resource depletion and the erosion of traditional cultural values by western influence. And so, after our return to Australia, we packed up and headed back to South Africa via Indonesia. We had originally intended to spend Christmas in Bali, but we quickly moved on from this increasingly commercialized island to the nearby island of Lombok. The vast numbers of Chinese graves there were a chilling reminder of the political 'pogroms' of the sixties, and we saw more of the by now familiar signs of environmental pressure and social change. Once again, we were shocked by the speed with which natural assets were being depleted and the pressures that were being placed on the environment through demands for commercial exploitation and western-influenced aspirations to consumer culture.

Lin and I realized that the affluent lifestyle we enjoyed in South Africa had cushioned us from the realities of life in the 'third world', and that the academic atmosphere of the rural university where we worked had diverted us from a true understanding of the problems faced by poor people with limited natural resources. Far from being just a holiday vacation, or a chance to expand my plant collection with some exotic specimens, our visit to Fiji had changed our perceptions so that we could no longer be content with merely observing and recording the physical characteristics of nature. We felt that we now had to try to take more of a positive stance in saving what was left of Earth's dwindling resources and helping people who so fundamentally depended on them. Lin always had tremendous strength of character and here again it bloomed. I had been in awe of her ability to stand firm on principle ever since we first met, and now, together, we were moving into a new commitment in life. There were other ramifications too, that might lead us into we knew not what. The uncensored television coverage we were exposed to overseas, and the many lengthy political discussions we went through in Australia had sensitized us to aspects of South Africa's state that we had not seen from our cloistered perspective in a little rural university. We were determined to make an extra effort in future to engage with our students on broader issues than just botany and geology and to pursue our academic work with more social awareness.

And so we set about securing major new grants for our respective departments in order to build up strong research schools, even though this went against apartheid education policy for our students. We also offered accommodation to students during the frequent 'lockouts' (when the university authorities would refuse to allow students into their lectures or living quarters) and we helped them to continue their studies off campus. We were lucky that we never fell sufficiently foul of the authorities to end up in prison as some of our colleagues did.

We had been living until this time in an old house in the town of Alice, next to Fort Hare University. It was classified as a 'white' area, and we had always resisted pressure on us to have a 'maid' or 'garden boy'. Aside from our daily contact with African members of staff and students at the university therefore, we had not been living in close proximity with African neighbours. When the government re-zoned Alice as a 'black' area in the homeland of Ciskei, we had to sell our house to the government and move out. We chose to move twelve miles away, up into the forested Amatola Mountains, where we settled in a village called Hogsback. Hogsback is an unusual area by South African standards, as it is high enough (4000–6000 feet above sea level) and far enough south that it is a temperate climate and even gets snow in some winters. The surroundings reminded Lin and I very much of the northern hemisphere, and we found an old stone house that had been ruined by fire and only partly renovated. The house was called 'Innisfree' and it nestled in a clearing at the forest edge, with magnificent views out over the lowlands of the Eastern Cape. Lin and I decided to take on the house and develop it further ourselves. Here, Lin was in her element, as she rediscovered a vast, rambling and overgrown garden that had been created originally in the 1930s by the first owner of the house. We also planned and built new rooms onto the house, doing most of the work ourselves.

The other unusual aspect of Hogsback was that the apartheid authorities seemed to have forgotten that it existed. African families lived side-by-side with Europeans on many of the (white-owned) properties, and there did not seem to be the same degree of concern about segregation and control of movement. However, because of this situation, black people seemed to have even fewer formal rights to land and property than elsewhere, and were thus often to be found in very impoverished conditions in their homes in the forest. Lin and I found ourselves living next door to a young couple named Lennox and Victoria Magadla, who lived in a mud hut with a corrugated iron roof. We got to know them very well over the next few years, and through them we became further sensitized to the plight of the disenfrachised majority in South Africa. We began to help the Magadla family financially, for example, by buying them their first car. Little did we know at that stage, that Victoria was later to become an important part of our 'family', after Lin and I had our first child.

By 1986, and in our mid-thirties , Lin and I were forging ahead with our careers and continuing with our PhD studies. Lin, who had earlier gained a distinction at Masters Degree level, was now lecturing in Geology at Fort Hare, and I was the right-hand man of the energetic and go-ahead Professor of the Plant Sciences Department, Ted Botha. We were now high earners and began to be irked by a tax system that took so much more from us as a married couple than it would from two single people. It seemed doubly unfair since we had only got married in the first place because the South African government would not have allowed Lin to stay otherwise. We both knew and had always known that the pieces of paper made no difference to our love and commitment to one another. We did our sums and discovered that we should be 25 per cent better off unmarried – and that a divorce cost the equivalent of just £200. So by mid-1986 we were no longer legally husband and wife, and the reality of our relationship changed not a jot! We passed the whole interlude off as a joke among our friends; but a deep unease about their reactions left us feeling too 'guilty' to tell our parents in Britain. It seemed too much and too unnecessary to explain, especially at such a distance when they could not see how our love was unaltered. I even kept our British marriage certificate (however illegally!) to avoid complications if we ever had children.

Up until this time we had always avoided the question of having a family. In fact, Lin was well known for her stated aversion to kids and for far preferring animals. But as Lin came into her late thirties we were aware of the biological clock ticking. We had been struck by the pleasure that our friends and colleagues seemed to be having with their children as they were smitten one after another by broodiness, pregnancy and the nurturing of their offspring. We had resisted for years. But now, while we never actually made the decision *to* try for a family, we became less careful with contraception during our lovemaking. It was as if we were still not quite sure about it, but if Lin should become pregnant then we should not be very upset.

Later that year we took a holiday to the tropical island of Réunion to see the volcanoes and enjoy the lush forests. In the magical ambience of Réunion, Lin and I spent time talking about our lives, our direction and hopes for the future. And, by the time we departed, Josie was conceived.

Yet when Lin discovered she was pregnant, it was still a shock for the both of us. We were so committed to our jobs and our material way of life, that the prospect of another human being to share it all with was at first unnerving. I quickly became resigned to the fact, and eventually quite excited at the prospect of a lovely little daughter – for it was sure to be a girl! But then I was not the one who would undergo the pregnancy, childbirth and lactation. Lin was more ambivalent. She could see the radical change this was going to mean in our lives and she began to have her doubts about going through with it. During the early pregnancy she suffered melancholy mood swings, and at one time she became so upset that she would go off for strenuous horse rides as if to invite the possibility of a miscarriage. We tried to rationalize our feelings in light of the hormonal changes that we knew to be taking place in Lin's body. But it was several weeks before I felt more secure in Lin's and the baby's safety.

Lin would not slack off her pace of work, however, and we continued to hurl ourselves at our teaching work and our PhD studies. In early 1987 I travelled to Germany to chair a session at the International Botanical Congress before rushing home in the hope that Lin had not gone into premature labour while I was away. Through ultrascans we had seen our baby developing, although we had declined to be told the sex of our child. We had felt the baby punching and kicking in the womb, and listened to its heartbeat. An amniocentesis showed that all was well with the baby genetically, and we converted the laundry of our home at Hogsback into a nursery for our expected new arrival. The predicted date for the birth passed and we grew anxious in anticipation. We had read all the books and done all the exercises. But nothing could prepare us for the full physical and emotional impact of the event that was about to occur.

Birth and Rebirth

March 27 1987 saw the start of a profound change in our lives. Heavily pregnant and two weeks past her due date, Lin went into work as usual, gave a couple of lectures and met me to travel home together. An hour later, I was working in the garage when Lin called me from the kitchen saying calmly that she thought her waters had broken. We set off for the maternity hospital eighty miles and an hour-and-a-half's drive away. Lin's contractions were evident during the journey, but she didn't seem at all perturbed, only quite mellow at the prospect of what was to come.

At the hospital, I had to wait on a couch outside Lin's room for most of the evening. We heard screams of pain from women below in the basement of the hospital and were told that this was where the African women gave birth. Naively we asked why they were not offered epidurals, and the nurses looked at us as though we were mad.

Eventually I was called in at around two in the morning to witness the birth. I had to stand behind a curtain at the foot of the bed, and was not allowed next to Lin or to hold her hand. The anaesthetist had 'missed the spot' with his epidural injection, so that Lin not only experienced the full pain of the delivery but had a dead leg on her left side too. She declined an epidural at her next birth! It was a difficult breech birth, and the obstetricians had to use a suction cup to twist the baby and extract her from the birth canal. Our daughter emerged wrinkled and jaundiced from the late delivery and with a large suction lump on her head. But we cried with joy and couldn't take our eyes off her. She was petite with an unexpectedly pretty almond-shaped face with slanting eyes and a perfect little mouth. We got some sleep while our daughter was taken away for tests, but by ten o'clock the next morning Lin had already had enough of being bossed around by the nurses and prevented from being with our child. So by midday, only ten hours after the birth, Lin had discharged herself from hospital and we were heading home with our tiny bundle to start a whole new life. We liked names that began with 'J' and could be abbreviated (our dogs were Jilly and Jackie) and so we plumped for Josephine. Josie's middle name is Alice, after the town we had first lived in next to Fort Hare University (itself named for Queen Victoria's daughter, Princess Alice).

Now that Josie had been born safe and sound, and both mother and child were well, Lin felt at last that she could break the news to her parents. And so, on the evening of the last day of March 1987, Lin rang her parents in the UK to tell them, 'Guess what? You're grandparents!' She explained about her worries for the baby (at thirty-six Lin was considered old for a first birth) and she told Peter and Irene that she had not wanted to worry them unduly during the pregnancy, especially if there had needed to be a termination early on. We were able to tell the grandparents that we would be bringing Josie to see them later in the year, en route to four months' study in the USA, and Lin found herself happily spending the rest of the phone call talking about all those matters of maternity that mothers and their mothers talk about. It was the first sign, after years of geographical separation, that we were starting to look back towards the UK, to our roots, and not outwards and away from our parents any longer.

Throughout the southern winter of 1987, our home at Hogsback was a cosy, baby-centred nest, with a fulfilling routine of feeding, nappy-changing and cuddling up together as the snow lay outside. However, there were signs that we had difficulty in adjusting to this state of affairs. I can remember us thinking that a baby should not have to cramp our lifestyle too much and that we should be able to treat Josie similarly to our pets. We begrudged losing our sleep and only rarely had Josie in bed with us. At first we may have let Josie cry for longer than we should before going to her. I often wondered whether this contributed to her being a more anxious child than her younger sister Megan, who was allowed far more licence after she was born.

Restricted maternity leave coupled with the pressure of her doctoral studies meant that Lin had to go back to work very soon after Josie's birth. This was the point at which we finally gave in and agreed to give our neighbour Victoria Magadla a job as our home-help and 'nanny'. Victoria slipped easily into the role of childminder and was a wonderful nanny during the first few months of Josie's life. Josie looks with curiosity at photos of herself snoozing contentedly in a blanket tied around Victoria's back. Lin too adopted this African way of carrying Josie, and found it was a good way to work and keep Josie happy at the same time.

Our happiness during Josie's first year of life was not complete, as I was facing problems at work. The plant sciences department, partly as a result of the work we did to obtain grants, was successful in turning out highly qualified black postgraduates, well equipped to work as scientists in the wider South African economy. This offended an administration that required of black students only that they should work as teachers in the 'homelands' or *bantustans*. Slowly and deliberately the department was squeezed through the cutting of staff to bring us into line. In protest I offered my resignation, and was amazed to find that several of my colleagues were willing to join in this stand on principle. When I pledged to give up nearly half my salary to fund a junior lecturer's post, the university authorities thought I had flipped; my resignation was accepted and I was banned from the university grounds. But at least I was able to spend much more time with Josie. I would leave her asleep outside in her shaded cradle by the study window, and I kept a piece of string attached to my toe so that I could rock the cradle while I worked on my PhD!

While Lin continued lecturing, looking after Josie and working on her research, I was offered a research post fifty miles away by my old head of department, Ted Botha, who had also moved in that same round of resignations from Fort Hare. We needed the money, but it meant leaving our beautiful home at Hogsback, and all the hassle of moving with a young baby. Still, we could hardly turn down this offer, and so we moved temporarily to Fort Beaufort in the lowlands. I was generously allowed to go ahead with the America trip during my first term in my new job at Rhodes University. Accordingly, Lin, Josie and I headed off for the States in September 1987, calling in on family in the UK as we went. Our parents were overjoyed to see us all. We travelled all over Britain and were feted by friends and family alike. There were plenty of the same jokes our friends had made in South Africa about how the eternally childless wanderers had succumbed at last. The warmth of our welcome and relief at finally getting away from the unhappiness of the work situation in the last few months at Fort Hare gave us a feeling of nostalgia for the UK. As we watched Peter and Irene, then Pat and Margery interacting so lovingly with Josie, the notion of moving back started to take root.

The next six months in Michigan were magical, and at last we were able to spend far more time together as a family. We could play with Josie for hours at home, and then explore the neighbourhood over the weekends with Josie strapped to one or other of our backs (although by now we used a baby carrier rather than a blanket – so as not to scare the locals). We made two short trips – to North Carolina and the Niagara Falls – but the excitement of these was nothing compared to our experiences on the way home from the States. I had agreed to stop off mid-Atlantic for a couple of weeks to collect plant specimens from around the volcanic springs of Iceland. And that is how we came to spend Josie's first Christmas in a hotel in Reykjavik, with only four hours of daylight each day.

On Christmas Eve Josie stopped eating and became feverish and irritable. This was the first time that we had seen Josie ill, and Lin and I were petrified. We rushed out to the shops for pills and potions and fussed over her every minute. On Christmas Day we called a doctor to the hotel, imagining all sorts of terrible possibilities. The young Icelandic doctor examined Josie thoroughly. We were amazed at the gentle and expert way in which he handled her, and she seemed soothed and comforted by his touch. He explained, in perfect English, that as far as he could tell, Josie had a cold, and she should be better in a day or two. Lin and I were vastly relieved, although a bit nervous of so simple a diagnosis. More significantly, we realized that we had probably at last made the mental adjustment necessary to stop thinking of Josie in the same way as our pet dogs! And sure enough, just as the doctor had predicted, Josie was back to her normal, bubbly, ravenous self within a couple of days.

There was one more bit of excitement to come before we left Iceland. I still needed to survey some steam vents in the north of the island. So we hired a small Lada and set off north into what quickly became a blizzard. Darkness fell even earlier than usual as clouds and fog enveloped us. The road became steeper and more tortuous, and we were soon on a full-blown mountain pass with sheer drops on the outside of each bend. The car's headlights were straining to cut through the ice-lashed gloom and we had to drive closer and closer to the edge of the precipice to avoid the snow drifts that were growing deeper and wider on each bend. We realized that if our way was blocked further on we might not be able to get back through these drifts as night overtook us. We hadn't seen a single other vehicle on the road, which did not look good, and so eventually we turned back. It meant we would lose precious time and money; but whereas in the past Lin and I would have thought nothing of spending the night cuddled up together in a car in the middle of a blizzard, now we had Josie to consider, and this changed things.

On our way home through the UK we stayed with my parents again. As we discussed our thoughts about returning to Britain to live, it was clear that they were delighted to think we might, at last, be coming 'home'. Seeing Josie with her grandparents made us realize that if we stayed in Africa, both Josie and our parents would miss out on important family ties as she grew up. We were serious enough about returning to start thinking practically – we needed to come soon if we were ever to get jobs in academia, as we were no spring chickens and every year there would be more well-qualified, younger (and cheaper) graduates to fill university posts. And then there was accommodation to think about. We looked around a few estate agents and were horrified by what was happening to house prices in the late eighties. In South Africa we could afford a big house with plenty of land to keep the ponies we loved; but what would be our options here?

Lin and I soon realized that London was a no-go area for us. North Wales, however, was immediately attractive. It was an area we both knew well from childhood holidays and loved for its rugged mountainous countryside; property was cheaper than in the South East; and it seemed a good place for a botanist to look for a job. Bangor was home to a number of environmental institutions, as well as the University of Wales's many life sciences departments. Lin even had family in the area; and her parents still kept a holiday caravan there, near where Lin had spent many happy weeks in her childhood.

By chance, some friends we met up with showed us a small advert for a house near Bangor that would suit us down to the ground. The house sounded fantastic. Plas Tan-yr-Allt was a big old stone and slate quarrymaster's house, with a lake and more than enough land and outbuildings to stable and graze some horses. It seemed surprisingly cheap and we decided we mustn't let the opportunity to have a look pass us by.

The house was tucked away up a steep stony track, and obviously had not been lived in for at least a year. The garden was unkempt, but the quiet serenity of the place was enchanting. To the east up the Nantlle Valley was the imposing bulk of Snowdon, the highest mountain in England and Wales. A few miles to the west were the gleaming waters of the Irish Sea. I was able to squint in through the windows to see beautifully proportioned high-ceilinged downstairs rooms, and at the back of the house was a conservatory, a real suntrap on the south side. I thought, 'This is the perfect place for us', and I took a few photos before heading back to Lin and Josie in Birmingham. Lin was ecstatic as I described the place and could not wait to phone the vendor. We were both disappointed, then, to hear that he had already accepted an offer and it was no longer for sale. Nonetheless, we left for South Africa with our confidence boosted – we *would* be able to find somewhere we both liked and could afford after all!

Back in South Africa, we felt less certain. Over here we were both sure of securing work that we loved; my career prospects were looking excellent already, and we were confident that Lin's could be as good as soon as she finished her PhD, although already Lin was looking forward rather to spending time with Josie and her beloved horses and pets and to being creative with the garden after so many years of intense academic work.

Josie was one by now, running about happily barefoot in the South African sunshine until she was nut-brown and with the soles of her feet hardened like those of her African playmates. Lin and I had always agreed that if we had one child, then we should have to have two. While we were concerned about how demanding two children might be, that seemed less important now. We were having a ball with Josie and the prospect of a second child was very appealing. We felt sure, too, that Josie would appreciate a brother or sister as close to her own age as possible to play with now and grow up with.

When Lin became pregnant for the second time, we were not aware of it at first. In addition to the pressures of commuting in opposite directions, juggling days of 'working from home' in order to look after Josie and struggling with finishing our PhDs, we were wrestling with indecision over our future careers and uncertainty as to where we would live next. On top of all this we lost our oldest pet. Our black cat Noodle had been with us for thirteen years. He was just as much a child substitute as our golden retrievers were before Josie's birth, but he was unhappy with the move to the hot, dusty streets of Fort Beaufort after so many contented years on our forested mountain plot at Hogsback. When Noodle went missing Lin became frantic and she would not rest until she had found our beloved cat. We searched the streets late into the night and again for the next five nights, but to no avail. By the end of the week, when it became clear that Noodle was probably gone for good, Lin was distraught. She cried herself to sleep and was too unwell for work the following day.

That morning I popped out for some shopping and returned to find Lin looking drawn and exhausted. I sat her down with a cup of tea, and Lin said, 'We're going to have to try again for a brother or sister for Josie.' The significance did not hit me for a moment, but then with a shock I realized that Lin had had a miscarriage. We hadn't even known that she was pregnant. I comforted her as best I could that sad day. I was certain that Lin's miscarriage had been brought on by her anguish over Noodle. For me it proved again how intense and deeply rooted was Lin's love for other creatures, and how shallow by comparison was my own emotional engagement with the world around me.

Later in the year, during the northern summer, we returned briefly to the UK for a conference. We took Josie to see her grandparents again, and while staying in Sutton Coldfield with Peter and Irene, I decided on an impulse to phone the vendor of Plas Tan-yr-Allt. To my amazement he told me that the sale had fallen through six months earlier, and that if we were still interested, we could have the property at last year's price. Lin and I were thrilled, and we needed little incentive to change our schedule so that we could fit in a trip to Wales to view the house together.

The very next day we found Plas Tan-yr-Allt cold and dusty after so long unlived in; it was clear that it would need masses of work to make it weatherproof and comfortable. But it satisfied every yearning that we had for a rambling old place in the mountains, with space for as many animals as we could ever wish for. Fate leapt in again a couple of days later when I mentioned our thoughts about returning to some old friends and colleagues at the conference. It just happened, so they said, that they were looking for someone to run the herbarium and biodiversity databases at the British Antarctic Survey (BAS) headquarters in Cambridge. We had worked together before, and they were sure they could offer me a temporary contract while we settled back in.

Lin and I were hardly keen to get into yet more long-distance commuting, especially as we were hoping for a second child soon; but we did want to move into Plas Tan-yr-Allt, to be near our families again and for our children to have the chance to know their grandparents and go to school in Britain. Although there were some excellent schools in South Africa and a marvellous climate and geography, in our experience then, the majority of white children seemed to grow up with a sense of apartness and superiority over their African peers, no matter how liberal their parents were. Black and white children might play cricket together in the streets, but it always seemed to be the white kid that was wielding the cricket bat, and the African youngsters who were running hither and thither to field the ball. We did not want our children to grow up with this mind-set. We saw, too, difficult times ahead. The economy was plummeting and there was a risk that, if we stayed much longer, we might get stuck there, unable to afford to return to the UK. With all this in mind, we paid the deposit on Plas Tan-yr-Allt and returned to South Africa with a new sense of direction and plenty of packing to do!

We handed in our notices, packed up most of our belongings and completed the sale of our house at Hogsback. The house sale had been a great stroke of luck and a bizarre story. A passing businessman saw the For Sale sign, wandered into the middle of Josie's first birthday party and immediately agreed to pay the asking price. We were tremendously fortunate that, because of his overseas interests, he was able to put a great deal of the funds straight into a European bank account, for in those days there were tight restrictions on how much money could be taken out of South Africa and we had risked losing much of the value of our house.

All the details of the move were tripping along nicely when, suddenly, everything changed. Just as we were due to load up the containers to be shipped back to Britain, a letter arrived out of the blue inviting me to take a very well-paid job as head of the botany department at the newly founded University of Namibia. The university was in Windhoek, capital of this stunningly beautiful country that was on the brink of independence and a new constitution. Lin and I just had to take Josie and go for a look.

We were already familiar through earlier visits with Namibia's extreme desert conditions and the awesome beauty of a country that felt almost like another planet. And as we drove north, our excitement grew at the prospect of having time to study the extraordinary wildlife and fascinating plants of the region. All Windhoek seemed to be aquiver with excitement at the forthcoming independence; and we felt this too, compounded by the principal of the university's enthusiasm for the country, its nature, and the excellent terms and conditions of the job on offer. And so it was that we decided to put our UK plans on hold for two years, and Josie spent most of her pre-school years in Africa, the continent of her birth.

Back in South Africa after our lightning visit to Namibia, we decided to let the UK shipment go ahead, confident that we could easily 'rough it' for a couple of years in Namibia rather than sort all that packing out again. And we ourselves flew back to Britain for the first Christmas that Josie was aware of and our first Christmas at Tan-yr-Allt. It was a wonderful time, restful days in front of log fires in the snowy Welsh mountain valley; and we wondered for a while about the wisdom of returning to Namibia.

Yet it was not a decision we regretted. The two years we spent in Namibia were exhilarating and eventful. Almost as soon as we arrived, Lin announced she was pregnant again, and Josie was pleased as Punch that she could now look forward to a brother or sister. Lin and I were hoping for another girl, but again we did not ask to know the sex of the child in advance of the birth. Lin's gynaecologist was well known in Namibia for his work on birth control in lions! He was quite used to dealing with mentally tough and physically capable mothers in this harsh, desert country, and he had no problem with Lin's insistence on working more or less up to the end of her pregnancy again, as she had with Josie.

Lin was now editing the Journal of the Geological Survey of Namibia. We continued to assist each other on fieldwork which took us all over Namibia, and usually we took Josie and the dogs along. During weekends and holidays we were able to explore further the rich diversity of the land: the fertile north, the eastern forest savannah, the arid desert and places that held such resonant names as Fish River Canyon and the Skeleton Coast.

With Lin eight months pregnant, we set off on a voyage of discovery through parts of Africa, the likes of which we had not really experienced south of the border. We encountered the San people ('Bushmen') hunting game with bows and arrows as they had for thousands of years. We came across elephant and giraffe, lion and leopard roaming free as they had always done in areas that were just wild open country, and not part of any national park or conservation area. We travelled through the northern tip of Botswana to camp in the Chobe National Park where we were woken in the night by elephants feeding in bamboo thickets right next to the tent. I was worried that they might accidentally trample us all in our sleeping bags, but Josie seemed unfazed and only fascinated by their munchings and grumblings. We watched for an hour their dark shapes looming against the starlit African sky, before they moved on to another part of the thicket.

Less enchanting were the endless bureaucracy and petty corruption that dogged our border crossings. We crossed the Zambezi on the ferry and drove down the atrociously pot-holed roads on the river's northern bank until we reached Victoria Falls. There was still a lot of tension in the region, as the South Africans continued to raid ANC 'safe-houses' in Zambia, and so we grew increasingly frustrated at the rusty gun barrels waved at us at each stop, and the money extorted from us while officials 'checked our currency allowances'.

But it was worth it. At Victoria Falls we enjoyed the stupendous sights and sounds of this wonder of the world as thousands had before us. I took Josie down into the mist forest fed by the rain from the falls, and we marvelled at the beautiful ferns and orchids, frogs and monkeys in the steamy, dripping fantasy land.

When we reached Lusaka, we found our way to the customs building where the Chief of Customs, resplendent in a uniform that made him look like an Admiral of the Fleet, welcomed us with open arms and paraded us before the rest of his staff. The Namibian border with Zambia had only just opened after many years of war. 'These are the first people across the border from Namibia!' the Chief of

Customs announced grandly, and the room erupted into applause as Josie sat in Lin's arms looking vaguely bemused. Our entry and vehicle papers were processed quickly and efficiently, and I was relieved that my dodgy passport passed muster again (in those days a South African stamp ruled out visits to other countries in the area and so I had judiciously 'doctored' my passport, so as not to cause trouble).

One night over dinner we were entertained by our namesake, Paul Russell, who was deputy head of the National Anti-Corruption Commission. An ex-Scotland Yard police officer, he was feared throughout Zambia, as not even politicians were immune from his powers. When he heard about our mistreatment on the road up from Namibia, he told us he would be sending an unmarked car that way very soon to sort out the main offenders. Paul also told me that if we were held up by officials elsewhere, I should just flash my passport with the name 'Russell' emblazoned on it, and let it be known that I was related to him. It wasn't long before we had the chance to try out this new gambit, at the first roadblock on the way out of Lusaka. The technique worked a treat and resulted in an immediate and polite invitation from the police officers for us to continue on our way unmolested! We progressed quickly along the Great East Road towards Malawi, with only an occasional hold-up at one or other of the fortified bridges along this strategic route. We had to maintain a strictly enforced 5 mph crossing each time in order to avoid further harassment. The one time we were sent back to do it again more slowly, the passport trick proved most useful again.

In Malawi we saw plenty of evidence of the war that was still going on in Mozambique. The road we were travelling on ran right along the border, and the houses on the Mozambique side were all shot up and bombed out, with thousands of Mozambican refugees camped in villages on the other side of the road.

Throughout the trip, Lin and I would stop off at various universities and projects to make contacts and renew old friendships. One highlight was being given a permit to spend a couple of days collecting plants on Mulanje Mountain, with Lin (well into her last month of pregnancy!) and I taking it in turns to lug Josie up and down the slopes in her back carrier whenever she became too tired to walk any further. We swam in the cool mountain pools and watched parrots and monkeys high up in the trees. We hardly saw another person, although sadly there was plenty of evidence of illegal logging in the forest reserve, with several hidden saw-pits in the depths of the ravines.

We headed north to Lake Malawi where we camped by the crystal-clear waters at Monkey Bay. Here, brightly coloured freshwater tropical fish darted and danced between the white boulders along the shoreline. Josie was fascinated by these fish, and I bought her a book about them. The pictures in the book and the sight of the fish in their natural habitat sparked Josie's interest in aquarium fish that endures to this day. She still collects fish in our pond in Wales, and dreams of swimming with the fish and being able to snorkel and dive to see them more closely.

All too soon we ran out of time. Our return journey included a short cut along an unclassified road that turned out to be the worst on the trip. The Land Rover was put through its paces, and I was worried that the lurching and bumping might be dangerous for Lin so late in her pregnancy. Josie, however, seemed to have a limitless capacity for enjoying the roller-coaster qualities of the ride and an ability to sleep at will, sprawled out on top of the luggage in the back of the vehicle.

Then, suddenly, it all turned rather sour. Josie would not eat her supper and was sick one night. She could not sleep and seemed to be going through feverish phases and cold sweats. In the morning we crossed the border into northern Namibia and took her to see a doctor at the ex-South African military hospital nearby. He was a young army medic, just back from a course in tropical medicine in Pretoria. He asked us where we had come from, and when we told him northern Malawi, he looked shocked. That area was known to harbour a pool of drug-resistant malaria mosquitoes. He frightened the wits out of Lin and me by suggesting that, although we had all been taking our anti-malarial pills, Josie may have contracted the drug-resistant form of malaria. We were horrified and immediately bundled Josie into the car for a non-stop dash back to the State Hospital in Windhoek, which we knew would be best equipped for dealing with this serious condition. Lin and I took turns driving the eight-hundred miles. We completed it in fifteen hours and made it to the State Hospital in the early hours of the morning. There, to our immense relief, the doctor on duty diagnosed Josie as having a 'head cold'. However, it would not clear up, and a few days later when Josie accompanied us to Lin's next appointment with the gynaecologist, he had a look at her and diagnosed a renal infection

– cystitis. Although we had been bathing Josie carefully every night in a washing-up bowl, she must still have contracted the infection somewhere along the journey as a result of some local contamination. Given antibiotics, Josie was right as rain in a couple of days. But we had been chastened once again, not only by the vulnerability to disease of a young European child travelling in Africa, but also by the erratic nature of the medical advice we had received.

With the imminent arrival of our second child, we knew that world travels with the whole family would have to take a back seat from now on. Lin even agreed, this time around, to take her maternity leave from a couple of weeks before the birth. On this occasion Lin was moved into the State Hospital in Windhoek before her labour started. When Lin finally gave birth, it was in the middle of the night and I dropped Josie off with friends on my way across town to the hospital. When I arrived I was overjoyed to find that we had another darling baby daughter, this time with masses of jet black hair. We were a bit disappointed with the nursing staff for having rung me so late that I was not quite in time for the birth, and they received a telling off from our gynaecologist who had also only just made it. Lin had done without the epidural this time, and the birth had been straightfoward, if rather painful. At least this time Lin was able to keep the baby with her, and no one was going to whisk her away as they had Josie.

We knew we were going back to Wales to live in a year's time and had already settled on the Welsh name 'Megan' for our new daughter. Josie started using the name as soon as she was introduced to her sister in the morning, and she seemed genuinely excited and fascinated by the new addition to our family. We had been worried that she might be jealous or resentful of this new focus for our affections, but in the first few days back at home with Megan, she showed herself to be very gentle and loving towards her baby sister.

By the time she was three, Josie was going to playschool and making friends of her own age, while Megan was seven months old and starting to toddle around, playing with the dogs in the garden of our home in Windhoek. Lin by now had achieved her PhD and was the first white woman ever to gain a doctorate from Fort Hare University. And in Namibia I had been elected Dean of the Science Faculty at the university, and was also on the council of the Wildlife Society of Namibia. I was increasingly being drawn into environmental issues in the country, and had already been involved in decision-making on halting the seal culling on the west coast, and roofing over the Eastern National Water Carrier (a canal that passed through a game-rich region of the country and killed thousands of animals every month). We had experienced the excitement of the independence ceremonies, during which I was nearly run over by a car carrying Yasser Arafat! And we had also had the sad and shocking experience of having one of our colleagues – Anton Lubowsky, a crusading civil rights lawyer – gunned down and killed outside his house in the run-up to the first free political elections in the new state. Anton had asked a group of environmentalists, including myself, to help the returning political party SWAPO to draft a post-independence environmental policy. We were gratified to see our ideas included in electioneering by the SWAPO politicians, and key elements of our advice were later included in the new national constitution.

For all the opportunities and responsibilities in Namibia, for all the excitement of life for us at this time, we were finding the pleasures of our family even more compelling. Lin and I were going to stick to our deadline of two years in Namibia, as our farmstead in Wales kept calling to us.

At Christmas 1990 we travelled over to the UK to check on the house and spend the festive season with our parents. Josie was nearly four and Megan was sixteen months. At home with my parents in Romsey we found that all was not well. My father Pat had been suffering from depression since he retired a couple of years before. He had not been able to adjust to the sudden change to a slower pace of life after leaving work, and more importantly he had got himself into a deep state of worry over the family finances as he moved onto a pension instead of employment income. Pat had convinced himself that he and Margery could not afford to maintain their modest lifestyle, and he had overreacted by cutting all his links with the fishing that had previously been his main interest.

Lin and I were horrified to discover what appeared to be a suicide note on his desk, hinting that he was planning to do away with himself when he went away for his annual shooting trip to Scotland. The suggestion was that he might try and drive himself to his death by deliberately crashing the car on the long journey north. Pat's doctor and Margery had done their best to convince him to go into hospital for treatment for depression, as he had in his forties, but to no avail. Lin and I were convinced that this "cry for help" was serious, and we hassled the authorities until Pat was admitted to a hospital where he could receive psychiatric treatment.

When we visited, he put on a brave face for the benefit of the children. But we could tell that all was not right. According to Pat, he had mostly been left on his own since he had arrived at the hospital, and if ever anyone did come to talk to him, it was usually a different person from the time before. He was fed up trying to explain his problems to new and disinterested people, who rushed off to their other duties at the first opportunity. He could not see the point of being there; but after some gentle argument, he agreed to stick it out for a bit longer. Pat walked us about the hospital grounds with a glum smile on his face and wished us well back in Namibia. I reminded him that it was only six months before we were due back permanently, and that the principal reason we were returning was so that our children could grow up near to their wider family, particularly to him and their other grandparents. We were sure that once we got back to the UK, we could brighten up Pat's life through increased contact with the grandchildren; and so we bade him goodbye as he stood forlornly in his greatcoat in front of the glowering old psychiatric hospital buildings.

The following week, I flew back to Namibia for the beginning of term. Lin and the girls were staying on for another fortnight with Peter and Irene. A day after I returned to Namibia, I received a late-night call from Lin. She told me that Pat had discharged himself from hospital and returned home the previous day, at about the same time as I had been flying back to Namibia. Margery woke the following morning to the sound of a gunshot, and Pat's absence from the bedroom. Pat had got up early, taken the double-barrelled 12-bore shotgun from his bedroom cupboard and gone around to the next-door neighbour's garden. There, on the doorstep of their house, he had turned the gun on himself and ended what for him had become an empty and pointless life.

I was at one and the same time grief-stricken, horrified and furious, so angry. Stupid, stupid man. You led a full and exciting life and were loved by a wonderful, devoted wife and some of the best friends a man could wish for. We later discovered that the family finances were in excellent shape, and that Pat could not have made better provision for Margery and himself in their retirement. The preoccupation with financial insecurity had been a complete delusion – one we learned that is common to depressive patients. Pat had prepared the paperwork for his death meticulously, and it became clear that he had decided on this course of action months before. I was racked with guilt as I flew back to the UK on the first available flight the next day. If only I had stayed on longer and made sure that he had settled into the voluntary work we had lined up for him. If only I had pushed still harder to have the authorities provide adequate care and counselling.

Lin and I comforted Margery and my sister Jeannie as best we could. They were both completely wrung out by the emotional turmoil of the first thirty-six hours since the tragedy, and were now sheltering behind the veil of stoicism that seems to run as a trait in our family. I had not experienced death at such close quarters before, but we derived from each other the strength that we needed to help us through the pressures of the days following Pat's death. Little did I know then that I would have to draw on the same inherited reserves to face the loss of my own wife and child, only a few years later.

We told Josie and Megan that their grandfather was dead, although we did not reveal the full trauma to them. Josie did not seem outwardly upset by the news, but she did appear to sense our grief, as she was quick to comfort us and offer her sympathy with little presents of flowers and drawings. She made a sweet card and posy to send to the funeral, although we did not take her along. This loss of the first of our parents made Lin and me even more determined to resist the allure of Namibia, including the lucrative job offers that were now coming my way there. It was made clear that I could expect promotion to professor as soon as my PhD came through, and I was getting more and more offers of substantial research grants and project funding from foreign embassies and donor agencies newly set up in Namibia. But the call of our roots was greater, and as the time approached for us to leave Namibia, we packed in a couple of last-minute trips out into the backwoods, to drink in the sights and sounds of this wonderful country. We camped in the bush in the Kaudom Reserve close to the Botswana border, and Josie played in the shallow water-filled pans that were filled with beautiful blue water lilies. Megan was toddling about by this time, and also loved to wallow in the cool water, in this country where shade temperatures above 40°C were not uncommon. It was going to be hard to say goodbye to Africa, but we wanted our daughters to carry home to the UK a sense of their roots in Africa and a reason to return there in years to come.

Just before we left something happened that gave the kids a bit of a shock and a first revelation that their parents were not necessarily invincible. One night I was awoken by a sudden stabbing pain in my ear. I was vaguely aware that I had reached up to scratch an itch in the same ear before fully awaking, but now it seemed as if something was running around inside my ear and biting me. The noise it caused me was deafening, although Lin could not see anything there. I was convinced that some sort of insect had been burrowing into my earwax, and that my probing finger had pushed it right in. I leapt out of bed and began jumping around the room, shaking my head and shouting in pain. It really felt as though something was eating at me from the inside of my head. I was almost delirious and Lin decided that she should bundle up the kids in their pyjamas, and whisk me off to the Accident and Emergency Unit at the State Hospital.

The night nurse declared that she could see absolutely nothing with her otoscope, but every time she poked around in my ear, the pain started again. At first I swear she thought I was malingering for some unaccountable reason. But then she agreed to try and syringe out my ear with hot water. When she started this process, the pandemonium got worse. I am usually quite a show off at grinning and bearing it, but this time I ended up running down the hospital corridor shrieking in agony and grasping my head with both hands as I tried to shake out whatever it was that was wreaking havoc inside my skull.

I looked up at one point and saw Josie and Megan, their faces white with worry, staring at me uncomprehendingly as Lin tried to calm them. She didn't know whether to be sympathetic or to burst out laughing, because if it really was only a flea, then I was being a terrible coward. Eventually the nurse phoned a doctor, who suggested that she kill whatever it was by syringing my ear with alcohol. And so I braced myself for the final battle. The alcohol was squirted into my ear and the insect went berserk. It fought for its life, cutting and slashing with what later I discovered were enormous pincers, until finally it succumbed to the deadly fluid. But not before I had whirled around the hospital again, like a voodoo dancer possessed.

Six months later when we were happily settled back in the UK, I felt an itching in my ear one night and scratched. Out onto the pillow, in a thin cocoon of earwax, popped a mummified beetle a full half-inch (13mm) long with pincers for mandibles like those on the back of an earwig – this was the little demon that had been fighting for its life inside my ear. I pickled the specimen in a vial, and used it to introduce my university lectures on the wildlife of Namibia, world famous for its two hundred species of unique desert beetles!

And so, with heavy hearts to be leaving Africa, but excitement at the prospect of starting a new life back in Wales, we 'came home' to Plas Tan-yr-Allt in the Nantlle Valley. During our first year back in the UK we worked flat out at every opportunity to renovate the house, and all that time I was commuting to Cambridge, returning to Lin, Josie and Megan only at weekends. Plas was a big, old, rambling farmhouse, full of damp and badly in need of fixing up. Lin had set straight to work to recreate the 'paradise' she had had at Hogsback. It was a hard battle fighting the Welsh climate, but she was determined. She stripped off the old plaster from the walls and lifted a damp wooden floor so that we could lower the level of the wet bedrock beneath. She even converted the coal shed into a downstairs 'guest suite' for aged relatives who could not get up the stairs. So our home life at the Plas was very busy. On weekdays Lin worked away indoors, keeping the damp at bay; while outside, she fought back the encroachment of the wilderness. I would return from work every weekend to take my turn at the cement-mixer or the rock-breaker!

Josie and Megan would throw themselves at me as I cast off my suit and briefcase – we would romp and play together and I would often make them a special supper before bed. It was great to sneak in the front door and surprise them early if I could. At other times, Lin would drive the girls to meet me at the train station some 18 miles away. This could be hazardous at night, as the car was so old that it was starting to break down regularly. Josie and Megs would be ready for bed in their snuggly pyjamas that had been warmed on the Aga. They would then cuddle up in a sleeping bag for the journey – then race in their slippers and dressing gowns to meet me off the train. They would fall fast asleep on the journey home and I would lift them from the car and carry them to their beds. It was always a challenge to see if I could do it gently enough not to wake them.

Josie and Megan shared a little back-room at Plas, with a view of the sea. Lin had painted it powder blue and it had the usual Beatrix Potter and bunny friezes around the girls' bunk beds. Josie chose the top bunk as she was the eldest. Both the girls had a chest of drawers with all their special treasures arranged on the top. They did not have a lot of toys – in a house like Plas, toys were somewhat redundant as there were so many interesting things in and around the house, with so much space to play and have adventures. Indoors there were rooms within rooms, interconnecting doors, cupboards, ladders and lofts. Outside there were the barns and stables, and an old pigsty that became the girls' 'cooking house'. Josie and Megan quickly became very independent and would often be off on adventures with the bigger girls living in the houses nearby, particularly Jessie next door.

Lin had her particular style of decor at Plas, a kind of 'out of Africa' colonial look, with old pale-wood furniture, faded floral upholstery and handwoven wall-hangings. African treasures and other mementoes from our travels overseas were scattered around. Lin loved colours to be mellow and easy on the eye and so she chose muted natural pinks and greens. Our furniture was a mix of second-hand pieces we had collected from old farm sales in Africa and then brought back to Britain with us. A tall dark-wood bookcase and desk with glass doors dominated the lounge. The girls kept all their games and jigsaws in the lower cupboards, while our natural history and travel books filled the upper shelves.

Lin had a natural talent for home-making. She was not particularly keen on sewing but nevertheless managed to make herself most of what we needed in furnishings. Plas was a large, cold house and needed a lot of cosying up – we got used to keeping the home fires burning in their lovely Victorian slate fireplaces. Lin had stripped and reblacked them all, and I stripped and renovated our early 1950s Aga in the kitchen.

Outside, the roses trailed up the house front, rhododendrons and hydrangeas lined the driveway and very soon Lin had transformed the wilderness all around Plas into a beautiful cottage garden, including vegetable beds, a horse paddock and a lovely wild orchard with pear and apple trees. It was a life of hard work to keep on top of it all, but great fun for us as we transformed this once empty and abandoned place into a warm and inviting family home. Any thoughts we had of selling up and moving to Cambridge to be closer to my job, were quickly dismissed after Lin came over to visit halfway through the year. However 'historic' it was, we could not summon up much love for the flat fenlands around Cambridge. So once again I started looking around for a job, but this time closer to home.

Despite my experience and enthusiasm, I could not get a job in Wales. And so, in 1992 I took a job as Environment Adviser with the British Council at their new headquarters in Manchester. This was much closer to home, but still too far to commute on a daily basis. I ended up staying in the cheapest flats I could find during the week, and even in a squat for a while. My bosses at the British Council were very understanding, and I was able to work extra long hours during the week, so that I could have long weekends at home.

Back at home Lin would wield the pickaxe or the sledgehammer during the week, and I would set to mixing cement and hefting slates at the weekends. Josie and Megan attended the local playschool and became immersed in the Welsh language for the first time. It was a moment of great pride, when Lin and I attended the playschool's 'Eisteddfod' of singing and storytelling, and we saw first Josie and then Megan boldly presenting their pieces in Welsh on the stage. It was obvious that their young minds were at a highly absorbent stage, and neither of them seemed to have any trouble picking up the language.

In 1992, Josie moved up to the local primary school in Nantlle, Ysgol Baladeulyn, and was taught in Welsh. She settled in quickly, thanks to the skill and care of her new class teacher Siân Thomas. Josie made new friends at the primary school, but still included Megan in most of her play. The older girls would often use Megan as their 'baby' for dressing up games around the house. Megan could always stick up for herself, however, and often proved to be the bravest and most daring whenever there was a challenge to face or a scrape to get out of. She was also good at playing happily by herself if ever excluded from the bigger girls' games.

The buildings, garden and fields were extensive enough that the kids could always find something fascinating and absorbing to do close to the house. But this did not stop them exploring further afield, over the slate tips and in the woods and copses near to Plas Tan-yr-Allt. They built dens out of slate blocks against the wild Welsh weather, and they lit little fires to cook meals for themselves and their dollies in these dens or in their 'cooking house'. This play kitchen was in an old slate pigpen near the orchard, and Josie and Megan would play there for hours with their friends.

About a year after we arrived back in Wales, we had got the house straight enough to turn our attention to the barns and fields. Josie and Megan were getting to the ages that we could seriously consider getting ponies for them to ride, and it had always been Lin's intention to have horses again, as soon as we could manage it. Now we had land of our own and stables for livestock too, the time had come to search out our very own ponies. We knew that we should need tough ponies who could withstand the Welsh winters, and the rough grazing. They had to be small enough so that the girls could soon grow to manage them, but it would also be nice to have one large enough for Lin to ride occasionally. A horse large enough for me would have to come later. The obvious answer was to have ponies that were adapted to the local conditions through years of breeding in the region – and so we settled on Welsh mountain ponies. Lin and I toured auctions and scoured advertisements in newspapers and magazines, for two ponies young enough to give us a good life with the children, and well enough bred and cared for to be safe for Josie and Megan to ride. And so it was that Tegid and Rosie joined the Russell family.

The girls' joy when we brought these ponies home was unbounded. I never failed to be amazed by the way that Lin, Josie and Megan would cuddle and kiss the ponies as though they were their very own big teddy bears. Lin had trained horses in the UK before we went overseas, and she had trained our horses Trixie and Rebel in South Africa. It was not long before Rosie and Tegid would come to Lin's or the girls' call, no matter how far away across the fields. They were young and spirited enough to tackle long treks across the hills eagerly, and they never required constant prodding or urging to carry on, like some of the riding school ponies we had encountered.

In 1993, Megan joined Josie at Ysgol Baladeulyn, and the girls settled into a routine of days at school together, and afternoons and evenings playing at home and helping Lin around the house and garden. I would be at home on Fridays, Saturdays and Sundays, and would tackle the heavier jobs, or the electrics and plumbing. If we ever had a free moment we took the dogs down to the beach or explored the hills of Snowdonia. In the winters we would cuddle up indoors – the girls liked nothing better than to dry off after a bath by sitting on towels on top of the Aga – and toast muffins in front of one of the open fires that we could light in just about any room of the house. If the snow lay for any length of time, we would sled down through the pony fields, or even break out our old skis and practise skiing the pony-field 'piste'.

My job with the British Council gave me plenty of scope for international travel again, and because of my African expertise I was soon on missions back to the countries of southern Africa that I knew so well. My job had changed from one of intensive study within a little-known area of botany, to one of broad concerns with environment and development in the 'Third World'. The personal gratification of promoting progress in a narrow branch of science had been replaced by a no less rewarding sense of satisfaction, that my work was now contributing to improvements in the environment and quality of life for many people in the countries where Lin and I had also lived and worked during our earlier careers. But it was all still keeping me away from home and family too much.

I longed to be able to be at home every night of the week to tell the girls their bedtime stories and have time with them at the weekends instead of devoting every spare minute at home to working on the house or garden. Why had we come back to Britain, if it was not to make more of family life, not less? We had always decried the 'yuppie' lifestyle of long-distance commuting and a 'weekends only' family life. And yet here we were doing exactly the same thing. I continued to try for jobs at Bangor University and elsewhere within daily commuting distance of home, but still to no avail. I would apply for a technician's job or a teaching assistant's post, only to be told that I was 'overqualified' – meaning 'too old' or 'too expensive'. I would plead that I did not expect to earn the kind of salary that I had before, but I had the sense that employers wanted younger staff they could control more easily than an older, more experienced person. It seemed, after several years of trying, that I was not going to 'break back into academia' after all, at least not here in North Wales.

Then in 1994, just as the British Council was undergoing some changes and I found that my job was no longer secure, out of the blue I was offered a prime academic position at one of Britain's leading universities. I was approached by Professor Ian Swingland, head of the Durrell Institute of Conservation and Ecology (DICE) at the University of Kent at Canterbury, where I regularly sent overseas students with British Council study grants. He had secured one of the first large project grants from the UK government's 'Darwin Initiative' (a funding programme to assist developing countries with species conservation projects) and he wanted me to come and run the programme for him. I would be in charge of training postgraduate students from Brazil, Indonesia and Zimbabwe, and Ian wanted to use my fundraising skills to secure further international aid to expand the programme, as well as using my overseas experience to help with teaching at the university. The money was good and the job prospects excellent at this rapidly expanding and highly respected institute.

We were now fed up with my having to be away for so much of the time. The children were both at primary school and needed more and more support from us. They were no longer compliant babies, but demanding young humans who were encountering all the normal problems of growing up and handling the pressures of modern life. I felt that I was missing out on so much of their development, and that Lin was having to shoulder too much of the responsibility of coping with the girls' needs.

When Lin and I visited Kent for a look at the university and to see what the countryside was like round about, we were pleasantly surprised. The rolling downs and dingles of East Kent hid pretty villages that seemed to have changed little since the Norman conquest. The verdant countryside and blossom-filled gardens spoke of a mild and gentle climate, which appealed to Lin after years of battling the elements on our North Wales plot. The area was known for its excellent schools, and it was only a few miles from France. And so, with mixed emotions, we finally decided to make the move to Kent. Selling Plas Tan-yr-Allt, however, proved not to be easy. Although all our work had increased the value and attractiveness of the house, we had had a few problems with neighbours occupying bits of our land, and few buyers were willing to consider a purchase that came with sitting tenants. It took over a year, during which I was abroad frequently, and Lin began to suffer some uncharacteristic depression, before we finally sold the house and found a place to live in Kent. We wanted somewhere small that we could live in and do up at the same time, in order to make a bit of extra money. We would then add this to the proceeds from Plas Tan-yr-Allt so that we could afford a place with land of our own in the long term. Lin was already talking about going back to work after the girls were settled into a new school in Kent, and this would make it easier for us to afford a place with land for the ponies. It took months of searching, but finally I discovered a peculiar late-eighteenth-century cottage for sale in the grounds of the old abandoned physical education college at Nonington in East Kent. Granary Cottage was a gatehouse, beside a much older Tudor manor house, and it faced onto a yard surrounded by barns and outhouses, with potential grazing nearby. We reckoned that we could get it renovated within a year or two to sell on so that we could move to a bigger place. And so, once again, we put off our pledge to settle down and stop fixing up old houses, and took on yet another renovation project to keep us occupied for the foreseeable future.

As the autumn term of 1995 drew to a close, we made the final arrangements to leave North Wales and move down to Kent. I hired a lorry and drove it up and down to Wales three times in as many weeks. Friends and neighbours in Wales helped us to fill the lorry, and after the gruelling cross-country journey from Nantlle to Nonington, friends at the Kent end helped us to disgorge the lorry's contents into the barns opposite Granary Cottage that we were generously allowed to use for storage. Little of our furniture would fit in Granary Cottage; but in any case, Lin would be getting to work with the pickaxe again before long, and so we intended to live our first few months at Granary Cottage in 'camping mode'. We spent Christmas 1995 in our new home, the house festooned in decorations, log fires ablaze. We gathered wood from the copse nearby, and the children started to make new dens and hiding places in the wood round about, just as they had in Wales.

An idea of Josie's 'take' on life during this last normal year of her childhood can be gleaned from the following extracts from her diary for 1995. It is a stark reminder of the impact of her later injuries – at the time of writing this book (summer 2000), Josie is aged thirteen but has still not regained the degree of written language capability that she displays here at the age of eight:

Jan 1: in the morning on new year's day we went to feed the ducks. One of them was white, and every time we threw her a piece of bread she catched the bread. We named the duck Snowy. On new years aftanoon we went to naners house and we had some mor presents. I had a pen and a book and some felt-tips. After that we caime home and went to bed.

Feb 28: on tysday we made pancaycs at school and at home. I had 8 and $\frac{1}{2}$ pancaycs

Apr 9: on Sunday me and megan and jessie made a theatr in the barn. We started to lern the show and we practised the show in the theatre

May 13: we helped Shaun moved into granary cottage. Granary cottage is our new house. We might be living there. It was a gate mans house

Dec 3: Today we moved into granary cottage and all we did today was we moved lots of stuff into the house and we got lots of grocerys. And we were going to chuc lots away cos we had so many things. After that we decided to burn it and I was going to watch, but then I went to play with Emily next door. We played with all of her toys. I looked after her becaus her mum went to have a wash. Then when me and Megan came back we had a china dolls te party. Then we listened to mewsic.

After Christmas we returned to bring the ponies down to Kent. We loaded Rosie and Tegid at Plas Tan-yr-Allt and there were tears all around during the final goodbyes. Lin was particularly upset to be leaving the beautiful home that she had worked so hard to make for us in the Nantlle Valley, and I knew what a wrench it was for her to leave the glorious mountains that were the backdrop to her daily life. Lin had started to put down deep roots in this harsh, captivating valley – she had even been voted Chairwoman of the Parents' Committee at Josie and Megan's school, despite her struggles with learning Welsh. I was sad for her and humbled by her devotion to me and the children, that she should give all this up for the sake of our being properly together again as a family.

But we had vowed to make a real go of it in Kent. This time we would be *together* for once and for all, and that was all that we needed to allow us to face any challenge in our new life and to overcome any hardship that might face us.

Death of a Dream

January 1996 began for the Russell family with business as usual: all of us in a headlong rush to cram in as much as possible and get the most out of our lives. Though Lin and I always complained that there never were enough hours in the day, looking back I now think that it was for the best that we lived our lives to the full in the way that we did. For two members of our family were soon to have their lives tragically foreshortened in a way that none of us, in our worst nightmares, could ever have foreseen.

Josie and Megan still had a lot of exploring and den-making to do in the grounds and buildings of the old Nonington College which adjoined our house. They had settled in at their new school in nearby Goodnestone at the end of the previous term, but they were now having to bring work home to do in the evenings. They had made new friends they wanted to play with frequently, and so there was always a gaggle of kids needing to be 'bussed' around to each other's homes. How some parents managed to include extra activities like ballet, Brownies, karate, music lessons and swimming in their children's schedules was beyond me! The Bruderhof religious community had bought the Nonington College estate and were happy to rent grazing to us on a field near to our house. And with the ponies now safely transported from Wales and installed in their paddock, there was also riding to be squeezed in after school during the short winter evenings.

Lin was as active as usual, taking a pickaxe to the inside of our cosy cottage, and to the flower beds on the outside. She forged ahead with the demolition of non-original walls and partitions on the interior, making way for planned improvements to the kitchen, lounge and bathroom. In the garden she was racing to get the whole plot planted with vegetables and ornamentals for the coming spring.

In February I arranged a VIP visit to Canterbury for the Zambian Minister of Environment (we were training several of his national parks staff at the Durrell Institute of Conservation and Ecology where I worked). In the same month I organized an environmental training course at DICE for an influential traditional leader from Zambia (Chief Chitambo IV). Freddie, as he preferred to be known, was the great-great-grandson of the chieftain who had looked after the explorer David Livingstone in the final months of his life. Freddie was used to doing the rounds of his 30,000-strong rural community in Kafinda, Zambia, on a pushbike. And so he was particularly appreciative one evening, when I prevailed upon my next-door neighbour Stuart Hardisty to chauffeur us all to a slap-up meal at a local restaurant in his Rolls Royce.

At work I was coming under increasing pressure to be involved in yet more conservation projects around the world. There were demands for me to fly off all over the globe, all within the first half of the year. Each was an important project that would raise the profile of the institute yet further, potentially bringing in more funding to help secure my job and others' at DICE. Yet why had the family moved from Wales, if it was not so that we could have more time together rather than less? Lin, as usual, was understanding. We knew that life was going to be a lot more expensive in Kent than in Wales, and so I needed the job security for us to do all the things we intended with the house. Lin insisted that she would be fine at home looking after the kids and working on the house and in the garden. But I vowed that, no matter how much extra it might cost my project sponsors to manipulate the air flights, I would be at home for Josie's birthday in March and Lin's in April. So began another crazy dash around the world that, unbeknown to me, would eat up half of the time I had remaining with Lin and Megan.

In March I jetted out to Indonesia to organize a workshop on the conservation of the world's largest lizard, the Komodo Dragon, which lives on small islands east of Bali. My counterpart in Indonesia (an ex-DICE student by the name of Ron Lilley) had to rush away to attend to the fatal hostage crisis in Irian Jaya in easternmost Indonesia, where members of his WWF environmental project team had been kidnapped by Papuan separatists. I flew back into the UK the day before Josie's birthday on 28 March, only to fly out to Peru the day after her birthday!

In Peru I worked with a team of senior personnel and professional associates of DICE, on environmental briefings for Peruvian government ministers and their staff. Our programme was supported by the energetic and dedicated British Ambassador John Illman, who, later in the year, was to become embroiled in the Japanese embassy crisis in Lima when one of his staff was taken hostage. John was assisting Peru in managing potential environmental threats from the vast new Camisea offshore gas field, and from rapidly increasing tourism to environmentally sensitive areas of the country. After a frantic round of briefings, meetings, lectures and receptions, we had the chance to visit the high altitude national park of Huascaran in the Andes, before flying back to the UK on 12 April, one day before Lin's birthday.

At this time, Lin had written a letter to Susan Owen, headteacher of the girl's school in Wales. It reveals a little of how she was feeling at the time: still homesick for Wales, but immersing herself in the tasks she loved, of developing the garden and renovating the house in our new Kentish home.

Dear Mrs Owen
Josie was so pleased to get your card and all the letters from her classmates. It was a lovely thought, thank you very much. Thanks also for the school photo – we have put it in the photo album Miss Thomas gave Megan. Do let me know how much I owe you for it – also if you have any of their last school photos – Sept 1995 – I would love to have one.

They both seem to have settled down in their new school – in fact after a couple of weeks there, their teachers said it seemed they had always been there. Josie is struggling a bit with her English spellings and misses Welsh a lot. They have both taken their Welsh books to school and have read to the whole class and of course we regularly have Welsh 'singing sessions' at home. It makes me very homesick!

I still miss the mountains, coast and general environment of North Wales and would gladly return if we could. But our cottage here is quite cosy and I'm getting the garden sorted now. It's very pretty now that Spring is here with all the primroses and daffodils about. I walk home from school with Josie and Megan – it's about two miles – almost totally across fields and woods, pretty and very 'English' – i.e. totally tamed and un-wild!!

We have been over to France a few times (it only costs £1 return on the ferry!). And Josie and Megs are doing French lessons with a friend. They find the pronunciation very easy after Welsh and enjoy it a lot.

Shaun at the moment is in Peru, has only just returned from Indonesia and is shortly to visit Tanzania again – so we still don't see too much of him!

I hope we can get to Wales soon. . . . Josie and Megs are longing to see you all at school again; they still call Nantlle 'our school'. So I hope we can all come up soon and see you. Till then, have a good Easter and once again thank you for the photo.

Best wishes, Lin.

After arriving back from Peru, I had a fortnight in which to de-brief on the first two trips, and to gather myself for the next two projects. In this intervening period something happened which shocked me into the realization that things really were becoming too much for me, and that for my own health and sanity I should try and slow down. On 25 April I had been scheduled to be present at University College, London, as an external examiner at a *viva* (the final oral presentation and defence of a thesis by a doctoral student). The study under review was a thoroughly executed project on the collection of fuel wood by women in Lake Malawi National Park, Central Africa. A very senior university professor was present at the *viva*, and the student who had worked for years on the project was now sweating out this final inquisition before hearing whether or not she would get her PhD. They waited and waited, and I never appeared. The appointment was in my diary plain to see, and I had prepared myself thoroughly by going through and assessing the thesis, before coming up with a range of questions for the *viva*. But I completely forgot to turn up for the event. When a secretary called to tell me late in the afternoon in Canterbury that everyone had gone home from the meeting in London, I burned hot with horror and embarrassment. I had never missed such an important appointment in my life before and I was mortified. I scrambled to repair the damage with abject phone calls to all concerned (I later attended a re-run of the *viva* where the student passed with flying colours). However, I realized with a jolt that I had taken on so much that my brain had simply overflowed. I was so overloaded that I could no longer effectively manage my life and work without running the risk of a major catastrophe. I had to do something about it.

I vowed to Lin that after the forthcoming two trips to which I was committed, I would take on no more overseas work for the rest of the year. I also came up with a new, strict principle for the future and for the family's sake: I would take on no more than two overseas trips per year, of no more than two weeks per trip. My administrative boss Dr Mike Walkey was, as always, completely understanding and supportive, and told me to divert my phone to his whenever anyone was after me for another consultancy or aid mission.

And so I left for Tanzania on 27 April, chastened by my *viva* experience, and determined not to let something like it happen again. Once in Africa I met up with two of my Tanzanian Masters degree students who were instructors at the College of African Wildlife Management situated on the lower slopes of Mount Kilimanjaro. We spent the next fortnight working together on vegetation mapping at the Mkomazi Game Reserve, as part of a major ecological project being carried out there by the Royal Geographical Society. I returned home in early May to find the Kent countryside welcoming in its mantle of green, and the surroundings of our home a riot of spring blossom.

Lin had worked a miracle in the garden. Flowers and vegetables were coming out everywhere. She had planted a lawn where before there had been only nine years' growth of brambles since the time when the house was last lived in. The kids were happy at school, and found constant excitement in their explorations of the countryside immediately around us. They had struck up friendships with the children of the Bruderhof religious sect next door, and were often to be seen playing with the distinctively dressed girls of the community in their long dresses, pinnies and headscarves.

One sunny weekend, the girls decided that we should have breakfast outdoors and so they set up the picnic table on the new lawn outside.

I had been in the bathroom trimming my beard right back to 'designer stubble' as I was due to go overseas again shortly and needed to look 'smart' for meetings with high-level colleagues in Portugal. As I emerged everybody laughed at me saying it looked as though I had shaved my beard off completely. If I was going to trim it back that much then why not remove it altogether? Lin said that it made me look younger, and the summer holidays were coming up for me to grow it back again if I didn't like myself clean-shaven. So, to the teasing taunts of the girls I nipped back into the bathroom and emerged a couple of minutes later having removed my beard of twenty years. Now the laughter was even more hysterical, especially as the lower half of my face was exposed as grey-white against the tan that I had picked up in Africa during the preceding month. Little was I to know that this change to a clean-shaven 'look' would correspond with a tragic turning point in my life, nor that the very act of shaving would henceforth become a poignant and daily reminder of those last few happy days that we all spent together.

I flew off to Lisbon for meetings at the British Council offices with the heads of Portugal's national parks and environment agencies. This was intended to promote a project that I had devised in collaboration with Portuguese-speaking friends and colleagues in the war-torn countries of Angola and Mozambique. The project would bring senior national park wardens from these countries to Europe for training to help them rebuild the parks and game reserves in their home regions that had been devastated by civil war. The plan was for them to have English language training at the British Council in Lisbon, practical training in environment and tourism management in Portuguese national parks, and theoretical training at DICE in the UK. I intended that this project should be part-funded by ourselves, the European Union and Portugal, and I had therefore to use my persuasive powers to the full with the officials that I met in Lisbon.

Drained by the fraught meetings and with a couple of hours to spare at the end of my trip, I walked towards the ancient fort of Torre Belem, across the glistening white expanse of pavement that caps Lisbon's western sea defences. I stood by replicas of the stone crosses that Bartholomew Diaz left at landfalls during his great voyages around the continent of Africa to the Indies, and which I had seen in situ in remote parts of Namibia and South Africa. I stared up at the awe-inspiring statues of the great Portuguese mariners and followed their gaze out to sea. The previous twenty years of my life had been spent, lured as I was by foreign climes, in a compulsive quest for excitement and adventure in the southern hemisphere. I felt a heady sense of accomplishment at what Lin and I had achieved, but there was another, more restful feeling. The sense of urgency and the craving for yet more experience had waned. Now I found my thoughts turning northwards as I gazed out to the Atlantic Ocean at the mouth of the River Tejo. I thought of home, and the love and warmth of family life that awaited me there. I knew that this was my last trip of the year and that the whole summer lay ahead of us for the family to work and play together. I was glad that I had made my pledge to 'stay home' at the expense of future career, and I was determined to honour this commitment. In the second half of my life, being together with my wife and my children would now come first. How could I have possibly known that this would be asking far, far too much?

I arrived back home in the third week of June 1996, to an ambience that justified all the sentiments I had felt in Portugal. The kids seemed blissfully happy in the verdant land that was rural East Kent in early summer. The 'Garden of England' is a place where grapes and peaches will grow outside over your porch, while tall hollyhocks and delicate delphiniums need never fear the gale-swept death that awaits them in north-west Wales. Josie and Megan were cheerfully content at their new school. And at home, they never tired of surprising their ever-widening circle of friends with their network of dens and secret hideaways meticulously constructed using the skills that they had honed on the slate tips of the Nantlle Valley in North Wales.

Lin was in her element at home. Granary Cottage was smaller and far more manageable than Plas Tan-yr-Allt and she was transforming the house in double-quick time. But the garden really was her masterpiece, as she had turned it into a lush and lovely cottage garden in just a few short months. We spent as much time in the garden as we could, and I began to turn an old brick sandpit into a lily pond so that the girls could have goldfish.

There was one slightly worrying event. Lin had begun work in the garden one day, only to discover that some of her precious pot plants had been stolen the day before. When we had hacked back the vastly overgrown hedges to allow light into the garden, we had revealed that there really was very little solid barrier between our plot and the public track that ran alongside the house. And there was no gate on our front entrance either. In Wales we had always done our own fencing and walling, but we could not see dry stone, pig-netting and barbed wire going down too well with our neighbours in the prettified surroundings of Nonington. Because I was so busy at work, we decided to get some estimates from contractors, for fencing that would give us a degree of privacy and security. As July 1996 began, therefore, we were receiving visits at odd times from fencing specialists for quotes, and other merchants came by to deliver building materials and sundry other items intended for the house renovation.

When I started work in Kent the previous year, I had bought an old Citroën 2CV to serve as a run-about, in order that Lin could keep our Subaru 1800 Estate car for use at home in Wales. The 2CV, which we called 'Dolly', had given up the ghost during the winter. Therefore, after Lin and the girls moved down to Kent, we decided to make do with one car only as we were now all living together permanently. We traded in the rusty old 1800 and bought a three-year-old Subaru Legacy 2.0 Estate. So that Lin could have the car for running the girls around, and so that I could 'fight the flab' and get some regular exercise, I had taken to cycling up the hill to Snowdown Halt, a mile and a half from Nonington, and catching the train to Canterbury. I would carry my bike on the train, then use it for the two mile uphill slog to the university. To make the journey through the potholes and over the kerbstones of Canterbury more manageable, I had bought a new mountain bike in town in May. However, as July began I found myself without a bike again. The back wheel had buckled under me one day when the chain slipped, and I was pitched headlong into the gutter while passing through a narrow Canterbury alleyway. The bike was back at the shop to have the wheel straightened, and I was therefore using the car to get to work, with Lin temporarily relying on friends for transport in the rare event that she ever needed it during the day. I was now dropping the girls off at school on my way to work in the car every morning, while in the afternoon Lin would collect them on foot, as I invariably arrived home much later.

Since the weather had improved, Lin in any case preferred to walk to school to collect the girls in the afternoon. She would take our youngest dog Lucy with her, and they would walk back along the country lane that stretched from Goodnestone School, through woods and fields to the Bruderhof Community's grounds behind our house. The track was called Cherry Garden Lane, and the girls quickly grew to love the walk, as it was far more fun than coming home in the car. Lin would walk the mile and three-quarters to school with Lucy on the lead (otherwise she would be off to chase rabbits) and the girls would meet her at the school gates for the ramble home. There was an eerie passage through a green tunnel of tall rape crop, then over a stile into 'Daffodil Wood', as the girls called it. They always looked out for the woodpecker's nest that they had spotted in one of the trees there, and then they climbed over a five-bar gate for the short walk along a back road before turning down Cherry Garden Lane. This rough gravel track led beside hedgerows and flowery cornfield margins where rabbits and pheasants scuttled about, past an isolated old house known as 'Mount Ephraim'. There, a path turned off Cherry Garden Lane and through a 'kissing gate' into the back of the Bruderhof Community's grounds. The path meandered past a tree with a swing where the girls would sometimes stop to play, then down to a poignant little graveyard in a wood where the old owners of the mansion interred their pets. Lin and the girls would take a shortcut through an ancient studded wooden doorway into the grounds of the uninhabited manor that backed onto our house. They would arrive home about three-quarters of an hour after leaving the school, depending on how long Josie and Megan had played on the way home.

In the secure and relaxed company of their mother and their pet dog Lucy, Josie and Megan always seemed to find something absorbing and interesting to do on this homeward jaunt. Josie recorded this by drawing, in June 1996, a map of the route they regularly took, with points of interest marked along the way. Looking at this map, drawn in Josie's untutored hand, always brings a flood of emotions to me. It is innocently naive in the charming way that it portrays the extent of Josie's world, and it also encapsulates a feeling of enjoyment of these surroundings. There is a sense in the drawing that Josie feels secure in her environment; she has never experienced anything ominous or frightening in the world around her. Perhaps she has some of her parents' worldliness and confidence. She certainly seems to have inherited her geographer mother's skills, as the map is surprisingly accurate in scale and proportion for a nine-year-old. So accurate, in fact, that every footstep can be imagined, as Lin, Josie, Megan and Lucy sauntered and gambolled to the point on the map where they would be met by the individual who would destroy Josie's innocence and trust, and who would extinguish in the other three life itself.

One evening in late June I had arrived home to a particular sense of elation and excitement in the house. The children were smirking gleefully and there was a knowing smile on Lin's face. Josie and Megan nonchalantly let it drop that we had a new dog. They giggled and squirmed with delight at the look of puzzlement and disbelief that crossed my face. We still had our old golden retriever 'Jackie' and our little bundle of mischief, the shi-tzu–spaniel cross 'Lucy'. And we certainly weren't in the market for another dog – especially without consulting Dad!

Next thing I knew, the kids had dragged me to Josie's bedroom where, also squirming with joy, was a small but powerful-looking, brindled brown mongrel, who was barely more than a puppy. The kids informed me that they had named him 'Stitch'. Here, in Josie's own words, is the story of 'Stitch':

Me and Lin were riding in the lanes and I saw something moving in the bushes, we went to see what it was, and it was a dog. We just thought that it was OK. So we went back home and get a lead, and an hour later we walked up the hill to see if it was still there. And it was. The dog was terrified. So we assumed that it was a stray. So we tried to put a lead on it. But it bit me. So Lin did it and we took it home. And when we took it home we gave it lots of food. We kept it for a few days 'til our friend Jazzmin got it. I called it Stitch, but Jazzmin called it Jasper. It was one of my best times, when I found a dog.

'Stitch' seemed to have been abandoned. There had been a group of young travellers camping in a copse adjoining the hedgerow where Lin and Josie had found the dog. But the travellers had moved on a couple of days earlier. Maybe 'Stitch' had run off, only to return and find his owners gone. Whatever the reason for his plight, 'Stitch' was not claimed during the next week. We informed the police and the RSPCA, and we put up notices in nearby post offices. However, after ten days of keeping Stitch at home, with an extra dose of doggy fun for the kids every evening, we asked Josie to put the word out at school that we were looking for a new owner for 'Stitch'. Luckily, the family of one of Josie's closest friends, Jazzmin, were looking for a dog. And so, during the first week of July 1996 the girls said their goodbyes to 'Stitch' and we delivered him to the Kelly household in Snowdown. Just before we left on this mission I took a photo of both girls posing with 'Stitch'. It was to be one of the last photos taken of Megan alive.

On the last Saturday in June, the summer fete season now in full swing, we all went to a local village show. As we bumped into various friends there, we got the feeling that we truly were becoming part of the community now. The following weekend saw us involved in the Goodnestone village fete. It was held, as usual, courtesy of the 'Lord of the Manor', Lord Fitzwalter, in the grounds of his estate. Goodnestone School arranged a pageant, and Josie dressed up as an American Indian maiden, while Megan wore a white dress as one of the Maypole Dancers. On Sunday Lin and I worked on plans for some alterations to the house. It was a listed building and plans had to be done carefully for the local authority.

At about this time, Lin wrote what was to be her last letter, to relatives in the north of England regarding arrangements for our summer holiday:

Dear Aunty Joan and Uncle Tom
I can't believe it's July already. This year seems to be simply flying by. The children are beginning to do end-of-term type things at school. Shaun has just come back from his latest trip – a week in Lisbon and is now hoping to be here until September anyway, when I think Peru comes up again. So we're trying to organise some holiday for us now! We'd all love to come to your cottage again if that's O.K. Megan is keen to be there for her birthday again – Aug 15th – a Thursday. So – depending of course on your plans – and the soft fruit season – would a date around then suit you? . . .
 We still have Jackie, our old retriever with us – she's well over 12 now and getting very ancient, as well as Lucy, the little shi-tzu of course who's a real live wire. Sadly one of our cats got run over here we were all terribly upset. He was with Megs on her bed at 8

am and at 9.30 am a neighbour came to tell us he was dead at the side of the road . . . We were so lucky in Wales being so far from any roads. I think I will have to put them in the cattery – for the first time when we go away – they'll hate it, but at least I know they'll be safe.

The ponies are fine – haven't been stolen yet! I'm giving a few riding lessons on them to pay for their grazing which is working out well. . . . Will you be going to the Lleyn Peninsula again this summer? We hope to spend a few days in our old caravan on the way back down from the north. It will be good to see everyone there again, but in a way I'm rather dreading being at the house again – yet not being part of it. It will be very strange. . . .

Shaun's contract has been renewed here at last – but only for a year – until April next year – so we don't feel at all settled here and are still looking for jobs elsewhere. We'll just have to see what, if anything, turns up. Our cottage here is still in rather a state, although I have reclaimed the garden which now looks very pretty – with sweet peas, delphiniums etc. – all the tall, Englishy garden stuff, that just got blown down or eaten by slugs in Wales! So I suppose there are *some* advantages – a few anyway!

Give my love to Anne and family. I'll give you a ring this weekend to see what dates would suit you best.

Much love Lin   xxx.

Monday 8 July was fairly chaotic for me at work as I was moving office to a different part of the building, at the same time as having a research project planning meeting with one of my Masters degree students from the Ivory Coast. I had to leave early as Lin and I were due at Goodnestone School for one of the regular parent–teacher meetings to discuss the children's progress. So that evening, we all travelled home together in the car rather than the girls walking home with Lin.

The following day, Tuesday 9 July 1996, is marked simply with a large black spot in my diary. How else would you denote the worst day of your life?

The day started as usual with our getting the girls up, breakfasted and ready for the car ride to school. Lin came out with us into the bright and fresh morning air, brushing past the dew-laden plants that now crowded the garden. I said I'd collect some things in town and Lin reminded me that the girls were taking part in a swimming gala in Canterbury that day. Tuesdays were usually swimming days and, as the girls went in a school bus to Canterbury, I often arranged to pick them up directly from the swimming baths. Lin frequently came into Canterbury to meet us on these occasions, and we might do some shopping or have tea at a cafe or in the park before coming home together. On this fateful Tuesday, we decided not to follow this routine, partly because I was still busy at work moving my office.

Josie and Megan had been trying out Brownies after school, and Lin had accepted an offer from her friend Liz Gregson to take them to Brownies with her daughter at about five o'clock that evening. So Lin told me not to worry if they were home late, and I told her that I would probably also be working late but that I would cook supper if I got home first. Lin kissed me quickly goodbye as we hurried off to school, and the last time I saw her alive was as she turned to walk back to the house through her lovely garden, with the dogs trotting happily at her side. At Goodnestone I dropped the girls off outside the school, where I last remember them clad in their pale-blue gingham summer dresses running off to join their classmates. The scene was the normal confusion of shoulder bags, gym shoes and lunch boxes, with girlish shrieks and giggles blending with the whine and rumble of car engines as parents wrestled their vehicles around in the confines of the no-through road in which the school was situated. This little cul-de-sac would soon become even more congested, as every parent took to driving their children to school in the aftermath of the tragedy that was about to unfold.

By mid-afternoon of that day, around the time that Lin would have been picking up the girls from school, I ducked out of work to get some things in Canterbury. I checked at the cycle shop but my mountain bike was not quite ready yet. I walked up through the pedestrian precinct of Canterbury town centre, stopping to get money at the cash machine of Barclays Bank, and then I returned books that the children had borrowed from the town library. I returned to the university campus to re-immerse myself in the work that had built up over the couple of days when I had been moving my office.

At about seven that evening I decided to head home, arriving at about seven-thirty to an empty house with only our old retriever

Jackie to greet me. I was slightly surprised, as I thought that if the family had gone to Brownies at five, then they should have been back by now. I assumed that they had stayed on for extra activities, or gone home with Liz Gregson and her daughter Lucy for a while. I vaguely thought that Lin might have rung me to confirm this, but there was no message on the answer machine. So I quickly set about making the dinner, hoping to surprise Lin and the girls with a tasty vegetarian risotto by the time they got home. Around half past eight the phone rang and I rushed to it, expecting Lin to be on the other end. But it was Liz Gregson who told me that she had called at five o'clock to take Lin and the girls to Brownies, but that the house was shut up with nobody at home.

A feeling of unease spread over me as my mind raced for explanations. I told Liz the only reason that I could think of for Lin's absence would be that Lucy had escaped off the lead and got lost. I knew from previous experience that Lin would scour the countryside in such a situation, and would not rest until Lucy had been found. I guessed that possibly she had been out for so long with the children, that they might have called on or been invited in to friends in the neighbourhood and stayed on to recuperate after rushing around the fields. Or perhaps Lucy had been involved in an accident and Lin had prevailed on someone to take them to the vets where the dog could be treated. I was rationalizing, but I could tell that on the other end of the phone Liz was worried. I said I'd telephone around to the local vets, and she said she'd call back a bit later to see what I had found.

As Liz rang off I turned to put the dinner on hold while my mind buzzed with possibilities. I found myself thinking beyond the vets idea, to the notion of Lin or one of the children having been involved in an accident. I started phoning the local vets, only to find answer machines with messages to the effect that none were open at this time. On an impulse I jumped into the car and drove along the road to Sandwich, turning up Cherry Garden Lane as twilight crept across the land. Why I thought they might still be somewhere along the route home from school I do not know, but I had to satisfy myself that they were not coming home late along there, after being held up for some reason. I was still clinging on to the escaped Lucy notion. As I entered the tunnel of vegetation that enclosed the entrance to the lane, it was darkening and I switched the car's lights on briefly to see ahead. I drove swiftly up the bumpy track in our Subaru Estate, and emerged at the far end without seeing a soul. I had driven without knowing it, just a few feet from where my family were lying in the bushes beside the track. I drove on all the way to the school at Goodnestone and then back again around the road through Chillenden to Nonington. I saw only a jogger resting at a road junction, but there was no sign of Lin and the girls.

It was now nine o'clock at night and I started an increasingly urgent round of calls, first to my local police station which put me through to an operations centre that told me there had been no accidents reported that evening in our part of East Kent. Over the next hour I rang hospitals further and further afield, but none had admitted anybody by the name of Russell, or fitting the descriptions of my family. Just after ten o'clock Liz rang back to hear my quavering voice on the other end of the phone telling her that Lin and the girls were missing. She shouted to her husband John to get the car out, they were coming over straight away, and as soon as she hung up I was on the phone again to my local police station. They remembered my earlier call and now seemed genuinely concerned. It was dark and the police were unhappy that a woman and two young girls were unaccounted for at this time. The officer took down my descriptions of Lin and the girls, and where their last movements might have been. I was asked the inevitable questions about whether we had had an argument, or might Lin have had any other reason to take the kids away without my knowledge or consent. I was slightly pricked by the insinuation in this question, but by now I was too worried to be overly concerned at the suggestion. The officer said that he would dispatch two constables to the house at once to get more details from me.

Liz and John Gregson arrived, followed by the police at about eleven o'clock. I started giving them more thorough descriptions and telling them what I had already done that evening to find Lin and the girls. I winced in front of Liz as the questions about the state of my marriage cropped up again, but she rolled her eyes as though she knew they were barking up completely the wrong tree. Once more my mind was racing ahead to try and work out what had really happened. It was late enough now that I felt no embarrassment at calling out the police, but I was still clinging to the notion that a benign explanation could be found for Lin's and the girls' disappearance. The worst thing that

I now considered was that one of them might have been involved in an accident. I tried to avert painful thoughts of one or other of the girls being hit by a car as they walked down the narrow lanes near to home. It was possible if they had been chasing Lucy, and for the same reason it might have been somewhere away from the normal school route home. I speculated that one or other of the hospitals that I had phoned had simply failed to pass on the latest admissions information to the receptionist who took my earlier call. So Lin could be waiting with one or other of the girls in some emergency facility. But why hadn't she called me? She had never let me worry like this before. But still it never entered my mind that something more sinister might have befallen them.

The questioning continued and frustration started to impinge on the feeling of fear for my family's safety that was now consuming me. How long would this go on before the police started to do something? The question was answered almost immediately as, at about half past eleven, a bus full of police officers skidded into the gravel driveway next to Granary Cottage, accompanied by a white van with a dog search team. Unbeknown to me, the local police had started the ball rolling on gathering the team for a search operation as far back as the time of my first phone call. The officers who had been questioning me went out to brief the search team, and at about midnight they set off in the direction of Cherry Garden Lane.

Now I was starting to go numb with worry. My defence mechanisms were switching in and I became quieter and less communicative. My brain was not allowing me to think beyond hospitalization for one of the girls as the worst possible scenario. I was hanging on in a kind of limbo, with the vague hope that someone would arrive with Lin and the girls smiling and embarrassed in the back of their car, and some sort of rational explanation for it all. I accepted another cup of tea from Liz and John and we spoke very little as we paced up and down outside in the driveway in the darkness. Lights glowed in police cars parked at the end of the drive, and radios crackled. Suddenly, at about one o'clock in the morning, another police car pulled into the parking area near to the houses. From the darkness emerged the same two local police officers who had questioned me earlier. One spoke quietly to Liz and John while the other asked me in a subdued voice to accompany him back into the house.

I went hot and cold all over; somehow I knew at that moment that the worst had happened. As we walked towards the house I trembled with dread. I had seen it in the movies a hundred times, and now this poor policeman was making the same moves, the same body language. We sat down at the kitchen table with me still clutching my empty mug of tea, hardly able to breathe. He spoke quietly and with a quaver in his voice.

'I'm sorry to have to tell you, Dr Russell, that we have found your family, not far from here, and they have been in some sort of accident. It's very difficult for me to tell you this, but I'm afraid none of them have survived.'

If I was numb before, now I entered a state of complete suspended animation. My external functioning switched on to autopilot and I drifted away into a kind of grey oblivion. I had trained my brain since I was a child to avoid anguish and distress by blocking out painful thoughts and turning instead to optimistic and cheerful ones. But now, mentally, I had nowhere to go, nowhere to escape. The enormity of what was being told to me removed with one crushing blow any chance of optimism or happiness in my life. My mind simply froze into a dreamy, unthinking void. I have a vague recollection of seeing myself, as though from the outside, performing as if I were in a movie. I could hear myself slowly asking the policeman: Where?... When?... How?... Surely not all of them?

He could only answer falteringly himself. He explained that the circumstances were suspicious, there seemed to have been some sort of attack. He said that in all his career he had never had to do anything so terrible as this. Liz and John Gregson shuffled into the kitchen, eyes red with tears; they had been told by the other policeman what had happened. They hugged me but I was cold and distant. I was still floating.

'Would you like some more tea?'

'No thanks.'

'We will have to ask you to come to the police station in Deal to answer some more questions.'

'OK.'

'We will have to seal off the house tonight, would you like to sleep over with friends or relatives?'

'No thanks, I'll come with you now.'

In my dazed state I started showing the police and my friends how to feed the cats and the dogs, and I asked them to be sure that there would be someone around to care for them and the ponies. John and Liz assured me that they would look after the animals, and then they pressed me to come back to their house with them. I sensed that they were horrified that I should be whisked off in the middle of the night to a police station in my present state. They wanted to let me get some sleep in the protection and comfort of their home, before releasing me into the impersonal aftermath of police and press that was bound to engulf me.

However, far from wanting sleep or human contact, I craved isolation and anonymity. It was as though I had suddenly been born an orphan into a cold, grey, alien world. I needed time and space to take in this bleak new landscape, and to decide whether to try and survive in it, or just to curl up and die.

These thoughts started to build in my head. I could not bring myself to ask any more detail of the police. In any case they did not seem to know, or were not telling, exactly what had happened to my family. Instead I turned in on myself, so that by the time a police car was detailed to carry me in the early hours of the morning to Deal Police Station, I huddled up in the back like a lost and beaten child. Once out of sight of friends and neighbours, and in the darkness of the car with only an unknown police officer sitting beside me, I finally broke down. I remember shrieking with pain, and the tears rolling down my face. I shouted and swore obscenely, which I never normally do. 'What has happened to them? Where are they? Why has this happened?' In the heat of my rage my train of thought suddenly became more rational. 'They were everything to me. Now they have gone, I have nothing left. Therefore there is no reason to go on living.' And I started whining, 'There must be an easy way out. Someone help me. Isn't there some sort of injection? It can't be too hard to find.' The police officers in the car were obviously deeply moved themselves. They tried to comfort me as best they could. But I could tell they longed for the cross-country journey down the winding East Kent lanes to be over. And in my delirium I too yearned for my life's journey to be over.

It was about two in the morning by the time we reached Deal Police Station. I was asked again whether I would like to sleep over with friends or on a sofa in the police station. Blankets were proffered. I declined and was ushered quietly into an interview room where I sat down for the first time with Ed Tingley and Pauline Smith, the family liaison officers who had been called from their beds at midnight to look after me. So began my relationship with the two police officers who would be my friends, confidants and protectors over the coming months. I told Ed and Pauline that I was willing to answer questions or give whatever details they might need to start building a picture of events leading up to the time of Lin's and the girls' deaths.

I sat through the night with Ed and Pauline, hugging a mug of tea and gabbling absent-mindedly about the lives that Lin and I had led. I was given the option to have the tape recorder switched on or off, and I said I didn't mind. I realized in a hazy and distant way that police interest in me might be more than just concern for the bereaved family member of the victims.

After three hours or so I was left alone with more tea and a blanket, and I drifted in and out of shallow and fitful sleep for an hour, with the sound of activity going on elsewhere in the police station. I had emerged from my brief suicidal phase, but I was too tired and drained to think about what might come next. I now seemed to be at the bottom of a deep pit, with no need to struggle. In any case I had the peculiar sensation that I need not worry, the authorities would look after me. They would throw down food and water into my hollow and I would just do what they told me. I could abdicate all responsibility for my future; I was an empty person.

At about six o'clock, Ed came in with a serious expression on his face. What he had to tell me came as a complete bombshell, and at once changed everything. He said that, although they had initially thought all of my family were dead, one of the children had in fact survived. She had been rushed to a London hospital during the night, and was now on life support in an intensive care unit. A shaft of light seemed to scythe down into my abyss and illuminate my future with a sudden clarity. One of my family had survived! My addled brain was galvanized with hope. There was a reason to go on after all. I could take control of my life again, because once more there was a purpose: get to the hospital and, in holding my loved one, hold onto my own life and sanity.

The police and the hospital wanted to know which one of my daughters had survived. Ed asked me to describe them, and I told him that Josie had longer hair, whereas Megan's was cut shorter. He phoned the hospital and was told that the child in their care had short hair and so it was most likely to be Megan. Preparations were made to get Ed and myself to London. As people started coming in to work in the morning the machinery of a major murder enquiry was getting under way. One of the county's most experienced and successful investigating officers, Chief Inspector Dave Stevens, had been drafted in to take charge of the case. He was organizing the staggering logistics of an enquiry that would involve hundreds of officers and, at that moment, the crucial field and forensic operation at the murder scene. However, there were now more layers of bureaucracy and people to be satisfied before decisions could be taken on the case. And so it was nearly nine o'clock before a car could be found for Ed to drive me to London.

The journey was most uncomfortable. It was a hot July day. The car was small, musty and noisy. My head throbbed through lack of sleep, and I felt clammy in the clothes that I had been wearing for the last twenty-four hours. We sat in traffic jams on our way into London, and from my hunched position in the passenger seat I stared unseeingly at other bored and frustrated drivers.

We arrived at King's College Hospital on Denmark Hill, South East London, and Ed parked the car in a no-parking zone. We were passed from Reception to the Head Injuries Unit of the 'Variety Club Children's Hospital', and led to the front door of the Intensive Care Unit (ICU). Other police officers were present and hushed discussions took place as I tried to peer in through the glass door. A nurse then ushered us into the unit and pointed across to the nearest bed. Lying on it and half submerged beneath a mass of pipes, wires and tapes, was a small, heavily bandaged figure. Her face was black and blue and puffed up like a balloon. Her eyes were tight shut, but by the freckles across the top of her nose above the oxygen mask, I knew her instantly to be Josie. I shouted out 'It's Josie!' before I was halfway across the room, and Ed looked startled. He had assumed that it would be Megan, and he could not see how I could be so sure who it was from such a distance, and with the child in such a state. Josie had been shaved in preparation for her operation, which had led to the earlier description of her having short hair.

I bent over Josie and my face creased into a smile as my eyes filled with tears. Here was my reason for living, and if all she did was breathe, that would be enough for me. I did not dare touch her, for fear of interfering with the spider's web of ducts and catheters trailing from her body; I knew that they were keeping her alive, and that was all that mattered. After a while of my gazing at her fixedly, Ed interrupted my concentration with a plea to come and meet the doctor in charge. We were only able to talk briefly and no one could give me any prognosis as to Josie's chances of survival. She had major skull fracturing and serious brain injuries and she was due to go into surgery for an operation to investigate and attempt to repair some of this damage. She would need scans and X-rays as well, and the doctors would only be able to give a partial prognosis by the following day. In the meantime, I was told, there was nothing I could do but await the outcome of the tests and the operation.

Ed took me to the hospital canteen for a drink and we started to discuss plans for the rest of the day. I was aware that the police needed to interview me in detail as soon as possible, in order to eliminate me from suspicion and clear the way for the rest of the enquiry. Ed explained that as the vast majority of woman-and-child murders are carried out by spouses or lovers, I was an automatic suspect and had to be eliminated from the enquiry as soon as possible. I understood fully that it was a matter of routine, and I undertook to assist the police to the best of my ability. People are often horrified that I was considered a 'prime suspect' at this most sensitive time, and are curious to know how it felt. At the time it did not worry me in the slightest, as I had much more important things on my mind. Of course I knew I was innocent of any crime and had no reason to fear interrogation. But being a suspect just wasn't a major concern for me, as I was now concentrating on organizing my life so that I could be near to Josie, even if she wasn't going to be with me for much longer.

My brain was starting to engage again, and I put the wheels in motion to secure a parents' room, so that I could be near to Josie in the ICU. Then I received a phone call via Ed's mobile. It was my neighbour in Kent who had bought the, as yet unlived-in, manor house next door to us. He worked in the Home Office in the Inspectorate of Constabulary, and had heard about the murders on the police grapevine. His was the first of many hundreds of sympathetic condolences that I was to receive over the coming weeks and months. It reminded me that my next and most pressing task was to ring Lin's parents to break the terrible news that their only daughter had been killed. I dreaded this task more than any, and I sat with Ed in the hospital canteen going over and over in my mind how I could possibly give them the tidings that would break their hearts. Ed explained that it was normal in such cases for a police family liaison officer like himself to be first to break the news; and that this was usually done in person with a house call. They had already arranged for an officer from the Birmingham police force to visit Peter and Irene in Sutton Coldfield that day. I felt that it would be shirking my responsibility for Lin's parents to hear of their daughter's death from someone other than their son-in-law. But as we were discussing this, we heard a report about the murder on the radio midday news coming over the canteen public address system. Ed looked taken aback that the news should have got out so quickly, and in sufficient detail that Lin's identity could have been recognized by friends or relatives.

A request then came through that I return to Canterbury, to begin the police interviews. It would also allow me to make a flying visit home to equip myself for a long stay at the hospital. The house had been cordoned off for forensic work and I would not in any case be able to return there to stay for many days to come. And so, after checking again that there was nothing more we could do at the hospital, we made the long, hot journey back to Canterbury, by which time I had composed myself sufficiently to speak to Peter and Irene on the phone.

As soon as I heard Peter's voice on the other end of the line, I could tell that he already knew. Irene had heard the item on the midday news as we had done, and was now in bed at home suffering from shock. The local doctor had been called and was looking after her, and in the mid-afternoon a police officer had knocked on the door to confirm the tragic news. Peter sounded as though all the stuffing had been knocked out of him. He could hardly speak, and his grief touched me so that I found myself faltering over the brave lines that I had rehearsed. I abandoned my attempts to console him over the phone and instead promised to ring him later with news of Josie as and when we received it. Peter promised in turn to come to the hospital to see Josie as soon as Irene was fit to travel (the police had offered to provide transport for them). I was learning myself that when you have lost the most important thing in your life, it is like a smack in the face and an insult to the memory of your loved one to be told to cheer up or that you will get over it in time.

Next followed a series of calls to my mother and sister, who were also in shock at the news, and to other close friends and relatives. The rest of the day was spent on the trip back to Granary Cottage where Pauline was allowed into the cordoned-off house to fetch some overnight things, including teddies for Josie. I sat outside in the car in a world of my own. The family home now just seemed like an empty shell in the distance and I had no urge to go back inside or face the signs of our life there. After making sure the animals were being looked after, we headed back to Canterbury. I then started with Ed and Pauline on the first of several long sessions of statement-taking, where I began to recount my and Lin's entire life stories for the enquiry record.

Later that evening we rang the hospital to see how things were going, and were told that Josie had been operated on and that she was in a stable condition. We were given a time for a meeting with the doctor the next day, when the results of the surgery and the other tests would be described to us. As it was now very late, I agreed to stay overnight in Canterbury. The police explained that media interest in the case was intense. Journalists and TV news teams had been descending on Canterbury and the Nonington area in droves and the story was on the front pages of all the next day's newspapers. To avoid the press, I was put up at a small hotel away from the centre of town. In the early hours, as I was turning in for the night I received a phone call from an old friend of Lin's in America. She had heard about the tragedy from her mother and sister in the UK and was already making plans to fly over to be with us at the hospital.

So ended the worst day of my life. I had experienced a wider and deeper range of emotions, in a shorter period of time, than ever before in my existence. My life had changed in a few short hours from one of stability and normality to one of deep anxiety and trauma. I had been projected into an extreme world of urgency and stress, un-familiar people and alien priorities. Before, I had always had Lin as my rock, to return to and rely on whenever things became too much for me. Now there was nobody to whom I could turn for that closeness and understanding. Instead, I had now to be the rock for myself, but most of all for my unconscious daughter, clinging to life in a hospital bed fifty miles from where I lay. Notwithstanding my tiredness, I slept little that night.

The next day we drove up to London early and found Josie, as before, swathed in bandages in the ICU. Her condition was described as stable, and so we waited for our appointment with the doctors. At the allotted time, Professor Charles Polky, the consultant neuro-surgeon who had led the team working on Josie the night before, entered the room. He was a tall and imposing figure, grey and bespectacled, and he obviously inspired awe and respect in the staff around him. He launched straight into an enthusiastic description of the damage to Josie's skull, with an occasional giggle like an eccentric scientist immersed in an explanation of his favourite subject. He had had to remove several pieces of broken bone, and cut back the damaged brain to intact tissue; in medical terminology 'she underwent debridement and excision of the severely damaged area of the brain underlying the comminuted left fractures'. The surgeons had had to make a long incision down Josie's left thigh to remove membrane surrounding her leg muscle, in order to use it to cover the torn cranial membrane over her brain. Josie had scratches and abrasions in many places on her body, including a torn right ear that had to be stitched. There were also bruises where the instrument that was used to beat her head had glanced off and hit her shoulders. Some of the others in the meeting glanced at me nervously in case the surgeon's manner was upsetting me. But in my career as a scientist I had met many colleagues like him, and I appreciated his candour. I had already started to experience the sometimes cloying sympathy of people around me, and I was thankful for Professor Polky's directness.

I had been told by people attending Josie the previous night that my surviving daughter was critically ill, with massive skull fracturing and serious brain damage. She was only being kept alive by life-support machines. It was 'a miracle' that she had survived at all; the police had already ascertained that she had lain for a long time with her injuries before being discovered. I was expecting, therefore, that if she survived at all, then at best I would be nursing a severely disabled person, possibly in a 'vegetative' state. I was prepared for this, but I was far less sure how I might handle a life or death decision. I was terrified that, as the closest relative, I might be called upon to consent to 'pulling the plug' on Josie's life support system, if it became clear that she was a hopeless case.

However, as Professor Polky moved from his explanation of the awful extent of Josie's injuries to a cautious prognosis for Josie's recovery, it slowly dawned on me that he was not talking about her chances of survival at all. He was saying that she would be likely to have impaired speech and language, some hearing difficulty and possibly some right-side physical disability. I couldn't believe what I was hearing. I cut in and started to press him on his statements.

'You mean she is unlikely to die?'

'Oh no, she won't die.'

'And you really think she will walk again?'

'She might have a limp.'

'But how can a person lose so much brain and not be severely disabled?'

'We see many cases like this, and as she is still young her brain will mend itself.'

'But how can you be so sure that her speech will be the only major problem area?'

'Because it is that specific part of her brain that deals with speech and language that has been most damaged. However, we have seen cases where the verbal capacity shifts to the other side of the brain as recovery proceeds.'

Suddenly my expectations were moved onto a whole new plane. Here, then, was the real miracle; that someone could suffer such terrible physical injuries and emerge with such a good chance of survival, and even recovery. Another specialist explained that Josie may only have survived because her skull fractures were so extensive. It meant that there was less of a pressure build-up in her skull as the brain swelled following the injury. Josie also had a very low body temperature when she was admitted to the hospital, and this too may have contributed to her survival, by reducing the swelling and the blood loss. The doctors must have seen the anguish slowly abating in my face as the meeting proceeded. They were quick to point out that Josie was not yet 'out of the woods' by a long shot, that her recovery would be long, drawn out and painful, and that there was always a chance of unforeseen complications and a relapse. However, I left the meeting greatly encouraged and with an intense feeling of gratitude, both to the doctors who had 'patched Josie up' with such skill and dedication, and to fate itself, which had spared my one daughter and now seemed to be pointing us both along a new path of hope.

Back in the ICU Josie was as before, and I alternated between periods of sitting with her and going with Ed and Pauline to a nearby anteroom where we continued with my statement-taking. This ICU served the Children's Hospital head injuries and liver disease patients: there was a tiny baby opposite Josie who was a liver transplant patient and had spent the entire first two months of his life in the ICU. His parents were already old hands at the routine of the ward and showed me what I could do to help the sorely pressed nurses. The nurses were pleased to accept our help on routine tasks around the ward as they were so overworked and stressed by the harrowing conditions in the unit. One of the medical orderlies explained how there was a high turnover of staff on the unit due to the stress levels. She said she herself was taking two weeks unpaid leave to go to Majorca, and she did not know if she could bear to come back to work there again.

From the moment that Josie had been admitted to hospital, she had been watched over by police guards. The police had concerns that the murderer might try to return to silence Josie, as she was the only likely witness to the crime. They were also worried about the intense media interest that was building around the case, and they wanted to prevent press intrusion. The officers who carried out this security duty certainly picked the short straw as they had to sit for hours at a time amid the hot and stressful conditions of the ward. They were not permitted to leave their posts without first arranging suitable cover, and yet I discovered that they had all volunteered for the task when hearing of Josie's predicament. They came from various police stations around Kent, but mainly from Dartford. The older officers, especially the women, were particularly sympathetic to Josie and quickly became involved wherever they could with assisting the nursing staff in ministering to Josie's needs. Several of the younger male officers had a far harder time coming to terms with the situation, and often could not bear to sit in the ward or get too close to the action. I found myself in long, subdued conversations with some of them, which helped to ease my stress and get things off my chest as well.

The name of the hospital where Josie was being treated was not made public, and the press were respecting this secrecy. However, my closest friends and relatives were being given the telephone number of the ward as they desperately tried to contact me to offer their sympathy and support. I found myself, therefore, fielding an ever increasing number of fraught calls from devastated friends and relatives who were still in shock at the news. Helping them to cope allowed me to put my own grieving on hold and to avoid slipping into deeper despair and desolation. There was not a minute in the day to stop and brood over my misfortune.

In any case, I felt strongly that mine was not a consequential hardship. The guilt of the survivor was festering inside me. I was asked if I would like to speak to people from Victim Support but I replied with uncharacteristic vehemence that I was 'not a victim'. The true victims of this crime were Lin, Megan, Josie and even poor Lucy. But I could never be characterized in the same manner. I had escaped scot-free from this calamity. Why did it have to happen this way? Lin was a better person than me; Josie and Megan had their whole lives ahead of them. Why couldn't I have been the one to be taken? I developed an irrational distaste for the term 'victim' as applied to myself, and I was developing the same antipathy for the word 'cope'. 'How are you coping?' everybody would say. It wasn't their fault. What else can you say to somebody in my position? They were trying to show their concern and sympathy. But, illogically, inside me I was more irritated than soothed by these attempts to help. I felt that I didn't deserve it.

We grabbed a bite to eat whenever we could in the hospital canteen, and it was a surreal experience to hear the reports of the murders and the police statements about my family coming over the radio news.

I continued to press for a parents' room so that I could be near to Josie overnight. The hospital authorities told me that I could have a room the following night, but this meant that I still had to find a place to sleep for the coming evening. Parents were not allowed to sleep in the ICU and my lack of sleep over the last forty-eight hours was catching up with me. I asked Ed and Pauline about staying over at a nearby hotel or guest house, and there was a pregnant pause. Ed said in a quiet voice, 'The chief investigating officer and the coroner want you to come back to Canterbury tonight, so that you can identify Lin's and Megan's bodies tomorrow.'

A shock of adrenalin flooded through my system and I grasped for a chair to sit down in. I had been yo-yoing back and forth between periods of hope and despondency. The hectic activity of the last few hours had kept me fully occupied and prevented my mind from wandering off into darker avenues of thought. But now I was plunged back into deep despair. I just wasn't ready for this. I had buried Lin and Megan in my subconscious as I fixed on Josie and her needs. And I had immersed myself in my duties to others around me. However, no amount of repression of my feelings and fears would save me from the agony of the task that I now had to face. The tears flow again as I remember my whimpered reply to Ed: 'Do I have to?'

As would occur many times in the future, Ed and Pauline were torn between their pragmatic duty and their sympathy for me in my torment. They explained how the closest relatives are usually asked to identify the bodies of deceased persons, so as to avoid the likelihood of mistaken identity. Pauline was deeply moved by my reaction, I could see she wanted to offer me a way out. But there was none. I knew I had to go through with it. And what was worse, they said that we had to find a second person to face the same trauma, in order to confirm the identification.

And so, after checking once again that there was nothing more I could do for Josie (she was still unconscious, but stable and 'not in danger' on her life-support machines), I travelled gloomily back with Ed and Pauline to Canterbury that evening. I was starting to shiver with horror at the thought of what I would have to face at the mortuary the following day. My tired body winced at the thought of another sleepless night at the hotel in Canterbury. But once again, fate seemed to throw out a lifeline. There, waiting at the hotel, was our old friend from South Africa who now lived in America and had made it across the Atlantic in double-quick time. She had found a place to stay with friends nearby and she was now ready to help in any way that she could. Here, at last, was someone I could be myself with, and with whom I did not have to put on a front. I spilled out my thoughts and emotions, and the dread that devoured me about facing the battered and lifeless bodies of my loved ones the next day. In my forlorn state I appealed to our friend to accompany me to the mortuary and I asked if she would be willing to be the second person that the police wanted for the task of identification. It was a terrible, selfish act to shift this burden onto her. I hated asking anybody to do anything for me, let alone this most awful of tasks. But I felt that I had no one left to turn to. I could see that she was shaken by my request, but she bravely agreed. And because of her sacrifice I turned in that night a little less terrified of the ordeal that lay ahead. I was thus able at last to snatch a couple of hours of blessed and restoring sleep.

The following day (Friday 12 July 1996) anxiety ate away at me as the preparations went ahead for the visit to the mortuary at the Kent and Canterbury Hospital. Ed and Pauline picked me up, and we met with Dave Stevens and the assistant coroner. They explained about the procedure before we made our way to the anonymous rear entrance of the mortuary. I stopped them to ask how Lin and Megan would appear, and it was explained to me that they would be swathed and that only their faces would be visible. The assistant coroner said that neither Lin nor Megan had any facial injuries. I stood outside with Pauline while the others went inside to make the arrangements. We were ushered into an anteroom next to the viewing area. Few words were spoken and the assistant coroner eventually asked if I was ready to go in. My cowardice welled up again and I asked for some more time to compose myself. My friend from America went in first with Pauline. After a minute or so she emerged stumbling on Pauline's arm, with tears rolling down her face. I averted my gaze, I could not go to her, I was holding everything back in reserve for my own test. Quickly I asked, 'Can we go in now?'

I was biting my lip with apprehension and trembling with fear as I entered the room. There, some distance across the room, were Lin and Megan, feet towards me, each laid on a trolley side by side. White sheets covered their bodies and the upper parts of their heads so that their hair was not visible (it would in any case have been shaved off to facilitate the pathologist's investigation). I had to shuffle closer to see their faces. There was no sign of damage or injury. Their eyes were closed and their mouths, grey-lipped, set in straight lines. They looked neither happy nor sad. Quite peaceful, just utterly and completely lifeless. I stared bleakly at them for a few seconds. I could feel myself losing control. I didn't want to do this. I didn't want to see them like this. This is not how I want to remember my perfect ones. Yet I knew in those few seconds that this ghastly image would remain with me forever, and defile my memory of them both. It was just too awful. I turned and blurted out to Ed, 'Yes that's Lin and Megan,' and ran for the door. Outside I cowered in the corner of the waiting room as the tears flowed and my body racked with sobs. Pauline and my friend tried to comfort me until I collapsed onto the sofa and covered my face. Slowly my anguish ebbed and I tried to pull myself together. The assistant coroner said, 'This is a very unusual situation and I have not had to do this before, but I'm afraid, Dr Russell, that we're also going to have to ask you to identify your dog'.

My weeping had calmed me, and with the worst part now over, I agreed to this next surreal experience. A side door to the waiting room opened and there, out in the corridor, was a stainless steel instrument trolley. On it, lying on her side with her head stiffly outstretched and her fur all wet and tousled, was Lucy. I gazed at her for a while and thoughts of the way that she must have died tried to force their way into my consciousness. I shook my head to expel them quickly and sighed, 'Yes, that's Lucy,' before returning to the waiting room.

I mumbled my gratitude to my friend and we shuffled out of the mortuary to the waiting cars. Guilt nagged at me again. I felt terrible at leaving Lin and Megan there alone to be returned to their cold metal cabinets. 'When will I be able to bury them?' I asked the assistant coroner. He explained that he wanted to retain the bodies for some time longer, and that it was normal for a second post-mortem to take place in cases of murder. This was often undertaken by a specialist other than the police pathologist, to ensure lack of bias. This was in case the murderer was detained and the defence lawyers required post-mortem results from an independent source.

In the afternoon we hurried back to the hospital in London. My friend from America was horrified to see the state of Josie, but as we discussed her condition with the nurses, one of them said, 'Oh she's breathing strongly by herself now, we can probably take her off the respirator tomorrow.' We looked at each other in amazement. 'In fact she should be coming out of her post-operative coma in the next twenty-four hours and then we can probably move her to the HDU over the weekend.' (The High Dependency Unit [HDU] is a room next to the normal recovery ward, where patients in a less critical condition than those in ICU can be monitored.) We could not believe what we were hearing. It was only three days since Josie had been admitted. We expected her to be in a coma for weeks. But now we were being told that she might be off life-support within hours.

With a lighter heart I set about getting myself installed in the parents' room which had become available since I had been away. The room was only a few metres from the ICU. It was airless and musty, and smelled of stale fish and chips and cigarette smoke. But this little haven was to be my bolt-hole and sanctuary for the next six weeks that I spent with Josie in the hospital. My task was made easier by my friend's presence. She started taking some of the phone calls, and she sat with Josie whenever I was called away.

I went back into the anteroom to do more work with Ed and Pauline on my statement. By now it had reached nearly eighty pages and covered almost our entire life stories. Our backgrounds and origins had to be explained: every problem we had ever faced; anybody in the world who might have had a grudge against any one of us; our financial situation in minute detail – all had to be included.

Early in the evening my friend knocked on the door of the anteroom and there was a tearful smile on her face as she peered around the door. 'I've got a surprise for you,' she said. We followed her back into the ICU, where I looked again across at Josie. Her eyes were no longer closed. Not really open either, just narrow slits through which her pupils glistened glassily. But her head moved and I found myself close up beside her whispering, 'Josie?' And to my astonishment her lips twitched back into the faintest little smile and her head moved towards me, but with eyes unfocusing. I looked round and beamed at the others. Those dratted tears welled up inside me again.

Pauline was overjoyed. I know that she had worried about me bottling up my emotion all week. She had not seen the tears that I shed at night when nobody was near. She had been overcome herself at the mortuary, yet she was relieved that I had finally let go, even though it was tears of anguish that I cried. But now there were tears of joy as we watched Josie's first signs of life, other than the electrical traces on the machines at her bedside. The nurses did not want us to stimulate Josie too much, as she was waking. And so, with a kiss on her forehead I had to leave her. In cases of such severe head injury the worry is that electrical activity across the broken nerve endings in the brain will induce fitting and epilepsy. Josie was, therefore, heavily sedated with anti-convulsant drugs. Nevertheless, the 'miraculous resurrection' that I had witnessed lifted my spirits and that night in my dank little room I got in a few extra hours of uninterrupted sleep.

The following day (Saturday 13 July) I woke up and headed for the ICU again, only to be greeted by another joyful sight. The oxygen mask was off Josie's face and the respirator machine had been pushed back. She was breathing on her own and she seemed contentedly asleep. My friend and I took turns once more, watching over her during the day and experiencing the wonder of her waking and smiling at us again on several occasions. I completed the bulk of my statement-taking with Ed and Pauline (they seemed to work a seven-day week with only a couple of hours a night for sleep). Then we assisted with the task of moving Josie, as predicted, to the HDU. Here she was in a smaller room with only a handful of other young patients. Life-support machinery was less in evidence, although standing by in case of relapses or complications with the patients. The walls were covered with bright pictures and paintings, many of them signed by pop stars and sportspeople who had come to the hospital to raise the children's spirits. Josie was provided with a special high-powered lamp that projected soothing coloured images onto the ceiling above her. This was supposed to exercise her vision and stop her getting bored.

Just before midday I went back to my room to spruce myself up. The police had provided a car and were bringing Lin's parents all the way from Sutton Coldfield to see us at the hospital. I waited for them at the entrance to the HDU and saw them approaching down the long central passageway of the ward outside. Irene hobbled towards me with a police officer supporting her on one side. She looked crippled with grief. Peter supported her on the other side and looked as though he had aged ten years. Their eyes were sunken and red with sorrow and we sobbed again as we embraced each other. I explained to them about Josie's appearance (she was still discoloured, swollen and bandaged) and I could see Peter and Irene bracing themselves for the entrance. As we ushered them into the HDU, they moved unflinchingly to Josie's bedside, greeting her with smiles and kisses. Josie returned the compliment with another of her dreamy smiles, which uplifted us all, and Irene pressed a little teddy into Josie's limp hand. They talked to her softly and encouragingly, showing not a sign of their inner turmoil, and I could see where Lin had got her courage and fortitude from.

After a while we left Josie alone and retired to the anteroom for a cup of tea. Peter questioned me on the events of the tragic day and told me again of how they had come to learn of Lin's death over the radio. He pressed me for more information on the police investigation and Ed explained as much as they knew. We knew that pressure from the media was building and that sooner or later we would have to face the press. I pledged to Irene and Peter that I would shoulder this responsibility and that they should not concern themselves with this aspect. Before they left for the journey back to Sutton Coldfield Peter took me to one side. He wanted to talk about Lin and we remembered her wonderful qualities.

'She was so strong, so unafraid,' we agreed.

'But,' he said plaintively, 'don't you think she was a bit naive to go walking alone with the kids in the countryside?'

I was stung with guilt at his cry from the heart. Lin and I had been used to such a free and easy life overseas. We had never encountered violence at first hand and we had returned to the UK with a rose-tinted picture of life as it was thirty years before, of our childhoods when we played in the woods without fear. If only I had insisted that Lin always drove or got a lift to school, then none of this might ever have happened. But as these thoughts rose up to torment me, so I realized as quickly that it was no use torturing ourselves with what might have been. For one thing, Lin and I were not the kind of couple who ever 'insisted' on anything with each other. Secondly, walking wherever possible rather than driving was a central tenet of Lin's green philosophy; and what had the world come to if we dare not even walk with our children the mile or so to school through the pleasant countryside of southern England? I was rationalizing, but my guilt was surfacing again.

Then I realized that Peter wasn't trying to apportion blame. He was struggling as we all were with a despairing lack of comprehension of the obscene deed that had brought his daughter's life to a premature end. I watched him walk slowly away, supporting Irene as they moved haltingly towards the door of the ward. Their lives had been blameless. Why should they be made to suffer so?

On the Monday I had a boost to my spirits, as Lin's best friend from Wales arrived to help in any way she could. She had been our next-door neighbour when we lived at Plas Tan-yr-Allt, and was Lin's closest ally and companion whenever I was away. With two friends now helping out at the hospital, life was suddenly much easier for me. We could take it in turns to be with Josie so that she was never without a familiar face nearby. I could start to juggle the pressures of the outside world that were building. There was to be a re-enactment of the crime back at Goodnestone, and the police were asking me if I could give a press conference to appeal for help from the public to find the murderer. I was already worrying about where I should bury Lin and Megan as I did not want them cremated. I had to cancel meetings that I had been due to attend in the coming weeks, and I had also to put in place cover for myself on the various projects with which I was involved around the world.

Letters from well-wishers across Britain and from further afield had started to pour in. I began a daily routine of spending an hour in my room going through the burgeoning mailbag, reading with sadness the terrible tales of loss and longing expressed in many of the letters by people who had also suffered family bereavements. Some of these letters were inspiring and uplifting and there were several from young children. I was also humbled that some very distinguished people had taken the time to communicate with me. My local MP from the Dover constituency wrote a kind and helpful letter, as did the Duchess of Kent. The Archbishop of Canterbury also wrote to me, giving his personal signature and adding his direct telephone number in case I wanted to reply. However, the letters that moved me the most were those from Josie's and Megan's two teachers in Wales, Susan Owen and Sîan Thomas. They both had such wonderful things to say about Lin, they obviously missed her terribly, and their words about Megan and Josie were not just the kind comments of teachers concerning their past pupils. Susan and Sîan had spent more time with my daughters than anyone other than Lin and myself. Their letters revealed the aching pain that they too were feeling over their loss.

There was one very important person who still did not know about Lin's and Megan's deaths. That afternoon, I met for the first time with the psychologist assigned to the team of specialists who would oversee Josie's recovery. She presented me with another bombshell for which I had not prepared myself: 'We are going to have to tell Josie that her mother and her sister are dead.'

Hurt But Holding On

I t had been a week since Josie was attacked. She lay in her bed in the HDU of Lion Ward, King's College Hospital, with drip tubes attached to her body supplying her with fluids and nourishment. She did not need respiratory assistance or blood transfusion any longer, but she was receiving heavy doses of anti-convulsant and painkiller. She could move her mouth from side to side, and she often clenched and ground her teeth. But she could not suck or swallow, and no intelligible sound had come from her mouth since she was admitted. She was incontinent and had to wear a nappy, and she had to be manhandled by nurses for her bathing and toilet. Her body was floppy and uncontrolled when moved, but she showed some resistance and struggled as best she could against the stimulation.

Josie's eyes were more open now, but still glazed with a heavily drugged appearance. Her facial swelling had lessened somewhat, and the enormous operation scar under the bandages on the left side of her head seemed neat and clean. However, there were two ragged punctures on the back of Josie's head beneath which the white skull bone was visible. The bone was badly bruised but not broken at these points, and the doctors were waiting to see if the edges of the wounds would repair and grow back over these openings without the need for skin grafts.

As Josie now seemed to be stable and not at risk of life-threatening relapses, the decision was made to move her from the HDU into the general recovery ward. For reasons of privacy and security, Josie was given a room to herself, the closest to the nursing station in the ward. It was surrounded by curtained-off glass walls and there was room for a couple of cupboards and chairs in addition to the bed. Dee Bowden, the ward's family support worker, had been hard at work organizing everything for me to stay comfortably at the hospital. She was able to squeeze a folding chair-bed into a corner of Josie's room for me. It meant that I could now stay right beside Josie every night, and that any friend helping me could use the parents' room. Josie was coming round and was showing more signs of restlessness and distress as her consciousness returned; I wanted to be near her in case she needed me at any time of night or day. And still a police officer always sat at the door to Josie's room.

A week after Josie was admitted to hospital, I was sitting talking to our police guard when the Children's Hospital's senior psychologist and a consultant neurologist approached. The day before we had discussed how we were going to break the news to Josie about the death of her mother and sister. The police were satisfied for us to proceed as we saw fit, and now was the time to go through with it. I had expected to be the one who would do this, but the medical and psychological staff advised against it. They wanted to be the first to break the news to Josie, so that they could take the brunt of any adverse reaction she might show. They explained that this would allow Josie to see me more as her comforter rather than her tormentor. However, I would be expected to follow up their initial breaking of the news with gentle reinforcement of the central message. There was to be no skirting around the issue.

Once again I felt guilty; surely this should be my responsibility, not that of a stranger? However, I eventually agreed to the plan. The specialists woke Josie from sleep and she lay on her side with her face on the pillow looking towards them. I stood behind the two as they crouched down beside Josie and started talking to her soothingly. They talked about the bad experience of the attack that Josie had suffered the week before. There were no euphemisms; no 'Mummy's not coming back for a long time', or 'Megan's gone to heaven'. The psychologist simply stated that Lin and Megan were dead as a result of the attack. At this, Josie hauled herself abruptly over onto her other side and faced the wall. She didn't cry, just kept on grinding her teeth and trying to go back to sleep again.

Then it was my turn to repeat the message to Josie. I followed through by telling her how devastated I was by the terrible events of the week before. I told her how sorry I was for her, but that she was getting better and I was by her side to look after her. I couldn't tell if Josie was really hearing or understanding me, and the presence of the other people in the room made it difficult for me to speak as I felt. I forced myself to carry on, telling Josie that Lin and Megan were truly gone forever and they would not be coming back. Finally it became too much for me and I wheeled away, bursting into tears again. Then my two friends both bravely committed themselves to the same process of trying to explain to Josie what had happened to her and her family. The specialists were sure that they had got through to Josie. I was unconvinced. I thought that she was so heavily drugged and sleepy that she would be unable to comprehend what was being told to her. I thought it just as likely that she turned away at the time of the initial explanation, so as to avoid the unfamiliar faces of the specialists pressed up close to hers. Whether Josie understood or not, we followed the psychologist's advice and talked about Lin and Megan in the past tense from then on whenever we were in Josie's presence. Over the next few weeks, therefore, as Josie slowly regained her awareness, she was left in no doubt that her mother and sister had really died.

By now various therapists had started coming to see Josie, getting her moving physically and mentally, and assessing her responses. Early attempts were made to get Josie to sit up and stand beside her bed, but without success at first. However, she was helped to sit in a wheel-chair for a few minutes, and she seemed to be at ease there. When awake in her bed, Josie had started to roll and thrash about as though she were already getting bored and frustrated.

On Thursday 18 July, nine days after Josie was admitted to the hospital, the first meeting was held of the full range of specialists who were to handle Josie's recovery. The team was headed by Dr Marion Crouchman (consultant neurodevelopmental paediatrician) who was to play the leading role in coordinating Josie's treatment, as well as liaising with the police. Other people present at the meeting included nursing staff and the family support worker, the occupational therapist, the physiotherapist, the speech therapist and the play coordinator. It was again emphasized that because of her injuries there was no guarantee that Josie would recover her speech. However, it was thought likely that due to the localization of the brain damage, Josie's intelligence and memory should escape relatively unscathed.

The physiotherapist stated that Josie could not sit herself up or stand at this stage, but that she had good head control. She had distinct right arm weakness as the surgeon had predicted, but her right leg seemed fine. She could 'fix and follow' objects with her eyes only poorly and her attention span was only a few seconds long. However, I was heartened by his confidence that Josie would walk and run again without too many problems. It was decided that from then on daily physiotherapy sessions would take place, and that occupational therapy would be phased in. It was also decided to start experimenting with food intake by mouth, so that Josie's drips could be removed. She was already showing signs of frustration with the tubes still attached to her, and she was now trying to rip them out at every opportunity.

So began a regimen that would govern our lives through the summer months of 1996 in Lion Ward. It was a hot and humid summer and I was now sleeping in Josie's airless room every night. She preferred to shut out the light and noise of the ward, and the door was, in any case, closed most of the time for security reasons. We needed fans to cool us during the night, and every morning I got into my 'battle kit' of light cotton shorts and tee-shirt to face the heat and toil of the day ahead, going barefoot about the ward. Washing and toileting Josie, dressing her and changing the bed, dealing with her physical struggling and her efforts to tear out her drip tubes, attempting to feed Josie by mouth and wheeling her around the ward strapped into a wheelchair: these activities kept me constantly on the go and, coupled with the mental stress, caused me to lose nearly two stone in weight in as many months. My waistline contracted to a diameter that I had not experienced since I was a student, and my new habit of shaving revealed an increasingly gaunt look to my face over the summer period. The few minutes spent shaving and relaxing in a hot bath each day were about the only quiet times that I ever got to myself. To this day, the act of shaving often brings back memories of how important those calm and solitary moments were for the maintenance of my equilibrium and sanity.

How I could have coped without Lin's two friends I do not know. They helped me immeasurably to shoulder the physical and emotional burden of caring for Josie during those traumatic first weeks of her recovery. They took it in turns to help out at the hospital, returning to their families for brief respite and recuperation every few days, before throwing themselves back into the fray again.

However, there was never any room for self-pity in the Children's Hospital. In fact what struck me immediately I ventured out into the general ward, was how minor Josie's predicament seemed compared to that of some of the other children on the ward. We had all these positive prognoses about Josie's recovery to give us hope, and every day we watched her became stronger and more vigorous. There were children alongside Josie, however, who had been in hospital for weeks and months. Some of them were in a desperate state, especially the patients with cerebral palsy who had to have repeated operations to relieve fluid pressure build-up within their skulls. The anguish suffered by the parents of some of these terminally ill children was dreadful, yet they all seemed to find such reserves of strength and courage to face their worst nightmares, and to be always positive and cheerful for their children's sake. Many of these parents were very concerned and helpful to Josie and me, and I felt ashamed at the growing hysteria in the newspapers over Josie's plight, when there were such unsung stories of bravery and selflessness being played out all around us in Lion Ward.

After two weeks in the hospital, Josie was losing the glazed and unseeing look in her eyes, but was still fairly heavily drugged and clearly not understanding much of what was going on around her. She was starting to sit up more strongly, and she looked forward to her wheelchair excursions around the ward and further afield through the labyrinthine passageways of the hospital. In her physiotherapy sessions she was being helped to stand and even walk unsteadily, with helpers always on either side of her to catch her if she overbalanced. As it was now clear that Josie was in the best of hands, I decided that it was time to face another bleak task that had been nagging at my mind for some time.

I had to find somewhere to bury Lin and Megan. I needed to start making arrangements for the funeral, as their bodies might be released with very little forewarning and I had to be ready to deal with the situation when it arose. First, therefore, I had to decide on a grave site. I had considered what Lin would have wanted, and I knew that she loved and missed Wales so much that it would have to be there. There was also the germ of an idea forming in my mind, that if Josie recovered we should return to live in Wales, as the thought of continuing in Kent after what had happened held little appeal. I knew that if Lin had died naturally of old age she might have asked to be cremated, and for her ashes to be scattered in the garden or on the mountains. But we had only ever discussed it in jest, and so I wasn't quite sure how she would have felt in such an extraordinary situation. I felt that I needed an actual place to go where I knew I could be close to Lin and Megan. I also felt that Josie would prefer this, although she was not able to comprehend or contribute to the decision at that stage. Lin's parents too were in favour of a traditional burial, and so I decided to look for a grave site close to our old home in North Wales.

On 23 July Ed and I travelled to meet Peter and Irene at the holiday caravan they owned at Llangadfan, near Welshpool. We all stayed there overnight, and the next day I pressed on alone to North Wales for a one-day flying visit to reconnoitre Lin and Megan's final resting place. Our next-door neighbour who had been helping me at the hospital was back at her home in Tan-yr-Allt. I first conferred with her to glean her knowledge of the local graveyards.

We discussed possible sites and then set off in the car, on a melancholy tour of the local burial grounds. The ones nearest to our old house were very austere and exposed to the wild Welsh weather. They were also very full and I learnt from one local rector that in some graveyards there was simply no more space for burials. We drove south from Tan-yr-Allt towards Porthmadog, and turned north into the beautiful Cwm Pennant, a blind valley that runs up behind one of Snowdon's subsidiary ridges. The road is narrow and gated, and criss-crosses a lovely mountain stream that descends the valley. At the foot of the vale, an unusual rocky landscape of hills and cliffs is covered in a patchwork of green pasture, russet bracken, dark heather and golden gorse. Buzzards wheel overhead, and there is also the ever present cry of seagulls from Cardigan Bay only a couple of miles away. Lin loved this spot. The unusual geology fascinated her and we often used to walk up the valley, or over and down into it from the hills around. We picnicked there with the children on many occasions, and Lin had always said that if we ever moved locally from our house at Tan-yr-Allt, this is the area in which she would have loved to settle.

The church that I remembered further up the valley seemed deserted and abandoned, and it turned out not to have a graveyard at all. We drove back despondently to leave the valley again, but as we neared the mouth of the vale we got a better view of the tiny church of St

Mary's at Garndolbenmaen nestling in a hollow by the river. Its ancient stone walls were grey with lichen and the graveyard was thick with long grass and summer blossoms. The bright red flower heads of orange hawkweed ('fox and cubs') danced and waved in the grass, and brought back more bittersweet memories. Although quite rare until recently in Britain, this plant was common where Lin and I worked in the northern USA in 1987, just after Josie was born, and the rich blooms reminded me of that happy time.

The centuries-old headstones in the churchyard lay this way and that, and the names on them seemed to link in an ageless way with many of the same names on the newer stones. We walked around the graveyard and found a large overgrown area in a corner that had not yet been used for burials. This looked like the perfect spot. There was a big bush of ivy growing over the dry-stone wall at this point, and I thought that it would provide an ideal shelter for whenever Josie and I might visit during inclement weather. It felt remote and timeless, wild and beautiful, and far from the hue and cry of the life I had to return to the very next day. And so the urge grew stronger to come back here with Josie – as well as Lin and Megan. I needed to look no further for a place to bury my loved ones, and so I asked around locally for the name of the rector in charge of the church so that I could seek permission for the burial. Late that afternoon I headed back to re-join Ed with Lin's parents at the caravan. I was able to report that I had found a place for their daughter which I was sure would meet with their approval, and the next day Ed and I returned to London.

We had been away for three days, and our friend from America and Pauline had been holding the fort. Not only that, but holding Josie too. As we entered the ward we were amazed to see Josie walking upright towards us, with Pauline supporting her on one side, while our friend pushed Josie's drip bottle stand and supported her on the other. Josie's face crinkled into a smile when she saw me, and I was overjoyed that she recognized me and seemed pleased to see me. Pauline explained that Josie had been getting increasingly restless and wanted to be out of bed and walking round as often as possible.

Thus began a period of intense physical activity for Josie, with us pursuing her around the hospital for hours at a time, as we tried to keep up with her walkabouts. She was still trying to tear the drip from her arm at every possible opportunity, and so we sought permission for her to switch over completely to food intake by mouth. Attempts had been made to feed Josie orally already, but she behaved like a naughty baby and more food ended up on her pyjamas than down her throat. We told her that if she wanted to get rid of the tubes, then she would have to learn to eat properly. After a few fights, and much to everyone's relief, the feeding drip was finally removed during Josie's third week in hospital. However, the irritating tube for the administration of drugs was still inserted into a vein on the back of her left hand.

During the third week at the hospital, the doctors tried a different kind of medication for Josie. At this point she was getting stronger and walking more steadily every day. But following the administration of the new drug, she had an alarming relapse. She started tottering about uncontrollably, with her eyeballs rolling. Her head would arch so far back that we would have to catch her to stop her from falling over backwards. Yet she still insisted on getting out of bed and staggering off through the hospital corridors, which further exercised us and the police security officers.

When this drug reaction began, we were plunged into gloom and worry again. We imagined that Josie's recovery had all been an artificial product of the drugs, and that these alarming symptoms might be the first true manifestation of the brain damage she had suffered. Thankfully, the symptoms receded when she was moved back onto her old medication again, but only after we had all received an alarming shake-up, and had learnt not to start counting our chickens in relation to Josie's recovery.

At the end of the third week in hospital, we were visited by Lin's old university friend Judy. She came to the hospital with her husband Brian and their two children Rachel and Simon. We prepared Josie to greet her old friends and she was thrilled to see them, all smiles and happy to play on the bed with the presents they had brought for her. Judy was en route to America where Brian had got a promotion with his company. As with all our visitors, they put on a brave face for Josie's sake, but as they left I could tell that they were deeply distressed by the spectacle that they had witnessed: the sad remnants of their old friend's family.

Josie was by now starting to wield a crayon in her daily play therapy sessions, and with persistent encouragement she had managed to draw a flower. She was very restless and easily irritated, and would not cooperate if it did not suit her. Her right-arm movement was improving and her walk was increasing to a run as she led us on her frantic sallies through the hospital each day. How her strength had returned was shown to us during the third week, when Josie had to go for another Computer Tomography (CT) scan. It was clear that Josie would never lie still enough for the scan to be performed successfully, and so she had to be drugged to knock her out for the procedure. Three hours after she left for the scan, we went back to the recovery area. Josie was just starting to come round and her eyes were opening. As we walked in, the orderlies were getting ready to wheel Josie back to the ward. The moment her eyes focused on us she decided that she was not going to wait, and she heaved herself mightily off the bed. We rushed forward to grab her as she fell, but, to the nurse's astonishment, she hauled herself up and flung herself headlong towards the door. And then we were off again, hovering beside her as she plunged back towards Lion Ward. Whether they were trying to cheer us up or not I don't know, but the medics insisted that they had never seen any patient, let alone a child, resurrect herself so soon after a general anaesthetic and walk away from the scene.

The doctors and therapists decided that Josie's frantic sessions of rushing through the hospital should be allowed to continue and that she should be safeguarded but not restrained. It was difficult to get her to settle, and so the best therapy was thought to be exhaustion – to let her run the restlessness and upset out of her system. Josie now knew her way around the hospital and she probed the corridors to their limits. She would run to the furthest reaches of the buildings, and beat against windows and fire doors if she was thwarted by a dead end or a locked entrance. Heartening, yet at the same time deeply distressing, was to hear Josie's voice starting to come back. She started to shout out disjointed and garbled words. But the haunted and animal-like sounds she made most of the time sent shivers through us all.

Once again, my emotions were on a roller-coaster. I was constantly forcing back the tears while I endured her anguished shrieks and moans as she grappled with fire doors and window catches. And yet there were moments of high comedy as she streaked ahead of her burly police security guards up the broad flights of stairs between hospital floors, leaving them panting and gasping for breath. Repressing the urge to swear profanely, they would round a final corner to find Josie seated on the top stair, grinning triumphantly and looking quite relaxed after her lightning climb.

It was during this fraught time that another urgent task called me away from the hospital for a day. The chief investigating officer, Dave Stevens, had been giving out regular bulletins on the case to the media, who were ever-hungrier for news of Josie and progress in the murder enquiry. Dave Stevens was a past master at interacting with the press. He had involved the media in publicizing several prior cases, and he believed strongly in using the power of newspapers and television to improve the chances of apprehending suspects and bringing cases to successful conclusions. He was himself the most highly trained negotiator in the Kent Constabulary, and had been involved as a mediator in several terrorism and hostage crises.

Dave Stevens had promised always to answer my questions about the enquiry and to hold back on nothing that I might want to know. There were some questions that I either did not have the courage to ask or wish to know, for example the exact details of the crime scene. And then there were questions that were so delicate that I had the sense not to ask them, because by knowing the answers I might have jeopardized the enquiry. But Dave Stevens was at all times completely frank and level with me, friendly and sympathetic, yet completely professional. He worked at least as hard as any of his 'troops', and he bore the heavy responsibility for satisfying the expectations of thousands of families now living scared in East Kent while the murderer was still at large. He had been masterminding an operation that involved hundreds of police officers and army volunteers, combing the countryside around Chillenden for the murder weapon. Hundreds of specimens had been collected for forensic examination, and thousands of homes were being visited in house-to-house enquiries. Information was sought among the Kent criminal community, which had also been outraged at this mother-and-child murder. Now DCI Stevens was mobilizing the full power of his press and public relations strategy.

I already felt a natural obligation to Dave Stevens to do everything I could to assist the enquiry, and I knew that this might entail some difficult tasks. In the last week of July, he came to me with the request that I meet the press for the first time. There was due to be a re-enactment of the crime on 30 July, when actresses would dress up as

Lin, Josie and Megan on the fateful day, and, leading a dog like Lucy, they would retrace the walk home from Goodnestone School to the murder scene. The media would be there to cover the re-enactment, and it would be filmed by London Weekend Television for ITV's *Crime Monthly* programme. Dave Stevens asked me if I would be willing to wait at Granary Cottage while this was taking place, and then to answer questions from the press after they had finished in Cherry Garden Lane.

It was with trepidation that I returned to the house. The police cordon tapes were still in place, but the forensic team had finished work there long before. The garden was as lovely as ever. Two of my postgraduate students had been cycling over from Canterbury and tending it, as they knew how much the garden meant to Lin. Our old dog Jackie and the cats were pleased to see me; they had been looked after by Stuart and Jane next door while I was away. I had been checking regularly on their well-being by phone, and the animals were even looking a bit fatter and sleeker as Stuart could not resist treating them with fresh butcher's cuts.

I walked along to the ponies, and friends from the Bruderhof Community came over to greet me in the field. They had been devastated by the murders, which had taken place on the boundary of their property, and they had endured some intrusive scrutiny from the police. Still they were, as always, very warm and welcoming to me, and quietly sympathetic as we caught up on each other's news. They had been taking care of our ponies, who looked well on the summer grass.

The house seemed cold and gloomy by comparison. Pauline had been back to tidy up in advance of my visit, and everything was neat. But of course there were signs everywhere of Lin and the girls. I had to avert my gaze from so many objects that reminded me of them; the pain of their loss was so raw, and yet I had to maintain my composure to face the press later in the day. I couldn't bear to face the question of what to do with all the things. Clothes, toys, pictures, utensils, all reminded me of Lin and Megan and our life together as it had been only three short weeks before, but which was now lost for ever.

I drank tea with Pauline and listened to the mobile phone conversations going back and forth, telling of the progress of the re-enactment. As the call came for me to go out and present myself to the media,

I felt little apprehension. I could see the tumult of photographers and journalists massing at the front gate, but I just felt jaded and resigned to it all. The sense of living life as though in a movie was back with me again and I could stand outside myself, watching almost with a sense of detachment as I fielded the questions. The journalists were courteous and deferential, and I became aware that many of them must have been moved by the re-enactment and visit to the murder scene. I posed for photographs, with my mug of tea still in my hand and Jackie sitting by my side, mesmerized by the phalanx of people facing us and the flash of camera lights. Afterwards, a couple of newspaper representatives were allowed into the house to question me in more detail, and I looked out some additional photos of the family to be released to journalists. Once it was all over I grabbed some clothes and a few familiar things for Josie, and after checking once more on arrangements for the animals, we headed back towards London as darkness fell.

While I had been away Josie had been continuing with her charging around the hospital. When I returned that night, she cuddled up to me and went to sleep in my arms. She had obviously missed me, and I was reassured by her actions that she was not rejecting me or blaming me for her plight. I felt that I had to do something to improve her lot at the hospital, and so we started to explore the idea of 'letting her out' for a bit. The next day I managed to get hold of a wheelchair, with a strap to hold Josie in and a nurse to accompany us down to a small garden at the back of the hospital. I had often noticed Josie gazing forlornly and uncomprehendingly out of the window of her room, at the industrial-looking backside of the hospital. At dusk it reminded me of a Lowry painting or a scene from the Charlie Chaplin movie, *Modern Times*. It must have seemed to Josie as though she had landed on another planet. But in one hidden corner was the tiny garden, and when we took Josie there she seemed more relaxed straight away. As we whiled away our time in this little haven, I could see over the tall walls to trees in the distance and I determined that we should try next to take Josie out for an excursion into the park.

The doctors agreed and so by the very next day I was given the go-ahead to take Josie to Ruskin Park, near the hospital. I wheeled Josie up Denmark Hill and into the park with our entourage of two friends, Ed and Pauline, a police security guard and a nurse. The doctors had removed Josie's main head bandage by this time, leaving just a dressing over the wounds on the back of her head that were taking longer to heal. She looked pitiful in her dressing gown in the wheelchair, with her pale head shaved and heavily scarred. No one on the sunny street seemed to mind; they must have been used to such apparitions in that place. We all started to smile despite ourselves, as Josie was straining forward in her wheelchair, grinning from ear to ear as she spotted dogs in the distance. In the park she became more animated still, as ducks and squirrels crossed our path. Next day, we decided, we should bring some nuts to feed the squirrels, and Josie agreed enthusiastically.

Josie was now able to indicate yes and no with a nod or a shake of the head, and she could also indicate positives and negatives through the use of marks and drawings in her therapy sessions. The sounds she made when distressed had become more articulate, and she was now shouting 'NO' more and more frequently. We joked about this obstinate 'NO' being the first word in Josie's returning vocabulary, and we were pleased to see it as another manifestation of her incredible tenacity and determination. She was not going to curl up in a corner and hide from her pain and her fears. She was now revived enough to fight back at whatever was causing her discomfort and her loss of independence – and if that meant giving those around her a hard time, then so be it.

This brought me to another task that I had to perform for the police. Josie's good progress meant that the investigating team were hoping to begin asking her questions soon about what had happened at the murder scene. Dave Stevens had gone to extraordinary lengths to educate himself and his team about interacting with child witnesses. But here was an almost unique situation in which a potential murder witness was not only young, but also 'struck dumb'. There were no textbook cases to inform the inquiry team as to the best way forward. The top specialists in the land were sought out to advise the police how to proceed, and Britain's leading expert on post-traumatic stress in children, Dora Black, was drafted in to assist with the enquiry.

Josie was already using a pencil in her speech therapy and play therapy sessions, and she had shown that she could do simple calculations and puzzles. The plan was to get her to signal her responses to questions by pointing to symbols or by making her own consistent marks on a sheet of paper. To start the ball rolling, I was asked to begin chatting to Josie about how much she could remember of her mother and sister from before the time of the attack. Josie and I sat down on her bed, amid the enormous pile of teddies and soft toys that was accumulating from well-wishers. I read to her from a picture book, and then in Ed's and Pauline's presence I tried to bring the conversation around to Lin and Megan. I pulled out some photos of our family, but Josie turned away at the sight of these and made off out of her room into the ward. Once again, I could not be sure if this was an adverse reaction to the photographs, or just impatience due to her painfully short attention span. It was still unclear whether or not Josie remembered anything at all about the circumstances that had led to her head injury.

Around this time we started taking Josie to the toilet on the ward, instead of making her use a bedpan. At first it was difficult and one or other of us had to assist her there. It was on one of these occasions that Josie first glimpsed herself in the mirror in the toilet. She froze and stared at her image as though she had seen a ghost. There, looking back at her, was a thin grey face, drained through weeks of pain and torment. Her head was shaved, and all her beautiful hair was gone. There was a long black scar arching about 23 centimetres from her temple over to the back of her head. Beside it was a depression over the part of her brain where the skull was missing. It gave her head a lop-sided profile and a misshapen appearance. Her ears also showed the signs of bruising and stitching from the time of her operation. Josie's lip trembled and she spun away with tears in her eyes as she rushed back to her room to hide under her pillow.

The surgeons had told us that notwithstanding Josie's 'skull deficit' (the area of missing bone) she would not need to wear a protective helmet. However, I was worried about her getting sunburn on her shaved pate whenever we were out and so I had already determined to get Josie a sun hat. As I watched her distress at seeing herself in the mirror, I knew that here was another reason to find Josie a hat as soon as possible. Back in the ward I asked Pauline what to do. As usual she had thought of everything, and she pulled a couple of summer hats out of the bag of clothes that we had brought from Granary Cottage. Josie grabbed for the nearest one straightaway, and from then on started wearing a hat whether she was indoors or out. It would be eighteen months before anyone apart from the doctor got to see the top of Josie's head again.

On 1 August Josie had been very active in the park and showed us how she could skip with a rope for a few turns. Ed and Pauline had started filming Josie using a small and unobtrusive digital video camera. The intention was to use this as evidence in the police enquiry and to try and record on film anything Josie said or did in case she started to show signs of remembering what had happened to her. We played back the first 'home movie' over and over on the camera's little screen, and we could not believe we were watching the same little girl who had been rushed to this hospital battered and beaten and on the edge of death only three weeks previously.

Josie's happy behaviour in the park was in stark contrast to her demeanour in the hospital. When cooped up indoors she continued with her headlong charges through the corridors and her beating against the entrances. She seemed inordinately strong; she had an appetite like a horse and she had developed a particular taste for yoghurts. The entrance to the mini-kitchen on the ward had a split stable-type door, and Josie would clamber over this like a monkey in her determination to get at the fridge and decimate the yoghurt supply.

The police had tightened security on the front door to the ward, after a journalist got in by posing as a parent. Now the door was locked at all times, with security code access and camera control. Nurses had to recognize anyone arriving at the front door before they would let them in. This restricted Josie's movements even more, but we did allow her to continue with her running races throughout the hospital at set times of day. On one occasion Josie got as far as the main front entrance of the hospital, where despondent-looking patients hung around in their dressing gowns to smoke cigarettes, before going back in to the enforced abstinence of the wards. Unfortunately, on that occasion, I had managed to park my car quite close to the front entrance, and Josie recognized it. She broke away from us and ran to the car, jerking and yanking at the door handle to get inside. She moaned and cried and we felt for her so, in her desperation to get away from this alien place. From then on Josie developed the worrying habit of stealing my keys at every opportunity and running off to the car in an attempt to force me to take her home. But she was still nowhere near fit enough to be discharged, according to the doctors, and the wounds on the back of her head continued to suppurate and showed no sign of mending. Professor Polky was worried that these injuries were taking so long to heal, and he could not rule out the possibility that they might still need a skin graft.

It was on our return upstairs from one of Josie's sorties to the car, that she first noticed a mural painting on the hospital wall of ponies in flowery fields. There was a white pony like Tegid, and a palomino just like Rosie. Josie screamed with anguish when she saw these pictures, and suddenly in a flash of light I realized what was torment-ing Josie so. I saw that she believed she had lost *everything*. Here she was in a strange and foreign place. She had to suffer pain and loss of dignity in her daily routines, and she was effectively a prisoner. She was surrounded mainly by unfamiliar people and worst of all she had lost her mother and her sister. Every time Josie tried to talk to me, she could not make me understand, her words were garbled and unintelligible even though we were certain that she knew what she was trying to say. But there was more. Yes she had me, but for all she knew, she had lost *everything* else in her life. Where was her home? And what did she love most if it was not her pets: her ponies, her cats, her dogs? Why had none of us thought to tell her that her home and her pets (with the sad exception of Lucy) were still there? I grasped her to me, sobbing out that her ponies were still all right. They were there at home waiting for her, and so was Jackie, and the cats Polly and Spindle. I knew then, as I had done with the park, that I had to get her there as soon as possible, to show her that the world she knew had not totally vanished. We started to make the arrangements immediately: permission from the doctors for a one-day visit home, a nurse to accompany us, friends to come to the house for Josie to play with; security measures to be put in place. Ed and Pauline would also come along and film the visit in case Josie revealed anything of importance on the trip.

The next day my mother and sister came to visit us at the hospital, and although this was trying for them, their presence served to calm Josie somewhat. They played with her and cheered her up, and, as I sat watching their brave efforts, the sound of my mother's soothing voice stirred deep-rooted memories in my subconscious, of times when I had been ill as a child and she had comforted me. Margery and Jeannie were exhausted emotionally and physically by the end of the day, as Josie had led them on one of her sorties around the hospital. But we were greatly buoyed up by their visit, as it seemed to help with the efforts to convince Josie that not everything had been lost that she remembered from her former world. For the same reason we looked forward to the second visit of Lin's parents Peter and Irene, which was scheduled in a couple of days' time. In the meantime we were going to take Josie home for the day.

So, on Saturday 3 August, Josie finally got what she wanted and was able to lead me to our car, open the door and get in. Josie's favourite nurse, Marlene, had given up her day off to accompany us, and she explained to Josie that we were only going home for the day. But Josie had a set and determined expression on her face, and we knew before we started that there would be trouble getting her back to the hospital at the day's end. I also harboured a deep and disturbing suspicion, which I kept secret from everyone else, that Josie might still be hoping to find her mother and sister at home after all.

The route to Granary Cottage was very familiar to me, and I had always previously felt a sense of comfort as I drove homeward from work into the secret embrace of the East Kent countryside. Suddenly this had changed, and ever since, when I have travelled through these lanes, I feel instead a sensation of darkness and fear. These backways and byways now hold for me a sinister air of foreboding, and I shiver with trepidation as I pass through them.

On this first journey with Josie back to Granary Cottage, driving my own car, this feeling of menace crept over me and was amplified by my worry as to how Josie would react to the homecoming. I was right to be apprehensive. We pulled into the back yard and Josie immediately got out of the car and walked like a zombie towards the house. She tugged at the door until I caught up with her to open it. Ed and Pauline were scrambling behind as they fired up their video camera to tape Josie's responses. Once in the house Josie stood staring at everything there that must have reminded her of her mother and sister and the life she had lost. She started upstairs with a wail growing in her throat, and burst into her bedroom. Her howling grew stronger and more anguished and she rushed through to Megan's room, grabbing one of her sister's teddies still on the dressing table. Then she plunged on into Lin's and my room, where Lin's clothes were still visible hanging on a rail. Josie was sobbing violently now and

Left: Lin aged nine in 1960.

Below: Lin and Shaun's wedding day at Exeter Registry Office, 19 April 1975 *(left to right)* Jean Russell, Anne Stacey, Margery Russell, Roger Stacey, Shaun and Lin, Irene Wilcox, Judy Green, Peter Wilcox.

Above: Campfire scene during Lin and Shaun's trans-Australian journey, November 1981.

Below: Lin with her own horse, Rebel, at Hogsback, South Africa, 1983.

Above: With Josie aged two months at Great Fish River Mouth, South Africa, 1987.

Below: Margery Russell with Josie and Victoria Magadla and her children 'Tallboy' and Bulelwa.

Above: Lin, Shaun and Josie on their first family visit to Plas Tan-yr-Allt before buying the property in 1988.

Below: Ysgol Baladeulyn 1994 school photograph, with teachers Susan Owen (*left*) and Siân Thomas (*right*). Josie is sixth from the left, centre row, and Megan is fourth from the left, front row.

Above: Lin, Josie and Megan with Lucy, picknicking at Llyn Dinas, Snowdonia, summer 1995.

Below: Granary Cottage, Kent, spring 1996.

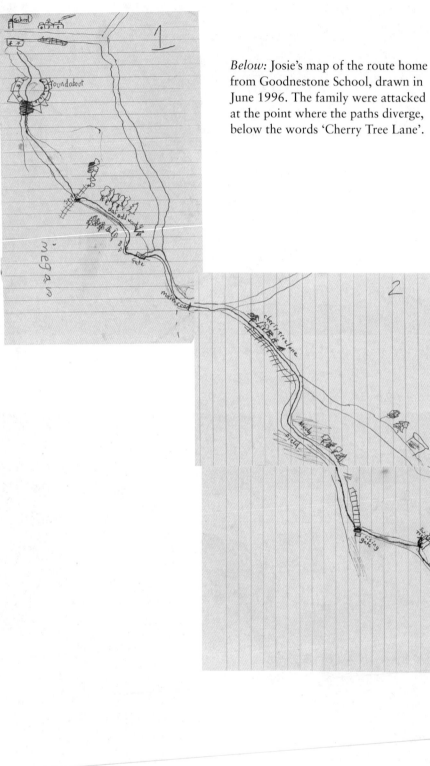

Below: Josie's map of the route home from Goodnestone School, drawn in June 1996. The family were attacked at the point where the paths diverge, below the words 'Cherry Tree Lane'.

Above: Josie and Megan on the beach at Dungeness, Kent, April 1996.

Left: Megan, about the time of her sixth birthday, at Plas Tan-yr-Allt in the summer of 1995.

Below: Megan took this photo in the garden at Granary Cottage in June 1996.

moaning like a wounded animal between her coughs and splutterings. Ed grimly pursued Josie with the camera while I vainly tried to soothe her. The others stood rooted to the spot in shock, covering their faces or turning away in distress.

Josie continued her lament around the house for what seemed like an age, as we longed for her to cry herself out. Outside, the Kelly family had arrived with Josie's school friend Jazzmin. I pleaded with Josie to calm down and that Jazzmin was here to see her now. Slowly Josie started to settle and after a while was ready to go outside to see her old friend. Josie walked slowly out, and Jazzmin gingerly approached her. They came close, and Jazzmin handed Josie a little present. A smile flickered across Josie's face as she recognized Jazzmin, and I suggested to them that they go along the lane to see the ponies. Pauline, Marlene and I accompanied the two girls as they walked slowly ahead of us, Jazzmin talking softly to Josie. All Josie could say by way of reply was 'uh' or 'mm', or similar noises. But Jazzmin was not fazed at all; in fact she acted as if she didn't even notice Josie's loss of intelligible speech.

We rounded the corner of the copse of trees that separated our house from the ponies' field. There in the distance were Tegid and Rosie. Josie looked across at them, with a quizzical expression on her face, as though she was not sure if these really were her ponies. But as they shambled across towards us, she ducked under the electric fence and moved quickly to meet them. She was smiling now and she reached out to greet her ponies with arms at full stretch. As Tegid came up she wrapped her arms around his neck and the tears flowed down her face. Pauline and I sniffed back our own tears and smiled through watery eyes at each other. It was such a relief to see Josie crying with something akin to happiness, rather than having to witness the horror of her naked torment as we had done in the house only minutes before. I left Josie with the others, and went back to the house to greet more of her friends who were arriving with their parents. We set up chairs and tables in the garden for afternoon tea and the children went off to join Josie at the ponies. I caught up on news with the parents and teachers from school. They had had the most harrowing previous three weeks, with headteacher Darryl Peek calmly and sensitively trying to help everyone through the tumult at Goodnestone School following the murders. Josie's teacher Lynda Roberts had borne the brunt of coping with the terrified and disorientated children in Josie's class, and with their shocked and bewildered parents. Lynda is one of those rare people who come to the fore in a crisis and who seem to be strengthened by adversity. She gave up all the hours in the day to help everyone around her, and her own inimitable brand of cheerfulness and encouragement was a major factor in holding together the frightened community that was Goodnestone School in the aftermath of the murders.

And so it was with the little community that gathered in Lin's garden on that Saturday afternoon. Josie returned from the ponies, flanked by her friends, nodding and gesticulating in response to their conversation. Linda greeted Josie with a big hug and then carried on as though it was a regular school outing. She soon had the girls handing out the tea things to the adults, and Josie joined in without hesitation. Josie seemed suddenly at ease as one of her old crowd, acting normally and not the centre of attention. This was greatly helped by the actions and attitudes of Josie's friends of her own age. Then and now, they seemed blind to Josie's changed appearance and her disabilities. It was as if they were interacting on a deeper level of understanding and compassion, as if to them the changes in Josie were purely superficial.

I was enormously relieved. The day had not turned out so badly after all. Josie was now enjoying herself with her friends, as they giggled over their enormous plates of party food. Josie had come home to where she remembered her mother and sister, and it seemed clear that she had truly grieved for them that day. I was convinced that the trauma and anguish she was displaying at the hospital were also part of this grieving process. Her misery was agony to behold. But somehow I felt that this was better than her becoming morose and uncommunicative and bottling up her emotions. As usual Josie was showing me the way. Her young and undaunted spirit was purging itself of pain. I wished I could do the same.

The afternoon ended and the guests made their way home. We cleared up, and then as predicted we had to face Josie's unwillingness to leave again for the hospital. There followed more weeping, arguments, rationalizing, cajoling, threats and bribes, and finally, as the light started to fade, we got away from Granary Cottage with our tearful charge. The lanes seemed more malevolent still as we sped away towards London, and I was glad that we were not spending the night back at the cottage. The day's experience did convince me, however, that for Josie's sake we should return there when the time eventually came for Josie's discharge from hospital. I hoped that Josie might be able to return to her old friends and teachers at Goodnestone School, at least until I had finally sorted out in my mind whether or not we should stay in Kent or move away from the area altogether.

The day after the visit, Josie seemed a little less fearful and distressed than usual. But unfortunately for her minders, she seemed instead to have become even more determined to get out of hospital and return home. She stole my car keys again and tore off through the hospital towards the front entrance near where she knew my car would be parked. She was now getting bitterly cross with us for keeping her captive, as she saw it, and it was only when Lin's parents arrived later in the day that she calmed down and forgot about escape as she played with them for a couple of hours.

Peter and Irene were delighted to see the changes in Josie and her vast physical improvement since they had last visited. I explained about what had been happening and how I would probably take Josie back to Granary Cottage after she came out of hospital. Peter and Irene were dismayed to hear of my plans to return to the house so close to the murder scene. But then I discussed with them my thoughts about returning to Wales. They were heartened by this possibility, as they knew that I wanted to bury Lin and Megan there. They felt as I did, that it would be good if Josie and I could be somewhere near to Lin and Megan for those times when we might want to visit them. And because they had a caravan in mid-Wales, Peter and Irene would see more of us there than if we stayed on in Kent.

I thought, then, that I might start making enquiries about places to live in Wales when I next visited. I knew that I would have to go back before long, as there were complex arrangements to be made in respect of Lin's and Megan's funeral, and all the formalities to be addressed in relation to their burial at St Mary's churchyard at Garndolbenmaen. Among these were the issues of getting Lin's and Megan's bodies to North Wales; the security and privacy of the funeral; and the special grave that would have to be dug so that mother and daughter (and Lucy) could be buried together. I had already thought that I would like to take Josie back to Wales for a short recuperative holiday when she came out of hospital, rather than going back to Granary Cottage straight away. Returning to the place that Josie knew and loved best, among her old friends in North Wales, seemed a better idea the more I thought of it. And the police too were happy that I slip away from potential media pressure in Kent when Josie was released from hospital.

In the meantime, however, we still had little idea of when this might be. The wounds on the back of Josie's head were still obstinately refusing to heal, and bone was still visible. Yet Josie's CT scan showed no build-up of fluid or blood clots in the damaged parts of her brain and she was growing ever stronger as her appetite soared. Josie was matching words with pictures in her therapy sessions, and this gave the police fresh hope that she would be able to help them significantly with their enquiries. With the help of the Dora Black Clinic, they started drawing up idiomatic question sheets and charts that would help them to communicate with Josie, and allow her to describe through images what was in her mind. The traumatic stress specialists advised that Josie should not yet be taken back to the scene of the crime. The idea was in any case repugnant to me, and I certainly had no wish to go there myself. The police were making regular checks on visitors to the murder site in case the perpetrator might return. They would make enquiries whenever they were unable to identify people as local residents.

Josie was generally calmer and easier to manage following the visit home, and she was having fewer emotional outbursts. In addition to receiving so many presents from well-wishers (we were having to pass some on to the hospital charity for sheer lack of space in Josie's room) she was becoming aware of the fact that she was being featured on television and in the newspapers. People pointed her out during our walks in the park. On one of these visits Ed and Pauline were filming Josie as she played on the swings and roundabouts (we were scared stiff when she first tried this, but there was no holding her back), when a mounted police officer rode up through the park. Josie was so entranced by his massive and docile horse, that he offered her a seat up in the high saddle. As Ed filmed the spectacle, many people gathered round and word quickly spread that this was the little girl who was the centre of interest in 'The Russell Murders'. At first Josie was shy, but after a while she began to play up to the attention of the well-wishers and to pose for the cameras that started to appear.

I realized at that moment that Josie was becoming 'public property' and that our relationship with the outside world was changed for ever. The pressure of public interest could easily become intrusive and burdensome, and would have to be carefully managed if we were to avoid becoming engulfed by this tragic notoriety.

Josie's recovery team were pleased with the general outcome of our visit home to Granary Cottage, and I received permission to conduct another such trip in a week's time. In the meantime, as Josie seemed fit enough, we hoped to brighten up her days by making a couple of excursions into the big metropolis of London. And here Pauline came up trumps again! Her husband had an old friend who was a senior yeoman warder at the Tower of London, and he arranged for us to make a special visit there.

So, during Josie's fourth week in hospital, I drove with Josie, our friend from America, Pauline and Ed, in through the main security entrance of the Tower, and we parked 'around the back' where the Beefeaters live. We were led on the most wonderful behind-the-scenes tour of this ancient edifice. Great studded wood and iron doors were opened for us, and we walked through dim passageways and up spiral stone stairways to emerge in hidden chambers and behind displays where we startled the general public on the other side of windows and screens. Josie was given the opportunity to see and touch exhibits that had played momentous roles in English history. Even she, however, felt so overawed by the invitation to sit on Henry VIII's throne that she declined the offer despite much cajoling. We indulged Josie's ravenous hunger with a massive plate of chips and lashings of tomato ketchup in the Tower Restaurant. And the day was rounded off, much to Josie's delight, by a trip to the souvenir shop where she chose for herself a teddy in a Beefeater's uniform.

A couple of days later we headed to Granary Cottage for the second time. On this occasion, Josie's return was less traumatic. She soon settled in and started playing with several more of her old friends who had turned up to see her. We organized a tea party in the garden again, and once more Josie spent quite a bit of time with the ponies. To liven up the occasion I had invited our old friend Steve Stratton. Steve is an entertainer, and he brought his piano accordion along to cheer us all up. He is a master of the singalong and he can put a swing into any party. But on this occasion even Steve gave up trying after a while.

He had been close to us in Wales and had a great affection for Lin and Megan. It was just too much for him to feign joy now. In any case, Josie and her friends seemed to be having plenty of fun fossicking around the garden and exploring the barns and stables of the old manor house next door. Steve and I sat and reminisced about the lives we had led in North Wales – the urge to return there grew stronger still.

During weeks five and six in the hospital, Josie's physical and mental state continued to improve, and she was managing increasingly complex tasks in her therapy sessions. We made two more day trips to punctuate the routine. One was to Kew Gardens, where I had friends and colleagues through my botanical background. We had a glorious day out in the summer sunshine, and Josie's behatted head bobbed back and forth among the exotic plants as she played to her heart's content with the friends who had joined us for the day. The other trip was to London Zoo where I also had several friends and colleagues through work. It was another wonderful day out, with a behind-the-scenes look at the way the zoo was run, and plenty of opportunities for Josie to cuddle everything from baby monkeys and a young giraffe, to snakes and giant hairy insects.

I felt an irrational twinge of jealousy at the physical attention Josie was lavishing on these creatures. As Josie emerged from her drugged state into greater self-awareness, she seemed to be developing an aversion for any sort of physical contact with adults – including me. It was an aspect that worried me then, and worries me still. I imagined that her deeply traumatic experience at the hand of the murderer might have led to a suppression of her affectionate nature, and made her hostile to any form of physical contact. But it was clear that Josie was still able to rough-and-tumble normally with friends of her own age, and it was this that made me think again about my pat psychological assessment. Josie recoiled from being hugged or kissed by adults, particularly her closest relatives. But I remembered that even before the murders Josie was starting to become averse to displays of sentimentality and physical affection from her relatives. I also remembered that I acted in exactly the same way when I was her age. I would baulk at being kissed by a granny or an aunt, and I would squirm my way out of any situation where I thought this was likely to happen. And so I hoped that I was reading too much into Josie's response, and that one day Josie just might kiss and cuddle her old dad again. As usual it was probably my own hang-up that was at the root of this sensitivity. Of course I missed the tenderness that I used to share with Lin, and the easy-going and demonstrative love that the children gave us. But I could not expect Josie, as a self-aware and image-conscious youngster, to substitute in any way for the affection that I had lost from my life.

And talking of hang-ups, I soon discovered what was to become my biggest area of denial and thought suppression. Thursday 15 August would have been Megan's birthday. I let it pass without recognition or acknowledgement. Josie, it seemed, had got over her sobbing fits whenever Lin or Megan was mentioned; I, on the other hand, was refusing to allow thoughts of my youngest daughter to enter my head. To do so would lead to my breaking down in tears, and the inner pain was so harsh and physical that it clenched my stomach and doubled me up. My unhealthy reaction to this response was to push memories of my perfect baby deeper and deeper into the recesses of my mind, where they stay to this day. If time can heal, then this is where I most need healing.

Six weeks after Josie was admitted to hospital, her head wound had at last closed over sufficiently that the doctors decided a skin graft would not be necessary. The wound still needed daily dressing, but by now we knew how to do this ourselves. I was keen to get Josie home as soon as possible so that we could take more control over our lives, and I was getting more and more frustrated at the lack of any move-ment on the hospital's part about a discharge date for Josie. I decided to take the matter into my own hands and I told the hospital authorities that I intended to take Josie home with me the next day. To my amazement and relief they agreed; but I had got myself into a pickle.

The following day, 20 August, Pauline had arranged another exciting day out for us. Her husband had friends in the Metropolitan Police's Marine Division, who operate the patrol boats on the River Thames, and we were to take a VIP trip in the Commodore's Launch. I could not simply cancel this trip, as we were due to be joined by two, truly, Very Important Persons – the police constables who had been present at the crime scene on the night of the murders, and who had sounded the alarm when they found that Josie was still alive. These young officers had experienced the full horror of that scene, and one of them (who had young children of his own) had cradled Josie's hypothermic body in his arms, as the police doctor drove them hell-for-leather to the nearest hospital in Canterbury. The officer was severely traumatized by his experience, and they had both been off-duty for some time and receiving counselling. Senior officers felt that it would be therapeutic for the two young constables to meet Josie and see what a wonderful recovery she had made. The Thames launch trip offered an ideal opportunity for this; although it was decided that for operational reasons, as well as to spare Josie any disquiet, she would not be told who they were. They would just come along as though they were our normal escort of security officers.

And so I set about organizing our hectic schedule for the day. We would take the launch trip in the morning, and then rush back to the hospital, where I had organized a farewell party on the ward for Josie and all her friends there. In the afternoon we would pack up and head home for Granary Cottage. And so it went. I finally got to meet the two young men who had played such an important part in saving my daughter's life. And although I could not acknowledge their actions openly because of Josie's presence, I tried to transmit in my handshake and my gaze, the incalculable debt that I owed to them. Our friend from America and Ed were with us, and Pauline filmed the trip, giving me a permanent record of this memorable and moving occasion.

It was a marvellous journey travelling up from Wapping to view the Houses of Parliament from the river, and then back downstream, beneath Tower Bridge and onto the lower reaches. We passed magnificent and famous buildings, seeing them from an unexpected perspective, and we also passed the vacant lot where the Millennium Dome was to be built. After viewing the Thames Barrier at close quarters, we headed upstream again, and Josie took the wheel for a while.

Suddenly we became aware of a commotion on the water. A speedboat had been hurtling up-river when it cannoned into a piece of floating debris, not far away from us. A hole was ripped in the back of the craft and it started to sink. The occupants, a man and a boy, headed the boat in towards the shore and shouted and waved to us for assistance. Once we were sure that the man and boy were not in immediate danger of drowning, the sergeant radioed one of his rescue teams to offer further assistance. While all this was going on, we had to cope with another drama on the launch. As soon as Josie had picked up the sense of emergency among the people on board, it had triggered in her a panic attack. She became very agitated and started to cry and cower in a corner of the launch. While the rescue was going on, we were also trying to comfort Josie and allay her fear. It was the first occurrence of a reaction that Josie would manifest many more times during the coming year.

The rest of the trip was mercifully uneventful, and we said our goodbyes and headed back to the hospital for the last time. There we enjoyed our lunch party with the nurses and patients who had become our friends over the preceding six weeks. I was once again sobered by the thought that some of the children there would not emerge alive from Lion Ward, while Josie was walking away with a smile on her face and a skip in her step. We vowed to come back and visit soon (Josie would have to return for check-ups) and we finally set off for home, six weeks to the day since Josie had been admitted to King's College Hospital.

Whether Josie remembers much of what happened to her in hospital, I'm not sure. I think that a lot of what she does remember is painful and humiliating for her, and she refuses to acknowledge or talk about it. For me, the period is burned into my memory as though with a hot iron. Much of my recollection of that traumatic time is stark and painful, but I can also remember the brightness of hope at each step in Josie's progress, and the wonder of witnessing Josie's resilience and fortitude throughout the ordeal. Behind it all lay the skill and determination of the doctors and nurses who repaired Josie, tended her body and her mind, and worked with her dauntlessly to fan those sparks of life and spirit into a breathing, walking, running and smiling girl again. To them I owe an immeasurable debt of gratitude, yet I know that they continue selflessly to do the same and more for other stricken children, every day of their careers. To them I say an inadequate – thank you so much for making my daughter better.

Desperation and Determination

The return home to Granary Cottage was a happier occasion than our previous visits. Our two friends from America and Wales were going to stay for a few days to help us settle in, and to help Josie prepare a surprise for me the next day, 21 August, as it was my birthday. Josie was keen to get home and settle back in with her pets and belongings around her. She now seemed to have accepted that her mother and sister were not going to be at home, but there was an incident that unnerved us during the journey. Josie suddenly became agitated at the sight of a car, the same model and colour as ours, going in the opposite direction. She craned her neck to see who was driving the vehicle, and then kept looking out for similar cars for a while afterwards. It was as if she had not quite believed everything we had been telling her all this time and was still hoping to spot her mother driving by: perhaps Lin had just run away, and we were trying to keep it from her with our preposterous stories.

At home, Ed and Pauline were waiting and they explained that a police guard would now be posted at our house. The murderer was still at large and the police wanted to take no chances with the safety of their most important witness. Officers would stay in a police car outside the house all night and patrol past at various times during the day. We were also shown how to operate a remote panic button that had been installed in the house. It was designed to summon police assistance rapidly if ever the guard was not present for any reason.

My birthday was a sombre event for my friends and myself. Josie insisted on brightening up the occasion with little presents that she helped to wrap, and a cake that 'the girls' baked together. The kitchen at Granary Cottage was still in a state of disarray since Lin's last demolition session, but we managed as best we could. Josie refused to be infected with any sense of melancholy, and she led the way in bringing a feeling of life back into the house, playing with our dog Jackie and the cats, and bringing Tegid and Rosie up to the house for grooming. The ponies' feet had not been tended for a while and so I made arrangements for the farrier to call in a week's time.

I savoured the short spell of relaxation on my birthday, as the following day we were due to be thrust in front of the cameras again. In the case of high profile crimes such as 'The Russell Murders', it was common practice for the police to use the BBC *Crimewatch* programme to appeal for public support in catching the perpetrator. The *Crimewatch* team had been gathering material on this case during the preceding weeks, and they spent the day of my birthday in the Chillenden–Goodnestone area, filming their re-enactment of events leading up to the murder. I had agreed with the police to be interviewed by the *Crimewatch* producer, and for Josie and me to be filmed in our garden at Granary Cottage.

The next morning I accompanied Pauline to a hotel in Canterbury where we were interviewed in a small room in front of the *Crime-watch* cameras. Pauline watched while I relived the events of the night of 9 July. I could see she felt for me as she had at the mortuary, and the questions became more and more intense until I broke down. The cameras were switched off, and then it was Pauline's turn to be interviewed. In the afternoon we returned home and the television crew set up their equipment in the garden. Josie and I were filmed chatting together as I pruned some plants in the borders. Josie was shy and kept her head down most of the time, with her face hidden by the floppy summer hat that had become her trademark. Eventually the crew got the footage they needed and we were left to relax after our nerve-racking day.

Ed and Pauline were coming round every day to make sure we were OK and to check on Josie's progress. I passed on to them the startling news that Josie remembered the swimming gala she attended on the day of the murders. I had mentioned it to her in conversation and she clearly understood what I was talking about. She even indicated to me that she had won a ribbon in one of the races. The police were therefore keen to start talking to Josie more seriously as soon as possible.

Various officials began to contact us about Josie's medical and educational provision, and to arrange for tests and assessments to be carried out. We were reminded that this was the last week of the school summer holiday. I didn't know at this stage whether Josie's academic progress would be sufficient to allow her to return to school in the near future. But what seemed very clear was how happy she was in the company of her school friends. This strengthened my resolve to find some way of getting Josie back to Goodnestone School, even if only temporarily.

During that first week back at home, there was no chance to adjust to a new, more sedate lifestyle, or to relax after the frantic pace of hospital life. The phone started ringing straight away, despite our changing number and going ex-directory, and I realized that any hope of a relaxing end to the summer holidays would be short-lived unless we could get away for a bit. Josie was disappointed that we had missed the summer holiday in Northumberland and Scotland she had been looking forward to so much. And so I had promised her that when she came out of hospital, we would get away for couple of days to Wales where she could see her old friends from school in the Nantlle Valley. Accordingly, at the end of our first week back at home, we drove up to Wales together and met Pauline there. We stayed in the holiday caravan in the back field at Plas Tan-yr-Allt, courtesy of Anthony Howland to whom we had sold the property a year earlier. Our next-door neighbour was back at home in the cottage next door and she helped to make our visit comfortable.

On the Saturday I arranged for Josie to meet and play with some of her old friends, while I continued making arrangements for the burial. I was put in touch with the Bishop of Bangor who cleared all the formalities in relation to the grave at St Mary's Church, Garndolbenmaen, including my wish to bury our dog Lucy with Lin and Megan.

On the Sunday, we visited Josie's old school at Nantlle and her teachers came over to meet us on their day off. They brought some of Josie's old classmates along with them, and while they were playing with Josie, I talked quietly to the headmistress Susan Owen and Josie's previous class teacher Siân Thomas. I had seen from their letters that they were deeply affected by the tragedy, but they retained their composure during our visit. I told them about my burial plans for Lin and Megan and that I was thinking about coming back to Wales to live. I could sense their depth of feeling as they offered to have Josie back at Ysgol Baladeulyn at any time. As they made this offer, I felt a great weight lifted off me. I was anxious about whether or not Josie would be able to continue her schooling. I thought she might have to go to a special school, or be taught at home. But I reasoned that if she could be incorporated back into the mainstream schooling system, then, of all places, this surely had to be the best. I could see Josie playing happily with her friends, and behind her the majestic bulk of Snowdon Mountain rising above the sparkling waters of Llyn Nantlle. Back with her old school friends in this wonderful environment, and with loving and dedicated teachers like these, surely that would give Josie her best chance of a secure and stable recovery.

There were tears in our eyes as Josie and I left Tan-yr-Allt on Sunday evening for the long drive back to Kent. I was unprepared for this emotion at leaving the place and realized how important these few relaxing hours had been. As we drove down the track away from the hamlet, I felt suddenly convinced of the correct path for us. I was going to bring Josie back to live and go to school again in the Nantlle Valley. We would be near to Lin and Megan, and we would have nearby our old friends and neighbours who had welcomed us so warmly, and among whom we felt most at ease.

The next day I went back into work at the University of Kent for the first time since the murders. I found that my office had been thoroughly turned over by the police and quite a few of my papers were missing. The computer had been accessed in my absence and there was a receipt on my desk listing the items that had been taken from the office. My colleagues were all very concerned and sympathetic about my situation, and I spent most of the day chatting to many of them in my office. When I met with my bosses, Professor Ian Swingland and Dr Mike Walkey, they immediately put my mind at rest about the integrity of the various projects that I was involved in. Other members of staff and postgraduate students had stepped into the breach and were shouldering various of my commitments. Ian and Mike explained that I was on compassionate leave as far as they were concerned, and that I should not trouble myself with work until I felt absolutely sure that I wanted to return. I was particularly worried that my contract was about to run out. If it had not been for the tragedy I would have been writing up proposals over the summer months, to initiate a new project or secure an extension of my old one. I told them of my intention to move back to Wales and, once again, Ian and Mike were completely supportive. They were convinced that they could find a way of keeping me on the payroll, even if I worked at a distance or from home. 'Just get home and look after that daughter of yours,' they insisted. 'We'll sort it out.' It was a great relief to know that my work commitments were being taken care of; but there remained a nagging doubt about my financial situation. I started to worry about how I might support Josie and myself if I had to go on to part-time employment, or if I had to give up work altogether to care for her.

An American PhD student of mine, Kent Cassels, whom I had known for several years before I came to DICE, had been deeply moved by our tragedy. He had come to help us at the hospital and had been helping to tend the garden at Granary Cottage while we were away. Kent still looked devastated when I met him at work. He was desperate to help us in some way, and offered to be our bodyguard as he was highly trained in self-defence! It was a touching mark of his concern, but I explained that we were already receiving special protection from the police. Nevertheless, Kent continued with his regular visits to our home over the months ahead, to help keep the garden in shape and to assist in any way he could. His interest was indicative of the deep affection that he held for our family, and he was just one of many friends who acted 'above and beyond the call of duty' over the trying final months that we were to spend in Kent.

Our next-door neighbours in Nonington had also been good and constant friends to us. They approached me at about this time, as they had heard me discussing the possibility of moving back to Wales. They offered to buy Granary Cottage from us at the price we had paid for it only months before, which was a very generous offer considering that Lin had removed half of the interior of the house and we had not put any of it back yet! The significance of this offer was huge, as it removed much of the immediate barrier to our moving back to Wales. The next step would be to find somewhere to live near to Josie's old school in the Nantlle Valley.

On Tuesday 27 August, Eddie our local farrier arrived to trim the ponies' hooves and reshoe them. We brought Tegid and Rosie to the house and Eddie started work on their feet. Ed and Pauline were standing by when I suddenly realized that Josie was nowhere to be seen. Pauline and I found her in tears, cowering behind a curtain at her bedroom window. She was flinching at the sound of Eddie's hammer beating nails into the ponies' hooves in the courtyard below. We comforted Josie as best we could and reassured her about the shoeing operation which she had witnessed several times before. Josie had always been difficult to convince that the hot-shoeing method was painless for the ponies. But this time it was obvious that there was something more deeply unsettling about the procedure she was witnessing. The sight and sound of that swinging hammer sent cold shivers through us as the implications of Josie's distress became clear.

The incident was duly noted by Ed and Pauline who, in addition to their pastoral support role with us, were watching Josie all the time for any clues that she might provide. I felt sorry for Eddie the farrier, as I knew that through no fault of his own he would be one of the automatic suspects in the murder enquiry. A man who used hammers for his living and was known by the police to have visited our home before, would be bound to come in for close scrutiny. His plight was no different from that of many of our other friends and acquaintances. The police were being absolutely meticulous in their investigation and would follow up the slenderest of possible leads. At times, I had been asked by the police about the most innocuous and unlikely of friends and neighbours, and it often seemed as though there was nothing I could say that would allay their suspicions. Friends would 'laugh off' the fact that they had been interviewed about their relationships with Lin and me, and they would tell me not to worry that they had been questioned at length about their movements on 9 July. However, I still felt guilty and embarrassed that they might think I had implicated them in any way.

At the end of August, Josie and I went to Canterbury with Pauline for the first of the sessions that she was to have with her new doctors, psychologists and educationalists. These sessions were designed to assess her condition so that the correct provision could be made for Josie's medical care and schooling. We met with the Kent and Canterbury Hospital Trust's consultant paediatrician who would be coordinating the team. This was the first adult male among the specialists who had been dealing with Josie since she emerged from her post-operative daze. Josie began the session playing happily with paper cut-outs on the floor. But as soon as the doctor began to do some physical tests to check her coordination, she became alarmed. When he approached her with his reflex hammer to tap her on the knee, Josie reacted with great fear and pulled away from him violently. The doctor was mortified by her reaction and it took several minutes for her to calm down sufficiently for him to resume his investigation. But by this time Josie had had enough. When the doctor began to grip her arms to test her muscular response, she burst into tears and refused to cooperate any longer. If we needed convincing of Josie's fears of physical contact and the close proximity of adult males, then this demonstration had provided ample evidence.

The police were still keen to obtain as much publicity for the case as possible, as long as the murderer was at large. One of my MSc students, Yolanda Maldonado-Holliday, was married to the chief gorilla keeper at Howletts Zoo near Canterbury. This zoo keeps the largest captive collection of gorillas in the world, and a special effort is made to maintain them in as natural a state as possible. However, Yolanda often found herself caring for orphaned baby gorillas at her home, and she had invited Josie and me over to meet her latest charge, Kwam, who had been rejected by his mother at birth. As the *Crimewatch* edition was being broadcast the following day, the police asked if we might allow press access to the zoo visit so as to pre-publicize the television programme.

We spent a delightful morning at Yolanda's home, where Josie played with Kwam, and Yolanda's two daughters. Kwam was in nappies and had a cot in Yolanda's bedroom, just like a human baby, but Josie quickly found that Kwam was about ten times as strong as his human counterpart. She was fascinated by his antics and she had got used to carrying him around by the time we all went over to the zoo in the afternoon to meet the press. We were joined by Pauline, and the photographers clustered around Josie and Kwam on the lawn at the zoo while I fielded questions from the journalists. Kwam was tired out by this stage and just fell asleep in Josie's arms. She refused to let them wake him up or harass him in any way, and she too kept her head down for most of the time, except for a few brief moments when the photographers snapped as many shots as they could. This behaviour established a pattern that Josie follows to this day, of giving journalists only as much as she wants to give, and if necessary giving them a good old runaround in the process!

The following day I travelled into Canterbury for my first meeting with the solicitor who was to play a central role in our lives over the next few years. After many years of living in Africa, where the welfare state is virtually non-existent in most countries, I was not aware of the UK criminal injuries compensation system. However, Ed and Pauline had been urging me for several weeks to hire a lawyer to pursue a claim on Josie's behalf. They explained that as Josie had been the victim of a crime, she was eligible for a state payout, and that I should waste no time in instituting a claim. I had reservations about this at first, not least because it smacked of large amounts of bureaucracy, with no certainty of seeing much return. In any case, I felt guilty about expecting the state to support us in any way, as I had not been a taxpayer in Britain for eighteen years of my earlier career. Both Ed and Pauline, my mother and Lin's parents told me not to be so silly and to think instead of Josie's future. If I was going to have to care for her, and take a drop in salary through working part-time only, then I should start to think seriously about these matters.

Taking their advice, I had half-heartedly let my fingers do the walking through the Yellow Pages in search of a suitable solicitor. My eyes had alighted on a small box advertisement for a practice that had experience in children's compensation claims – Harman & Harman of Canterbury. Now I was meeting with the senior solicitor in the practice – Sarah Harman. She was slim and elegant and very smartly dressed, but immediately put me at my ease when I entered her office. I sensed her deep natural sympathy, and I could tell straight away that it was good fortune that had brought me to this firm. Sarah knew all about our case from the press coverage, and she already knew many of the major players in the drama – for example, Dave Stevens and the coroner – as a result of her years working in the Canterbury area. She led me through the intricacies of the criminal injuries claim procedure, explained the years that it might take to achieve a satisfactory result, and told me not to worry about money as she would be willing to take this case on an absolute minimum cost basis. The suggestion that I was not too sure about, was that I should also make a claim for compensation on the basis of any 'post-traumatic stress' that I might be suffering in the aftermath of the murders. I told her that I didn't feel as though I was suffering anything more than the normal grief of a bereaved husband and father, and that I had declined to have any form of counselling or psychological support. Sarah urged gently that I at least allow myself to be assessed by a specialist to give us a more independent view of my state of mind. She explained that Josie too would have to be assessed by medical, psychological and educational specialists in support of the claim, but that it should be possible to make use of much of the assessment work that had already been conducted at King's College Hospital.

I came away feeling that another weight had been lifted from my shoulders, and that I could happily place all my trust in this highly competent advocate. When I got home, Ed and Pauline were pleased that I had found a good lawyer. They told me that Sarah was from a highly respected family in the area (her sister was the MP Harriet Harman), and that she had a reputation for committed crusading on behalf of her clients. In the afternoon, we were visited at home for the first time by Tania Allen who was to be Josie's speech therapist, carrying on the excellent work with Josie's verbal skills that had begun at the hospital. Tania would be coming to us or we would be visiting her every couple of days for the entire time that we remained in Kent.

That evening we sat down to watch *Crimewatch*. Josie had been on the front page of several of the day's national newspapers again, and the programme was being trailed extensively. I was struck by Nick Ross's words as he introduced the programme: '... a case unprecedented in British criminal history'. This echoed what Dave Stevens had told me, and I could still not quite believe it. Surely murders were being committed every day of the week in Britain? Why should the tragedy that had struck my family be so different from the traumas afflicting so many bereaved relatives in other parts of the country? Maybe I was influenced by my fatalism, built up through years of living in Africa where vast numbers of children and their parents are struck down daily by the mindless violence of war, flood, famine and disease. I also had a sneaking suspicion that the press interest in this case was not only the result of Dave Steven's artful media relations, but also had more than a little to do with the fact that Josie was photogenic and that her image helped to sell newspapers.

During *Crimewatch*, Josie's image was again used to tug at the heart-strings of viewers. The footage of my interview was also used, but thankfully only up to just before the point at which I broke down. Dave Stevens made a cool but impassioned plea for assistance from the public to catch the killer, and the programme must have had a great impact, because later we were told that it had elicited one of the largest ever responses to a *Crimewatch* appeal, with many hundreds of phone calls to the studio and the incident room over the days following the broadcast. One poignant aspect to the programme, in hindsight, was the involvement of the presenter Jill Dando who narrated the case details and interviewed Dave Stevens. She herself was to be tragically murdered on her own doorstep only three years later.

Two days later, my next-door neighbour from Wales was back with us, helping out at Granary Cottage. We were all invited by Pauline to attend the graduation of her son John from the local Police Training Centre. It was an enjoyable time, watching the passing out parade and listening to the Kent Police Band, but we were then surprised by a specially laid on ceremony to present Josie with a giant teddy bear and a cheque for £1200. John and his friends had raised the money for Josie through charity events and appeals among several police forces in southern England. It was an incredibly generous gift; Pauline and her family were really pulling out all the stops for us.

Early in September, Dave Stevens came to see me with another request. He wanted to put out a special appeal for information on the case, in the country's most widely read newspaper – the *Sun*. He stated that the paper was starting a nationwide campaign to clear up several high-profile unsolved murders, and they wished to start the ball rolling with 'The Russell Murders'. The *Sun* would put up a £20,000 reward for information leading to the arrest of the murderer; Dave Stevens would provide an update on the investigation; and I was being asked to write a letter appealing for public assistance to the enquiry. Dave guaranteed that my letter would be published in its entirety, without editing. This is the letter that appeared in the *Sun*:

Dear Sir
I am hoping that you will be willing to publish this letter in whole or part, to appeal to anyone who may be able to throw further light on the senseless killing of my wife and child in Kent two months ago.
  My life has been shattered and I don't know if I will ever be able to rebuild it again to recover a fraction of the happiness that we once had. It is still too early and too painful for me to hold my

dead wife and child in my thoughts for more than a few seconds at a time – especially after having had to identify them lying side by side in the mortuary, the worst experience in my life.

Lin was twice the person I was, the complete wife and mother. I shall love her forever. Megan was so young and so perfect, she carried so much of Lin's and my hopes and dreams; only to have her life deliberately snuffed out by another human being. Mostly, whenever thoughts of the attack enter my mind, I try to thrust them away because I can't bear to think of the anguish that Lin or the girls must have suffered watching even our dog being battered to death, let alone each other. At other times I find myself wanting to know more, to help me rationalize the evil and prepare myself to explain it to my surviving daughter Josephine.

Soon after the attack, when I thought my whole family had been lost, I wanted to take my own life. But my strength to carry on has come from Josie who, although brain damaged, is tackling the task of re-learning to speak from scratch with cheerfulness and determination.

During the six weeks of her rapid physical recovery in hospital, Josie showed no signs that she remembered the events surrounding the deaths of her mother and sister. I hoped that she might have been incapacitated early in the attack, and therefore spared the horror of witnessing the actual killings. In fact, she so often scolded me for looking downcast or sad that I started to believe that she was already coming to terms with her grief. And this in turn helped me to rally whenever I found myself slipping back again into deep despair.

Since returning home however, Josie is giving many signs that she can remember the attack. It has unfortunately become plain that the experience has changed her forever. She was always happy and carefree, with no fear of people or places. Now she often recoils in horror from well-wishers who approach us in the street, or bursts into tears and hides if someone comes to the house. She sometimes cowers and shivers in a corner if a car goes slowly past the house at night. I watch over her every minute, even when she goes just yards from the house, and this also sensitizes her to the peril of our situation.

Otherwise, in order to have some time to tackle the mountain of work from officialdom that has engulfed me as a result of these murders, I have to leave Josie in the care of people who can offer her sufficient protection were she to be attacked again. We have a police guard outside our house every night, and police presence often for hours during the day. This is also a reminder of the potential threat to our safety, and we cannot settle back into a normal life until the need for protection is removed.

There is a similar feeling of insecurity amongst the population of the district where we live. My local postmistress summed it up when she said 'the children don't come for their sweets any more'. The killer of my family has created fear throughout the community of East Kent and none of us will be able to walk happily in the country lanes, nor let our kids play out of our sight again, until the murderer is caught.

As I wait still for permission to bury Lin and Megan and our dog Lucy, and as I live in hope that the murderer will be found and an explanation emerge, Josie and I live in a kind of limbo – unable to comprehend or come to terms with the past, and unable to think ahead to any kind of meaningful life in the future. A letter I received today summarizes the thoughts of so many well-wishers:

Please know that so many people are wishing you both well in your recovery and are very much hoping that this man will be caught soon. The whole country holds its breath for you both.

At the latest count Josie and I have received over 600 cards and letters of sympathy and support. My heart goes out to those who have related stories of loss and bereavement. I want to thank friends and colleagues, and the hundreds of complete strangers from around the world who have written to me. And I especially want to thank the people of the village of Nonington where I live, and the other villages nearby, who have given Josie and I so much support and encouragement. It is them who will be most helped to return to some kind of normality when the killer is caught.

If the person who did this was unable to control themselves at the time of the murder, then it could easily happen again. And for the sake of everybody's safety, including the murderer himself, it is essential that he be caught or give himself up as soon as possible. Anyone who was a witness to events surrounding the killing, or anyone who knows who it might be should give up this informa-

tion to the police, even anonymously. I can't believe that nobody
knows who carried out this crime except the murderer himself.
If someone does know, then if there is a drop of conscience or
humanity left in you, please contact the police – or, if you prefer,
the newspaper – as only then will Josie and I be able to escape
from fear and begin to rebuild our shattered lives again.

Shaun Russell

On the evening of the day that the newspaper came out (9 September),
Josie had gone to bed and my friend from Wales and I were in the
living room at Granary Cottage discussing the affairs of the day. We
moved into the kitchen for a cup of tea, leaving the copy of the *Sun*
on the living room table. Up until this point, we had carefully vetted
Josie's access to newspaper reporting of her case, not least because we
wanted to avoid her distress at the many pictures of Lin, Megan and
Lucy that had been appearing in print. Josie came down unexpectedly
from her room and spied the paper with her mother's and sister's
photos on the front page. Unbeknown to us, she opened it up and
found an even larger colour photo of the whole family inside. And
beside it was the e-fit picture of the crime suspect, with the word
'Murderer' in a banner headline above it. Josie came into the kitchen
clutching the paper indicating: 'Yes, that's him... that's the man who
did it.' We were shocked to see Josie with the paper, but sensitive to
the potential significance of her declaration.

I phoned Ed to report the incident, and voiced my reservations that
Josie's response might have been conditioned by the positioning and
headlining of the image. It must have been irritating to the police that
she had now been exposed to this image, before they had asked her
to describe her assailant in detail. It was, however, suggestive, and
prompted the police to move ahead more quickly, to bring in a police
artist to work with Josie on her memories of the killer.

Dave Stevens had been taking advice from Sarah Helps, the clinical
child psychologist at King's College Hospital, and Tania Allan, the
speech therapist in Kent, on how to structure Josie's interviews and
what kind of questions the police could ask her. He was also still
receiving advice from the Dora Black clinic in London, which specialized in helping children who were witnesses to violent crime and who
were suffering from post-traumatic stress. Eventually, Dave gave Ed

and Pauline the go-ahead to extend beyond general conversation about the recent past, and begin probing Josie's memory of the attack. In the last two weeks of August, Ed and Pauline had taken Josie out on several treats to relax her in their presence. In the first couple of weeks of September they began to sit her down formally in the evenings at Granary Cottage and to video Josie's responses to their carefully framed questions.

We soon found that it was better for me not to be present, as Josie misbehaved more frequently and tried to avoid the questions if I was in the room. It mirrored her behaviour at the hospital where, because of her familiarity with me, she was more likely to be naughty in my presence. But there was also the sense that she was reticent to discuss these private and personal matters in front of me. Possibly she wanted to protect me from the upset that it might cause me. She had seen me break down several times and she had slowly come to realize that beneath my stoic exterior I was hurting too. Josie was putting on a brave face for most of the time, but it didn't take too much for Dad's facade to crack. Whether it was genuine concern or simply her embarrassment at seeing her father in tears didn't matter; Ed and Pauline soon learnt that Josie was more attentive and cooperative when I was banished to the kitchen!

By this time Josie had enough words to say 'umm' (yes) or 'no' to a question, but Ed and Pauline also made use of a specially designed 'dictionary' of images that Josie could point to to elaborate her answers. Pauline had gone to a lot of trouble to build a scale model of Cherry Garden Lane and the murder scene itself, so that Josie could pinpoint actions and the timings of events. She had designed and crafted small, lifelike figures of Lin, Megan, Josie and Lucy, and the murderer with his car. The model was finely detailed, right down to a tiny hammer representing the one used in the attack. It was a chilling sight when I first saw this model, but Josie was fascinated by it, and played with it like a doll's house set. She grew in confidence as she saw Ed and Pauline hanging on her every word, and she would move the figures around and repeat the sequence of events animatedly and with little evidence of concern.

I had already referred in public to the 'love–hate' relationship that we shared with Ed and Pauline. Always our shadows, it was impossible to forget the serious intent of their presence. However, the 'love' side of the equation was always the stronger. My admiration for Pauline grew greater by the day. She had kids of her own, and by this stage had come to understand Josie so well that she knew just how much probing she could take, and when was the right time to bring the interview sessions to a close. Ed also had children of his own and he was like an affectionate big uncle figure to Josie. But he too knew just when Josie needed a stern word if she was playing them up deliberately, or when she was misbehaving out of boredom or laziness.

As the interviews continued, it became clear that Josie remembered most of what had happened on that fateful day. Ed and Pauline often emerged ashen-faced and solemn from these sessions, dazed by what Josie had been telling them, but also humbled by the matter-of-fact way in which she provided the information. Josie usually looked relieved when she came away from these discussions, but we got the distinct impression that it was only because she wanted to get back to her toys again, rather than for any other, more unsettling, reason. It certainly seemed as if she understood the importance of her testimony and that it was her 'duty' to help the police in this way. I felt the same, and so I was pleased with the way that she handled these potentially very traumatic interviews. I have even to admit to a sneaking sense of pride at the way she wound up Ed and Pauline on occasion. It proved yet again that Josie was exerting her will on the world around her, and that she would not let what had happened cow her spirit or crush her individuality.

The police interviews with Josie had provided enough detail of the murders that Dave Stevens decided to go public again with a press conference on 10 September. This time I accompanied Ed to the police incident room at the Knackington Headquarters of 'Operation Scribe' (the Russell Murder enquiry). The press were lined up again in full force, and Dave revealed some of what Josie had been telling the police. However, he kept back key parts of Josie's testimony, so that he would have leverage when the time came to interview likely suspects.

I explained to the journalists how Josie had been handling the interviews and updated them on her progress with speech therapy, my thoughts about her going back to school and our returning to live in Wales. Josie's picture duly appeared on the front pages of the national dailies again, and all the stories focused on Josie's description of how the family were accosted by the murderer. Many of them also featured information on a hammer that had been found in a hedge close to the murder scene. The suggestion was that this might be the murder weapon. I found myself in complete agreement with the senior investigating officers that this was probably just a hoax. From its position it was inconceivable that the hammer could have been missed in the detailed field search carried out immediately after the murders, and the tool had provided no relevant forensic material. I also learned that somebody local had told the police where to look for the hammer after a seance evening with a ouija board. I had already learnt from the less savoury content of my postbag that high-profile and sensational tragedies such as ours brought cranks and perverts out of the woodwork. I put the hammer hoax down to a sick joke on the part of someone who wished simply to gloat over the drama that they hoped it would cause.

Friday 13 September was far from unlucky for Josie and me. We had chosen that day to take Josie back for a visit to her schoolmates in their classroom at Goodnestone School. As with the teachers in Wales, the staff at Goodnestone were very keen to have Josie back in their care, and seemed unfazed by the prospect of having a virtually speechless child in their classroom. I had been having discussions with the headteacher Darryl Peek about setting up an exploratory visit, and Josie's class teacher Lynda Roberts was also eager to welcome Josie back. Accordingly, we went into school halfway through the morning, and Josie was ushered quietly into the classroom. The majority of the children were overjoyed to see her, but I could see apprehension on some of the faces. Lynda and the other staff, along with trained child psychologists and counsellors, had been ministering to the needs of the more deeply affected and traumatized children (and parents) since the time of the murders. It was good, therefore, to sense the anxiety in the class dissipating as Lynda quickly assimilated Josie back into their activities. The children could see that apart from her hat Josie looked just the same as before.

I left Josie happily joining in with her peers, as I went upstairs for another conference with Darryl Peek. I told her that I was now sure that I wanted to take Josie back to Wales to live, but that it would probably take months for me to find a place to live within striking distance of Josie's old school. In the meantime I was keen for Josie to come back to Goodnestone with her old friends and teachers. I had pressed Darryl and Lynda on the question of their having a child in class with a severe speech and language impairment. They surely had enough to cope with as it was? And why should they make all the extra effort when we were likely to be leaving for Wales in the not too distant future? But they were both adamant that it would not be a burden for them, and in fact it might even help to ease the situation in the class by allaying the fears of the other children and building a happy and settled classroom spirit again. Darryl explained that she had started clearing a way through the formalities required to allow Josie back into the classroom. She had some battles ahead of her, for sure, but portents were good as we had already received a very supportive letter from the head of the County Education Authority, which made it clear that no stone would be left unturned to provide Josie with the support she needed.

We were expecting the first set of formal assessments by an educational psychologist the following week. This was intended to provide Josie with the special-needs statement required for her future educational provision. When that came through, Josie would be likely to have a 'special-needs' assistant to help her on a one-to-one basis in the classroom. Darryl had already arranged that one of the school teaching assistants (Julie Kelly, Jazzmin's mother) could start coming to our home to give Josie preparatory home schooling. Clearly she had been pulling strings on our behalf, in addition to coping with the difficulties of the new school term in the aftermath of the killings. Here was yet another person to whom I would always owe an enormous debt of gratitude.

Josie and I spent the weekend of 14–15 September in Romsey, Hampshire, with my mother and sister. It was another brief chance to get away from the continuously ringing telephone at Granary Cottage, and to relax in the company of two understanding and compassionate women who always put our comforts first, no matter what difficulties they were facing in their own lives. My mother takes the *Express* newspaper and so we were amused to read in the *Sunday Express*, a story about our friend from America who was helping Josie and me at home, with a fuzzy photograph of her sitting in the background during our trip to Howletts Zoo. We joked about me being seen with this mystery blonde and reflected on the fact that Josie and I were now famous enough that the newspapers were resorting to printing stories not only about us, but about our friends too.

We returned to our first visit from an educational psychologist who began to assess Josie's responses to a set of standard tests, in order to prepare her special-needs statement. It was particularly difficult for the specialist as many of the tests required spoken or written answers, and of course Josie could not respond in this standard manner. There were more speech therapy sessions with Tania, more routine inter- views with Ed and Pauline, and Julie Kelly started to come in regularly to give Josie home schooling. I took Josie over to Goodnestone School again for another morning in her old classroom, and then had a meeting with Dave Stevens and the coroner, who updated me on progress with the second, 'independent', autopsy, and indicated that Lin's and Megan's bodies could be released to me in a fortnight's time. We even found time for dinner with friends. What with shopping, cooking, cleaning and tending the garden in addition to everything else going on, life seemed as hectic as ever. I met twice more with my solicitor Sarah Harman that week and had to agree when she suggested to me that I had not had time, nor was I allowing myself the time, to grieve properly for my lost family. She prevailed upon me to speak with an eminent psychiatrist in London, who would assess me for symptoms of post-traumatic stress syndrome and I arranged to have an appointment with him the following month.

The last task that week was to take Josie back to King's College Hospital for a routine check-up. It felt strange walking back through those familiar and rather forbidding corridors. But our step was lighter in the knowledge that we were going to see old friends, and that there was nothing more painful in store for Josie than having a plaster pulled off. Josie's rearmost head wound had all but cleared up by this stage and we were given the go-ahead to reduce her pill intake to zero over the next few weeks. We chatted with the nurses and doctors who had become so much part of our lives during the summer, and they were all delighted with Josie's progress. And we were sad- dened by the continued presence on the ward of children who had been there when we left, and who were still struggling bravely against life-threatening illness.

On Saturday 21 September, Josie and I wandered over to the Bruderhof mansion nearby, where the religious community was having its annual Open Day for local residents. They were overjoyed to see us, and Josie renewed friendships with some of the children she had played with there before the murders. It was the first time that we had been out in public together locally, and many of the residents of Nonington approached us to express their sympathy, and their pleasure at seeing Josie looking so well.

That Monday, 23 September, we were visited at home by Dora Black. Dora had been assisting the police over the preceding weeks, and Dave Stevens had relied on her for much professional psychological input to the case. He wanted her to meet Josie personally, to assess her state of mind and ensure that the interview techniques they were using were appropriate and non-stressful. Josie was a bit put out by this very smart and elegant lady arriving at the house and beginning to ask her all sorts of sensitive and personal questions. And I was hard-pressed to justify to Dora why I had declined to have formal psychological counselling for either of us. I explained that neither of us was at ease talking about personal matters with strangers or medical professionals. I told her that we had found much succour in talking things through with Ed and Pauline, and that our friends and relatives had acted as informal 'counsellors'. Dora was still worried, however, as in her wide experience, most children who had been through traumas like Josie's showed more adverse symptoms. She could not believe, for example, that Josie was not having nightmares; and she suggested that Josie was not showing 'appropriate emotional expression' and that she might still be in a state of brain-damage-related 'euphoria'. Reluctantly I agreed to Josie attending the post-traumatic stress clinic in London for some sessions of play therapy and psychological observation.

I had now settled on 5 October for Lin and Megan's funeral, and so I had to get back to Wales to make all the last-minute arrangements. During the last week of September, I took Josie back to Tan-yr-Allt once more. I delivered her to play with old friends, and went off to meet with the local undertakers – Pritchards of Tremadoc – to whom I had entrusted the burial arrangements. They would have to travel down to the Canterbury mortuary two days before the funeral, to bring back Lin's and Megan's bodies, and Lucy too.

I wanted a small private funeral at the Garndolbenmaen graveyard, and the police were in favour of this so as to be able to control any media interest more easily. But I was aware of the large number of friends, relatives and neighbours who would want to pay their respects to Lin and Megan. And so I arranged for a public service of remembrance to take place in the chapel at Nantlle on the morning of the funeral. The burial would then take place at St Mary's, Garndolbenmaen, during the afternoon.

In between the various meetings it took to arrange all this, I spent some time looking in estate agents' windows to see if there were any suitable houses for sale in the Nantlle Valley. I knew that keeping house as a single parent would be a demanding task, and I was therefore looking for a smaller property than we had been used to. A two-bedroomed cottage with a manageable garden was now the target, and I knew before I started that to find such a place with paddocks for the ponies would be nigh on impossible at short notice. However, while we were staying at Tan-yr-Allt, I learned that one of our old neighbour's cottages was on the market, next door to Plas Tan-yr-Allt. The only drawback about this was the proximity to the house where we had lived before we moved to Kent, and so the area was filled with memories of Lin and Megan. In addition, the cottage had no fields of its own for the ponies, although there was the possibility that we could rent a field not too far away. Otherwise the cottage was perfect. It was tucked away quite privately up its own gravel track and had a small and pretty garden. When I suggested the possibility to Josie, she was pleased as Punch about the idea, because, if we could secure the property, she would be living next door to Jessie again. Josie and Megan had grown up with Jessie, like a big sister living next door. Jessie was taking Equestrian Studies at a nearby agricultural college, and would be the perfect partner for Josie with her horsey interests if we moved back with our ponies.

Josie had also always looked up to Jessie's mother as a dependable auntie figure living nearby. And so it seemed a nigh-on perfect solution for us to be able to move back to the cottage next door to Plas Tan-yr-Allt. Josie seemed to have no qualms about living so close to our old home, and so I resolved to contact my solicitor about making an offer on the house, as soon as we got back to Kent.

October began – a blur of activity. More police interviews, more speech therapy and more time at Goodnestone School for Josie. I met with educationalists to discuss progress on Josie's return to school, the police to make the final arrangements for the funeral, and my solicitor, Sarah Harman, for further briefing on Lin's estate in probate,

Josie's compensation claim and our house conveyancing. At this meeting, Sarah also mentioned to me that she had been contacted by the media with a view to 'securing access' to Josie and me for personal interviews and photo coverage of our story. Sarah explained to me that the case had become so notorious, that there was a considerable build-up of media pressure for an 'inside interview' with me about the events of the tragedy. I had an inkling of this as a result of the increasing number of letters that were reaching me from well-known television and newspaper journalists, and from the editors of national newspapers. Some of them mentioned payment for access; but because of the pressures of daily life at this time, and because I was happy for the police to control the contact that I had with the media, I had been simply filing these approaches away with the hundreds of letters of condolence that Josie and I were receiving.

But Sarah was very concerned about my financial affairs. She knew that my contract at the University of Kent was about to end. She knew that Josie and I were moving back to Wales and that I had no job there. She had explained how it would be unlikely that I could access the proceeds from our Welsh house sale for years, if ever, as they were now tied up in the probate affairs surrounding Lin's estate (as she died intestate and legally not married to me). She also warned of the years it might take to secure Josie's criminal injuries compensation. Sarah told me that I should start to think really carefully about how I was going to care for Josie and her special needs, given our parlous financial future. She explained that it was now a sad fact of life that 'stories' such as ours were worth large amounts of money to the national media, and that we should at least consider some of the offers that were coming through. I told her that I would, and that in the meantime she was welcome to explore the possibilities further.

Another important meeting took place at the beginning of the week, when several of the specialists now charged with Josie's care gathered together. It laid the groundwork for the ongoing therapy that Josie was to receive, and the further tests that needed to be carried out in support of her special-needs educational statement. I was somewhat dismayed to see the number of experts now being drawn into the loop on Josie's case, as I knew that she would baulk at many more sessions like the last one in Canterbury. Specialists present at the meeting included the consultant paediatrician, a speech therapist, occupational therapist, play therapist, clinical psychologist, consultant child psychiatrist, local education authority representative, and a social services representative. Mercifully only a few more formal tests needed to be done, some of which could take place in the classroom once she had settled back in at Goodnestone School.

On Thursday 3 October we packed our bags and headed for Wales again, to prepare for the funeral. By the next day, friends and relatives from as far afield as Cornwall, Kent and Tyneside had arrived at Tan-yr-Allt or were staying nearby. It was good to see them again but there was no party air about this gathering. There were attempts by well-meaning friends to jolly things along, but this led to friction with others who were not in the mood for levity. I was quite relieved that most people let me sit by myself in the corner and not join in. My head was too full of anxieties about the day of the funeral and memories stirred by the presence of these friends, for me to share in pleasantries and light conversation. In fact, the only person who appeared to be enjoying herself was Josie. She was happy to see all the old friends and to enjoy the spread of good food that our neighbour had laid on for everybody. Josie ran around impressing the adults with her magic tricks and refusing to let anybody be sad if she could possibly help it. Again, I could not decide whether these were the actions of a little girl who simply could not understand the significance of the events going on around her, or if Josie was deliberately blocking them out and compensating with 'euphoric' behaviour as suggested by the psychologists.

In the middle of all this, I received a call from Sarah Harman to tell me that one of the national newspapers had printed an article about our enquiries concerning the value of 'Josie's story'. Sarah was abject in her apologies; she knew that I was in the middle of preparing for the funeral and that the last thing we needed was bad coverage in the newspapers. This was even more important because of the sympathy card that the police were playing in their media relations, in order to draw out further information on the killer from the public.

Having got to know Sarah over the preceding few weeks, I could see how the situation had arisen. She was passionately committed to our case and had vowed to get absolutely the best deal possible for Josie from the Criminal Injuries Authority, and any other sources of support she could find. She had even refused to take proper payment for her services and was treating ours almost as a *pro bono* (unpaid) case. Her faxes to the newspapers had explained our financial plight, but must have piqued a newspaper editor and precipitated the admonitory article. Sarah was contrite. She offered to hand over our business to another lawyer, but I would not hear of it. I had one hundred per cent faith in her commitment and skill and did not want to lose her practical (and emotional) support. Sarah did, however, ask that I should let her find another lawyer specializing in media affairs to handle this aspect of our lives, as she felt out of her depth in this area; and I agreed to this. This experience forewarned me that one 'played with the dragon's tail' at one's peril – we would have to tread extra carefully in future in our dealings with the press.

On the morning of the funeral, Josie's euphoric behaviour continued as we drove up the valley for Lin's and Megan's memorial service at Capel Baladeulyn, Nantlle. Because there were so many familiar faces present, Josie seemed again to be enjoying herself, running around and between the guests, leading them along the rows of floral bouquets and posies, and pointing out interesting designs and pretty condolence cards. There was one particularly touching tribute in the form of a teddy-bear-shaped arrangement of red and white carnations from the pupils of Ysgol Baladeulyn. There were also messages from friends we had made in far-flung corners of the globe and long in the past, and I wondered how they had learned of our tragic news and been able to ensure that their floral tributes and dedications reached us on this sad day.

The chapel was packed with about 150 people, and Josie and I sat at the front with Peter and Irene. The police had ensured that only two representatives of the media were present in the church, one each from the local paper and the Press Association, and their cameras were kept at a discreet distance from us.

The Reverend Dewi Roberts led the service. Dewi's own children attended Ysgol Baladeulyn, and his son Robert had been in Megan's class. When I went to see Dewi to make arrangements for the service, he told me that he had never had to conduct a funeral for people so young or who had died so horribly. But this young minister rose to the challenge of the oration with enormous grace and strength, as men of God so often seem to do in a crisis that is felt by the whole community. His elegy was deeply moving and he had barely begun before my tears started to flow once more; they continued for the rest of the forty-five-minute service. It was an overpowering feeling of love and sympathy that I sensed from the little community in that packed church. People from different backgrounds and even a different mother tongue to Josie and myself, who welcomed us without reserve when we came to settle in this valley. They shared our grief openly, and I was once more convinced that it was to this place that Josie and I must return.

There is space here for only a couple of extracts from Dewi Robert's inspirational address at the memorial service:

Today in this service we are remembering the most innocent: a child's life; and the best: a mother's love and dedication. There is nothing in this world more precious than a child's life and a mother's love.

I remember the first time I saw Megan. I can recollect the way she smiled at me. It was her way of acknowledging me. And I remember her eyes. Megan's eyes were full of character. They were expressive eyes, intelligent eyes. They almost sparkled, she was so full of life and vitality. She was a real treasure.

Whenever I saw Lin, it was always with the girls. I often saw them cycling to or from school. Lin had a great zest for life, she enjoyed life to the full.

Words cannot express how we feel about this awful and wicked tragedy. We realize that we do not know how to truly sympathize with you as a family, for this tragedy is outside our own experience. But we certainly feel for you and wish that you might know that our hearts are with you at this time. Sadly, in this world, we know that the best and most innocent are sometimes the ones who suffer most.

There have been many prayers said for you in this part of Wales in school, in church and in the community at large. We continue to pray that you may be sustained in your grief by one another as a family and by your closest friends. We pray that you will be given grace and strength to sustain yourselves in your lives together, and be able to rebuild your lives again in peace and quietness wherever you will choose to live. And I pray that as a family you will become stronger and even closer together through this tragedy, and that

Josie will recover from any emotional and physical scars, and in time know a truly fulfilling life. May your fond memories of Megan and Lin sustain and uplift you. May those memories become stronger and deeper as time goes on. And may all the bad memories fade away and become distant.

The hymns in the service included *All Things Bright and Beautiful* and the Welsh hymn *Iesu Tirion Gwel yn Awr*, which refers to the prayer of a young child. Our friend and neighbour from Kent, Stuart Hardisty, read three beautiful short poems that he had written specially for Lin and Megan and brought tears to the eyes of most of those present. Afterwards Josie and I spent some time with friends and relatives outside the church, before leaving for a quick lunch with Peter and Irene and to prepare ourselves for the burial service in the afternoon.

About thirty of our closest friends and relatives congregated at three o'clock in the village square at Tremadoc, two miles from the grave-yard, where the funeral cortège of hearses and mourners' cars was waiting. We drove slowly up to St Mary's Church and filed inside to wait as the coffins were brought in. On Megan's smaller coffin was the same wrenchingly poignant teddy bear of red and white carnations that we had seen in the morning.

The Reverend Dewi Roberts assisted the Rector, Canon William Jones, at this smaller, private ceremony. My emotion welled up again during the Canon's moving speech, and through the prayers and hymns that followed, which included *Morning has Broken*. Throughout the service Josie gazed quizzically at the coffins. My mind was in turmoil again; should I have let her see Lin and Megan at the mortuary after all? How could her traumatized nine-year-old mind possibly comprehend that the vibrant, living, breathing mother and sister she had so recently taken for granted as eternal presences in her life, were now lying lifeless in these shiny wooden boxes? The feeling grew stronger as we filed out after the coffins, which were borne compas-sionately by local men who had volunteered for the job. The caskets were lowered gradually to the bottom of the grave that had been excavated for them in the spot I chose weeks before. The grave was dug doubly deep, to allow for Megan's coffin to be placed on top of Lin's. I learned afterwards from the gravedigger that there was space for me too, in case I chose to be buried with Lin and Megan at a later date.

I could hardly control the shake in my hand as I took the earth from the undertaker's trowel and scattered it on the coffins. When it was Josie's turn to cast the earth, she approached so close to the edge of the three-metre pit, that I worried for a moment she might slip in. But then I saw that she was looking long and hard into the grave. There was a pause as Josie continued to stare, unperturbed by the muffled sobs of those around her, who were turning away and clutching each other in their grief, unable to bear to watch this child's last farewell to her mother and sister. Did Josie finally realize at this point that her mother and sister were really gone? It makes me feel better to think that she did.

As we walked away from the grave to the waiting cars, we were only vaguely aware of a local journalist photographing us from behind the cover of a gravestone. There were cameramen behind a police cordon near the cars, but we appreciated the fact that the press had kept a respectfully low profile, and no attempt was made to follow us to the funeral tea after the burial.

The funeral tea is a traditional feature of burials in Wales, and ours was held at the Tremadoc Hotel back in the village. About forty of us sat stiffly down to tea, sandwiches and cakes, but it was not long before Josie was injecting a little of the wake spirit into this alcohol-free gathering. She was determined, as usual, not to see people sad, and so she began to buzz around the tables, chatting in her rudimentary way with the guests and showing them some of her magic tricks. It was like the tea party on our first return to Granary Cottage. Josie's enthusiasm slowly infected the assembled company, so that by the end of the afternoon the conversation had become quite merry and the hubbub in the dining room belied the sad reason that brought us there.

With the funeral over, I too could relax a little. I felt I had done my best for Lin and Megan, and that they were now safe in a place to which Josie and I could always return to be near them. It was only a matter of time before we would be back here to live, and I wouldn't feel quite as estranged from my wife and daughter as I had when they were in their cold steel boxes in the mortuary at Canterbury. And the sight of Josie, relaxed and smiling as she played with her friends from Nantlle, further intensified my desire to make the move back to this area as soon as humanly possible.

The following day, Sunday, we relaxed at Tan-yr-Allt with some of our friends and relatives. There was a large amount of sensitive and moving coverage of the memorial service and the funeral in the newspapers, but they had struggled to explain Josie's behaviour. As I was to find over and over again in my contact with the media, some papers made up the stories that they thought would be appropriate, such as the piece that had 'tears falling from Josie's cheeks'. Others were more discerning and noted that Josie seemed to be 'in a world of her own'. The *Cambrian News* noted Josie's 'inappropriate smile' flashed at photographers on our arrival at St Mary's Church. There were even references to Josie's clothing, particularly the floral Dr Marten's boots which she had chosen to wear for the ceremonies. Several papers referred to the fact that up until this time I had 'maintained a remarkable composure' in public, but that at the funeral I had finally broken down. I felt the double-edge to these comments, which might connote admirable behaviour to some people, but make me seem cold and unfeeling to others.

Beneath the piece about the funeral in the *Sunday Mirror*, I noticed another article. Under the headline 'Killings Linked to Rachel's Slaying', it described the similarities between 'The Russell Murders' and the 1992 killing on Wimbledon Common of Rachel Nickell. Rachel had also died in the month of July, and in front of her young child, attacked while walking her dog in a peaceful country setting. Unsurprisingly, police investigating both cases had exchanged information. What caught my eye was the information that Rachel's partner André Hanscombe had written a book about his experiences and those of his child who witnessed the murder. I resolved to get a copy of the book as soon as possible, because here at last was a person with whom I might be able to identify, and whose story might hold some counsel for our situation.

DCI Dave Stevens had always told me that he would answer any of my questions and help me in any way that he could. He had already had to put up with indiscretions on my part, for example when journalists 'doorstepped' me and squeezed out more information than I should prudently have revealed. Yet he never became angry with me nor reprimanded me. He had told me that they were using a forensic psychologist to build up a picture of the killer. The specialist was based at a northern university and had come to Operation Scribe after assisting with the Jade Matthews murder inquiry on Merseyside. Like everybody else I was still struggling to comprehend what sort of person would have committed the heinous attack on my family, and so I put aside my reticence for once and asked Dave Stevens if I might meet with the forensic psychologist.

It is not normal practice to allow relatives of the deceased to meet with or question the forensic psychologist in a murder enquiry. In fact great pains are often taken to protect the identity of profilists as they may be at risk themselves, especially if they become successful at 'fingering' violent suspects consistently. And in my case, for all I knew I was still a suspect myself, albeit a low-priority one at this stage. However, although I could see that he was reticent, the DCI was true to his promise, and so one sunny afternoon in early October I sat down to tea in my back garden with Dave Stevens and the forensic psychologist. I began by asking him about the techniques employed to build psychological profiles of killers and he obliged by explaining the approaches used. But he was not so forthcoming about the specific profile of the man wanted in our case; maybe this was still classified information at this stage. He was even less forthcoming about himself and his own background, possibly for the reasons of security mentioned above. Instead he used this line of conversation to turn the questioning round on me, so that by the end of the afternoon he had thoroughly scrutinized my background and feelings about all that was happening. I felt strangely cheated, and I had a sense of unease that this just might have been a set-up to probe me further as a suspect. Afterwards, I put this down to my own paranoia, as Dave Stevens was at pains to dismiss my concerns. I rationalized that while psychologists inevitably have to ask questions of you in their jobs, they seem often to have an aversion to being asked questions about themselves!

On the morning of 8 October, Josie had the first of many sessions with the police artist. The early sessions were spent winning Josie's confidence by doodling and playing around with paints and crayons. After several such meetings, the artist was able to begin preparing some drawings of the murderer, based on Josie's memory. The resulting images were similar to the e-fit produced earlier by a witness who had seen a man driving away from the scene of the crime. It is possible, of course, that Josie's description might have been influenced by her memory of the e-fit that she had seen in the newspaper previously. However, she only glimpsed the e-fit on one occasion as far as we know, and she did not have access again to that image until well after the police artist had completed his work.

That same afternoon I caught the train up to London for my first session with the psychiatrist Dr Christopher Jarman, who was to assess me for my post-traumatic stress submission to the Criminal Injuries Compensation Authority. Dr Jarman was very friendly and put me at my ease at once. I responded by doing as I imagined one was supposed to do with a psychiatrist, and poured out everything I could think of about my parents, my prior life, my loves and hates, weaknesses and hang-ups. Dr Jarman made the point that I seemed to be almost naively transparent and uncommonly eager to expose my innermost thoughts. He was used to his clients being a lot more guarded in what they revealed to a stranger – I later found that he was a leading forensic psychologist and had interviewed several murderers during his illustrious career, which might explain that!

I told Dr Jarman that I did not feel the need for counselling or formal psychological support, and that I could not honestly say that I felt I was suffering from post-traumatic stress. All I would admit to was my intermittent sobbing fits ('grief attacks'), and the dominance of Lin and Megan in my dreams. I conceded that I might be repressing my memories in an unhealthy way, because whenever I woke from sleep for any reason I could see that I had almost invariably been dreaming about Lin and/or Megan. I rationalized that my body was compensating for my refusal to hold Lin and Megan in my thoughts during my waking hours by letting them live instead in my dreams.

Dr Jarman worked through the symptoms of post-traumatic stress disorder with me:

1. flashbacks and recollections of the tragedy;
2. sleep disturbance (dreams and nightmares);
3. acute distress on being reminded of the trauma;
4. repression of the memory and avoidance of the memory triggers;
5. compulsive reliving of the events in one's mind;
6. diminished interest in daily life (lethargy, detachment, isolation and withdrawal);
7. impaired occupational functioning and lack of initiative;
8. shame, guilt and self-blame;
9. preoccupation with revenge;
10. sexual dysfunction, e.g. impotence.

And to my horror, I had to admit that I was manifesting just about all of these symptoms to a greater or lesser degree. Dr Jarman also noted something that would be repeated to me by friends and professionals alike over the next few years, viz. that because of our frantic pace of life, I had not yet had sufficient time to reflect on my appalling loss or to grieve properly.

That meeting notwithstanding, I had become increasingly embarrassed about my continuing absence from work, and so I insisted to my bosses at the University of Kent that I was fine, and that I could begin lecturing again. Accordingly I began to ease myself back into some limited teaching at DICE, giving some lectures on nature conservation to the Masters degree students in mid-October.

On 11 October, Ed, Pauline and I took Josie up to London again, for the first of her psychological observation sessions at the post-traumatic stress clinic. On the way into London Josie started showing signs of a panic attack, and she became particularly distressed in the underground car park near to the clinic. Walking along the street towards our appointment, Josie hung on to me fearfully and kept dragging me into doorways out of the way of oncoming strangers. At one point she broke down in tears in a doorway, and would not emerge for several minutes until Ed, Pauline and I had tried everything we could think of to calm her and entice her onward. Thus Josie was upset and doubly shy during her first session at the clinic, and this same pattern repeated itself during her next visit a week later.

When we returned for this second session, Josie's panic attacks on the journey and in the street outside the clinic were even worse than before. It was painful to see her so disturbed and I came to the conclusion that the visits to the clinic were causing more stress than they were designed to relieve. It was out of character for me to voice dissension on any aspect of Josie's treatment by the professionals, but the sight of her distress moved me to make my feelings known to the clinic staff. By mutual agreement, therefore, the attempts to study Josie were called off.

Since leaving the hospital, Josie had gradually become happier at home and more stable and settled in her behaviour. Through her continuing interviews with Ed and Pauline she became used to talking with them about the murders, and she did not seem to have any problem about 'discussing' Lin and Megan with me. Ed and Pauline began to raise the question of taking Josie back to the site of the murders, which at first I found unconscionable. However, as Josie showed little in the way of antipathy towards this suggestion, and as it could provide further vital clues for the police enquiry, I eventually acquiesced to the plan. We had found that Josie worked best when alone with Ed and Pauline, without me to distract her, and this was a convenient excuse for me to avoid having to accompany them to Cherry Garden Lane. I was not yet ready to visit the spot where Lin, Megan and Lucy had died. So Ed and Pauline went with Josie in their car, to show her the murder scene. They drove slowly past the spot in Cherry Garden Lane and asked her questions as they went, at the same time videoing her responses. Josie seemed fairly disinterested during this first time back to the site, and when they returned I was relieved to learn that she did not seem to have been upset by the trip.

Josie's schedule continued to be full, with thrice-weekly speech therapy sessions, and tutoring at home and during her regular visits to Goodnestone School. During half-term in the fourth week of October we took the opportunity to return to Wales again for a few days' break. We visited the grave and made our first efforts to tidy it up and prepare the soil for planting some flowers. I met with my local solicitor in Caernarfon to progress the purchase of the vacant quarryman's cottage at Tan-yr-Allt. I also met with Josie's old school teachers again, this time to institute formal preparations for Josie's eventual return to Nantlle School.

After these few pleasant days spent 'at home' in the Nantlle Valley, we were as sad as ever to have to make the long journey back to Kent. But this time there was a compelling reason to return. The next day Josie was to start school again at Goodnestone. And when I took Josie to school on the morning of 29 October, she joined her classmates just as though it was a normal day. As she slipped into her seat in the classroom, beneath drawings on the wall that she and her sister Megan had done earlier in the year, the teachers and I fought hard to hide our emotions from the children and from each other. We all realized the enormous significance of this moment. It was a potent symbol of Josie's return to a degree of equilibrium in her existence, and a signal to all around her that she would not be thwarted in her striving to regain a life of balance and normality. A lot of people had worked very hard to make this moment possible, not least the little girl who was looking up expectantly at her teacher to begin the day's activities.

The days were now even more full. Josie was at school all day, and her class teacher Lynda Roberts continued to give her all the support she needed. Particularly significant was the contribution made by Josie's special-needs teaching assistant, Angie, who worked closely with her in the classroom throughout the whole of the remaining time that Josie spent at Goodnestone School. Art had always been Josie's favourite subject, and it was in this area that Angie found a rapport with her that allowed them to pass many happy and productive hours together, drawing and painting, making models and other handicrafts. But after school there was little time for rest, as Josie had to continue her visits to the Seabathing Hospital at Margate where I had started taking her for speech therapy. Then there were her continuing interviews with Ed, Pauline and the police artist.

At the end of October, Dave Stevens released further information to the media about the revelations that Josie had been making in her interviews with Ed and Pauline. Through the use of Pauline's models of the murder scene, Josie had helped the police piece together the sequence of events leading to the attack.

In the first week of November, pictures were released of the models that were being used to jog Josie's memory, and this caused a fresh flood of letters from people who were convinced that it was not right that Josie should be put through the ordeal of having to relive the events of the tragic day over and over again. Yet Josie seemed to accept this task, and was not outwardly upset by Ed's and Pauline's questions. In fact she seemed to derive some degree of pleasure from being of such help and importance to the police. However, this did not stop the minority of disapproving letters that have continued to arrive in my postbag to this day. For example, scrawled in red ink across a newspaper photo of Pauline and the models of the murder scene, one correspondent wrote: 'A cruel experiment. Shaun – stop it now. I feel sure LIN would not wish it to go on. Let the dear, brave little girl leave this cruel association in the past, and with you find some happiness. What a crazy, cruel way to spend money. The psychopath will give himself up, or be found in time.'

The papers also ferreted out the news that Josie had been back to the murder scene, that she would likely need another operation on her skull to insert a protective metal plate, and that she would have to face an identity parade at some point in the future. In fact, Josie had already practised the procedure of an identity parade when Ed and Pauline took us to the Kent Constabulary's ID parade suite in the Medway area. There, she had played a game of hide-and-seek with teddy bears in the police station, and then identified specific teddies behind the one-way see-through mirror of the ID suite. This was to get her used to the formal identification process that she would probably have to face at some time in the future. It was clear that Josie understood the significance of the task that awaited her, because she was very anxious about the one-way mirrors. She tried to scratch off the silvering to make sure that it was not possible for someone in the parade room to see through to her. And as we left the suite, she turned and ran back again for one last look to assure herself that the murderer could not see her, even if she could see him. We could tell that Josie was not convinced, and the brave way that she tried to conceal her fear from us tugged at our heartstrings again.

A happier event during this first week of November was a visit to a leading London restaurant for a slap-up meal courtesy of the owners. Albert and Michel Roux, the brothers who run the famous Le Gavroche restaurant in Mayfair, had read of Josie's story, and Albert's partner Fay had sent Josie a beautiful teddy bear with an invitation to come for a meal at the restaurant. Josie really took a shine to this teddy and christened him 'Al-bear' when she heard me pronouncing Albert Roux's name. When she asked me if we could meet these nice people, I agreed to take her up to London for a meal at the exclusive restaurant. It was an unforgettable occasion, and we dined like royalty. We sat at a table near to Max Hastings, the editor of the *Evening Standard*, and Fay and Albert entertained us with stories of their lives in the milieu of haute cuisine. The atmosphere was warm and friendly and we were even invited to see behind the scenes in the shiny, spotless kitchens.

When this restaurant visit was mentioned in a national newspaper shortly afterwards, we realized that our every move was now being watched and that almost everything we did was considered news-worthy. Dave Stevens's own news machine was running at full steam in an attempt to keep the profile of the case high in the public mind, and so I was given the go-ahead to speak to the press again. As the *Sun* newspaper had put up the £20,000 reward and publicized the case very thoroughly, it was arranged that their crime reporter Mike

Sullivan and top celebrity photographer Arthur Edwards would come to the house after school on 8 November to talk to me and take a few photos of Josie. Mike had suffered tragedy in his own life when his sister was murdered and so I had felt a degree of empathy with him during our previous encounters. It was the same on this visit and I opened up my inner feelings to him without reserve. A pattern was starting to emerge during these interview sessions with journalists. I would naturally try to be polite and helpful and give the media representatives what they wanted for a good story. I am sure that it often resulted in me revealing more than I should have done from the point of view of police strategy. However, as I had to sit down and address the issues and emotions surrounding the whole experience of the tragedy on these occasions, the sessions began to take on the role of therapy for me. I was not having counselling from anyone else, other than occasional private discussions with close friends. But those were never as incisive as the encounters with newspaper correspondents, as friends would always want to spare my feelings. And so, although I would often end up breaking down during these conversations with journalists, I would usually come away with a sense of relief and the feeling that in some small way my pain had been lessened through this catharsis.

After my meeting with Mike Sullivan, we wandered with Josie down to the horses' field to get a few photos. Josie was eager to please by posing on her pony Tegid, and she started to do gymnastics on his back like a circus performer. It was amazing to see Josie so physically capable and fearless, and Arthur moved nearer to get some close-up photos. Arthur Edwards is famed throughout the trade as the doyen of celebrity press photographers. He is known as 'The Old Warhorse' to members of the royal family, and he had become noted for his images of Diana, Princess of Wales. However, notwithstanding his stature and skill, Arthur seemed not to know about the dangers of equine electric fencing. We were separated from Josie and Tegid by a strip of electrified tape used to fence off the paddock. And before I could shout a warning, Arthur had swung one leg over the fence and was straddling it as he focused his camera on Josie. The inevitable consequence was that poor Arthur received a bolt from the blue where it hurts most, and the air was certainly blue for a few moments afterwards! We all fell about laughing, not least Josie, and I couldn't help feeling that the old dictum about the dangers of working with children and animals had been proven true yet again.

We looked out for a resulting article and photos of Josie in the *Sun*, but on this occasion there was no immediate publication, and we never saw the photos appear in print. We found this often to be the case in our future dealings with the media. If other news was of higher priority, then our story might get pushed off the priority list and go cold as it was overtaken by events. At other times the reverse would happen, and a story would appear when we were least expecting it, often containing old or 'stale' material, both written copy and photos. An example of this occurred the day after our visit from the *Sun* journalists. A full two-page spread appeared in the *Daily Mail* about the murders, and lots of personal information about Lin and me and our family life was published. Dave Stevens had phoned me up late the night before, when his press officer had picked up that the article was about to appear. The paper had gathered lots of information about us through questioning friends and relatives in Kent and in Wales. Dave warned me that the information I had revealed to him during police interviews, about my divorce from Lin in South Africa for tax purposes, was about to become public domain.

The problem with this was that, to spare their embarrassment, Lin and I had never told our parents that we were technically divorced. I had been psyching myself up to face this task, as I knew that word would eventually get out. Many of our friends in South Africa knew the situation, as it had been common practice among double-income spouses there to divorce for tax purposes when the system discriminated against married couples. But the newspaper article precipitated me into earlier action than I had anticipated, and I spent a couple of painful hours late that night on the telephone, explaining to my mother and to Lin's parents why we had become divorced ten years before in South Africa. It was inevitable that Peter and Irene would see the article, as the *Mail* was their own daily paper. As it happened, they were very understanding. They had become resigned many years before to the fact that their daughter had a very strong mind of her own, and had never set great store by the 'sanctity of marriage'. They remembered sadly that she had even kept her pregnancy and the birth of their first grandchild Josie from them until after it had occurred. They consoled themselves with the knowledge that, as at the time of Josie's birth, Lin was sensitive to her parents' feelings and her first priority had been to spare them any unnecessary worry or embarrassment.

Another piece of old news that set tongues wagging and caused distress to our friends and neighbours, was the speculation that Lin and Megan had been killed as a result of mistaken identity. An entrepreneurial businessman who lived near to us was known to have made a few enemies as a result of his bold business ventures and flamboyant lifestyle. The person in question had even admitted to me that he had been visited in the weeks preceding the murders by a man professing to be interested in his house (which was for sale) but who turned out to be a violent criminal. He was sure that it was the same man who had later been found dead with two colleagues in the notorious 'Essex Range Rover Killings'. My businessman neighbour also had a wife and young daughter, and, like Lin, they regularly took their dog for walks in the surrounding countryside. The bizarre speculation had grown up that the businessman's wife, daughter and dog had been targeted by a hitman, and that the attack on Lin, Megan and Josie was the result of mistaken identity. Dave Stevens was quick to dispel this theory (it had been investigated and dismissed weeks before). But the prevalence of speculation and conjecture in press articles increased as the weeks went by while the police investigation ground on with no immediate signs of drawing to a conclusion.

The days of November passed quickly, and the nights drew in. The policemen who guarded our house were having to endure ever-colder conditions in their car outside at night, and on 21 November I noted in my diary that we invited them into the house in the middle of the night, as frost had encrusted their car. I might also have invited the policemen in in order to calm Josie, for she sometimes became frightened on hearing a car engine close to the house late at night (the freezing bobbies needed to switch their engine on occasionally to run the car heater).

It is hard, when looking back, to appreciate the paranoia that gripped the district in those days while the murderer was still at large. The police continued to be concerned that the criminal might try to return to silence Josie, especially as their success in distilling her evidence had been so widely publicized. I find it almost comical to remember now, that I kept a weapon close at hand in case I might have to battle an intruder (a sharp-tipped African stabbing spear, an assegai).

And I knew the exact location of my Grandad's First World War bayonets, in case I needed to grab for them in the dark. One person close to the case had even offered to provide me with quite unlawful means of personal protection – CS gas, which, however, I declined.

During the day Josie continued at school as normal. I noted in my diary in November that she had come home one day and said the new words 'all', 'can' and 'packet' in quick succession. She was at last starting to move beyond simple words such as 'no' and 'OK', although she still only used words of one or two syllables at the most. In the evenings she continued her work with Ed and Pauline or the police artist, or went to Brownies, although now without her sister to accompany her. Josie also attended her friend Victoria's birthday party at the village hall, and Ed and Pauline took us skating for the first time at the ice rink in Gillingham. This latter visit sparked Josie's interest in a pastime that she has enjoyed ever since.

Josie carried on with her school swimming trips, and swam outside school hours as well (she was achieving greater and greater distances and was already becoming a stronger swimmer than me). We made a weekend trip to Romsey to see my mother and sister, and Josie swam in a friend's pool on an unseasonably warm day. We were all amazed by her strength in the water and her fearlessness on the diving board. I watched her playing in the pool with our friend's daughters, Rebecca, Hannah and Nicky, who were around Josie's and Megan's age. She seemed to be enjoying herself so much that I felt sad again, and even broody that Josie did not have a sister any longer to share in her life and enjoyment. Once again I tried to ease the pain with the harassed parent's rationalization that at least I would not have to face years of sibling rivalry. But it only seemed to make me feel worse, and I would have given a lifetime of putting up with sisterly squabbles if only I could have my Megan back again. I can remember shrieking with laughter that evening at the video clips on the TV programme *You've Been Framed*. I was struck by the fact that it was the first time since the murders that I had abandoned myself so, but my mirth was tinged with guilt. I felt that it was somehow wrong to be laughing when there was still so much to cry about.

The bill for the funeral expenses arrived, and Peter and Irene insisted on paying it. The sale of Granary Cottage moved ahead and was completed late in November. The purchase of the cottage we wanted at Tan-yr-Allt was also continuing without a hitch, and these incredibly fortunate, well-timed circumstances often made me feel that 'someone' was watching over us and giving us a run of good luck after what had gone before. The new owner of Granary Cottage kindly offered to let us stay on for the next month while Josie finished her term at school in Kent, and until we could get organized for the move back to Wales. Things were now moving so fast that we seriously expected to be back in Wales in time for Christmas.

Of course, the newspapers picked up the story of our return to Wales, and we had our first experience of photographers snooping around uninvited, trying to get pictures of Josie going to and from school. So far, most newspapers had abided by the 'deal' with Dave Stevens to leave us alone in return for regular news releases and press conferences. However, as the case went quiet while officers laboured away behind the scenes sifting through the expanding mountain of statements and evidence, so 'Josie Fever' grew and the demand for news and photos of her increased.

By now, I had been deliberating for many weeks over whether to do anything with the newspapers. My solicitor Mark Stephens had been keeping me informed of offers, but up until this time had been advising me against doing an 'exclusive' deal. I still felt uncomfortable about selling our story to the newspapers, because of the matter of principle about exploiting our misfortune and cashing in on the family tragedy. And I could see that to agree to an exclusive would involve us in all sorts of extra strains, particularly in relation to the other newspapers. There was, in any case, no time to spare for such things at the moment, but I had at least been discussing the issue with my closest friends and relatives to gauge their opinions. The amounts of money being offered were substantial five-figure sums.

I was surprised to find that all the friends and relatives I asked said that I should go ahead with a newspaper deal. I think that people around me were genuinely worried that I was taking Josie back to a very uncertain financial future in Wales. They seemed deeply concerned that we would have insufficient to live on, at a time when Josie might need all sorts of extra input into her upbringing. There might be a need for special or private schooling for example, and ongoing medical support in the future. We had no certainty at this stage of receiving substantial criminal injuries compensation, and several relatives urged me to accept a newspaper offer. They thought that it was intolerable that we should have to accept a serious drop in standard of living through no fault of our own as a result of the tragedy. They wished instead for Josie to be compensated for what she had lost, by having better rather than worse financial provision than previously, and they frequently offered to tide us over any money problems that we might face with help from their own resources.

Mark Stephens had already made all these points to me; he had children of his own and had also been deeply moved by our situation. He had become as involved as Sarah Harman in trying to get the best 'deal' for us, and he later became a (non-paid) trustee of the Josie Russell Trust Fund. Mark had noted the hassles we were starting to get from the media, and he told me point-blank that Josie was now of such enormous national interest that the press might start to obtain their stories by coercive methods if I refused to engage with them sufficiently. Or they would simply start to make the stories up as we had already seen happening. Britain's privacy laws were so weak, explained Mark, that we would have very little redress if an inaccurate story was published about us. Mark echoed Dave Stevens's advice to give the media a little of what they wanted as often as possible, and that by careful management the worst effects of press intrusion might be minimized. And, Mark reasoned bluntly, if we were going to be hassled anyway, then why not get paid for it?

I had prevaricated over this question for the best part of three months, but it was an event in late November that finally helped me decide on my course of action in relation to the media. I was watching television one night and on came an interview with Colin Stagg, the man who was acquitted of the killing of Rachel Nickell. He had been released after a judge found that the police had collected evidence against him in an improper manner. The interview spurred me to do as I had intended a couple of months earlier and get hold of the copy of the book written by Rachel Nickell's partner André Hanscombe. The next day I went into Canterbury and found a copy of *Last Thursday in July*. I took it home and read it from cover to cover. The story of the Wimbledon Common murder was horrific, and I found many parallels with my own situation in the tortured writings of the author. André Hanscombe had fought his way through the tragedy, and he continued to live with his son Alex who had witnessed the murder of his mother when he was aged four. What shone through was André's deep commitment to protecting his son from the frenzy of press interest in the aftermath of the murder. He and his parents-in-law went to extraordinary lengths to stave off journalists and photographers, refute articles that were written about them, seek written apologies from newspaper editors who misquoted them, and pursue legal redress where they felt they had been misrepresented. André seemed to be driven by an intense desire to protect his family's privacy in their grief, and he had the youth, the principles and the commitment to fight his corner.

What was shocking and sad was how little headway he made. Not only did the newspapers and the broadcast media seem to do very little to address André's concerns, they seemed almost deliberately to print damaging and insensitive material as though to spite him. The book made it seem that if you decided to put up the shutters and not cooperate with the UK press, then the overwhelming weight of ghoulish and prurient public interest might spur the media on to beat those shutters down, with little or no recourse for the hapless victim. I was dismayed to learn that André Hanscombe eventually left the country to live with his son in France, and I could not help but imagine that the press had had a role in driving him out of the country.

And so I decided that the lesser of two evils would be to engage with the media in as balanced and cooperative a manner as possible until Josie became old enough to decide for herself whether she wanted her picture taken or not. I did not have the spirit or the principles of André Hanscombe, and my days of crusading against injustice as in South Africa – when I was the same age as André – were over. I felt old and jaded and not in the mood for a fight. So I instructed Mark Stephens to accept an offer, though not necessarily the highest one, but from a newspaper that would be likely to give us the most sensitive and sympathetic coverage. I suggested either the *Express* or the *Mail*, simply because, although I had never regularly taken a newspaper myself, my mother read the *Express* and my parents-in-law the *Mail*.

At the end of November Ed and Pauline brought us over some cardboard boxes, and we started the long and painful job of packing all our things for the move to Wales. We were lucky to have had the use of the barns next door to store many of our belongings, as the accrued detritus of our lives and the contents of Plas Tan-yr-Allt with its five bedrooms and barns would never have fitted into three-bed-roomed Granary Cottage. And now we were moving back to an even smaller two-bedroomed cottage in Wales – the time had come for a radical sort-out.

The decision to move back to Wales had been taken under duress, but now things were moving so smoothly I had time to reflect on that decision. Although I was giving up my job, and although it would probably be a long time before I could settle into a pattern of working from home and attracting sufficient income to get by financially, these considerations had become secondary. I was no longer interested in pursuing my career as my first priority; I was instead focused on establishing ourselves in a stable, secure and non-stressful home environment that was also practical and manageable. So what if we had less space than before? It would be a lot easier for me to clean and maintain. I would have my work cut out caring for Josie and keeping house on my own, and eventually moving into part-time working from home. The problem of grazing the ponies was still there (we never for one moment countenanced selling them), but I felt confident that I would be able to rent some cheap grazing near enough to home that we could continue to have the ponies relatively close by.

We had to start throwing out most of our accumulated possessions. There were four enormous piles: a pile for the essential things that we would have to take to Wales; a pile of valuable items that would not fit in the cottage – sofas, beds, sideboards, piano and so on – that would have to be auctioned off; a pile for less valuable items that we would donate to charity shops and friends; and finally a pile of worthless items that would simply have to be taken to the dump. There were some very tough decisions to be made during this sorting process. A lot of items of considerable sentimental value had to go, particularly in the line of furniture and clothing, either because they simply would not fit into the cottage in Wales, or because the memories they elicited were too painful.

I was forced to jettison my entire collection of plants (my herbarium) which was of considerable scientific value and had been assembled over thirty years of collecting in forty different countries of the world. It was heartbreaking because in the small amount of the collection that I had managed to go through I had found several species new to science. It was likely, therefore, that there were many more lurking there in the musty packets and boxes that I had to relegate to the skip when clearing out Granary Cottage and the surrounding outbuildings. But the whole time I kept telling myself that anything to do with work could no longer be my priority. In placing Josie first I would have to put my scientific life and career behind me and concentrate on a home and family life where work would assume a lower priority in the future.

The four piles grew more or less equally, although the rubbish pile was significantly larger than the other three. It was both horrifying and at the same time strangely liberating to realize that we would be going to start a new life in Wales with only one quarter by volume of all our prior life's possessions.

The pace of life did not slow for a minute. I was acutely aware of the lengths to which the University of Kent had gone to keep me on a salary after my contract had expired, even though I was rarely able to get into work. All UK universities were struggling terribly with funding cuts at this time, and the vice-chancellor Professor Colin Sibson had been supremely generous in supporting me out of contingency funds during this period. But I felt that I had to give something back and so I had been preparing a proposal for a new project that would secure UK government 'Darwin Initiative' funding for Peruvian nature conservation officers to train at the University of Kent. It was hardly the ideal time but, nevertheless, the proposal turned out to be a success.

Around this time we completely forgot to turn up for one of Josie's speech therapy sessions at the Seabathing Hospital in Margate. It was the only time that we ever missed the appointment, and Tania was at pains to put us at our ease over the mistake. She explained that she often had more of her clients who didn't turn up for appointments in a day than the ones who did, and that people often omitted to phone saying that they couldn't make it.

Amid all this purposeful activity, I still found time to go with Liz and John Gregson to see the Sandwich Carnival. It was a dark, cold and rainy night, but the streets were lit up by the bright lights of the carnival floats. One of the lorries carried Josie's Brownie troop, and the girls were all arrayed in fancy dress for the occasion. Josie and Lucy (Gregson) were dressed up as dogs (Josie as her favourite dalmatian breed) and they thoroughly enjoyed themselves travelling around town on the back of the lorry to the sounds of the marching bands.

Josie's happiness on that night was in sharp contrast to her mood three nights later. On the evening of 3 December I sat down with her to explain a letter that had arrived earlier in the day. In it, the specialists at King's College Hospital explained formally how Josie would have to have another operation to 'close her skull defect'. This meant inserting a carefully crafted titanium plate beneath the skin of Josie's head and screwing it to the skull to cover over the hole that remained there.

I tried as gingerly as possible to introduce Josie to the idea of this operation – I had already been preparing her with discussions on the safety aspects of a plate, and the sense in having one, as well as the routine and painless nature of the operation. But when Josie saw from the letter that this talk of another operation was serious, she burst into tears and flew into a terrible rage. She hurled herself at me, screaming and kicking and then retreated to her bedroom where she cried herself to sleep as she ignored all my attempts to console her.

I had been kidding myself that maybe this second operation was not absolutely essential after all. Perhaps the bone or cartilage might just grow back across the hole in Josie's head? But now it seemed that was wishful thinking, and that the operation would have to be gone through with after all. I decided on a holding strategy, and that we would wait until we were settled back in Wales before sorting out the arrangements for this next traumatic period in hospital for Josie. The next day she was better with me, but showed her simmering displeasure during another visit to the medical centre in Canterbury where she was due to have a hearing test. She was most uncooperative, and Pauline and I felt ashamed at her rude behaviour with the unfortunate audiologist. We apologized as best we could and headed home, hoping that the specialist had been able to get some results from the tests so that we would not have to return.

At this time we received our first payments from the Criminal Injuries Compensation Authority. Lin's parents received £5000 each for the loss of their daughter. I received £5000 for the loss of my wife Lin and £10,000 for the loss of my daughter Megan. I also received £2630 for the cost of the funeral, which I reimbursed to Lin's parents. These were the so-called standard amounts that immediate family members receive automatically for the loss of close relatives as the result of a crime. This money came at just the right time to subsidize the house purchase in Wales as the money from the sale of Granary Cottage had to go to pay off the mortgage and was not enough to cover the Welsh house purchase. It also paid our removals bill back to Wales, and it meant that we were solvent in time for Christmas back at Tan-yr-Allt.

My solicitor Sarah Harman led me through the compensation documents and outlined her strategy for claiming for Josie's loss of her mother's services, her post-traumatic stress and her personal injury. She also took me through the process for claiming my post-traumatic stress compensation and for the loss of earnings that I would incur through having to look after Josie until she was 18. Sarah had just received supporting documentation from specialists who had assessed Josie for post-traumatic stress, her physical and emotional state, and educational capability. These documents were harrowing to read. Although we had been overjoyed at Josie's progress so far, it seemed that I had lulled myself into a false sense of complacency over her achievements. Josie was back at school in the daytime, and I had got to know her new form of speech and gestures so well that we communicated with little difficulty at other times. However, the stark figures and graphs of the assessment sheets told an altogether more depressing story. 'Profoundly dysphasic', 'densely aphasic', 'a preserved lexicon [vocabulary remembered from before the attack] of only about 20 words and phrases' were various descriptions of Josie's speech and language capability. Josie was said to have 'very little or no expressive language'. Even her non-verbal cognitive functioning was at the lower end of the range for a child of her age (her non-verbal IQ score was 80; 100 is average). This was most distressing when she had been well above average and in the top quartile of her class according to her school reports before her injuries. Josie was projected to need one-to-one support throughout her school career and was expected to show impairment of her speech and language skills right through into adulthood. It was as though the specialists had never really explained to me the full significance of Josie's disabilities and impairments. Or maybe I just hadn't asked them firmly enough, out of fear of the truth. I took encouragement from the fact that Josie had moved up from an equivalent mental age of four to five years when assessed at King's College Hospital, to the level of a six- to seven-year-old now (she was nine). To me that meant she was getting better fast, and I tried to blank out the more ominous predictions in the reports of 'permanent residual impairment' and 'delayed post-traumatic stress symptoms'.

On the evening of 4 December I watched proudly with several other parents as Josie attended her enrolment at the Brownies. She had been due in this same hall only a couple of hours after she was attacked on that fateful July afternoon five months before. It was a symbol of her 'resurrection' and will to continue on a path back to normality that she was now receiving her enrolment badge.

But any thought that Josie might be returning to a life of normality was quickly dispelled. The following day Ed and Pauline took Josie back to the murder scene for a second visit, this time on foot. On their return I could see by their faces that it had not been a successful visit. Josie seemed fairly relaxed and unperturbed, but Ed and Pauline explained that at the murder scene she had been evasive and un-cooperative. She had hovered around the site, gathering flowers from the hedgerow for a posy in a kind of displacement behaviour, but she would not approach the exact spot where the attack had taken place. She was reticent about answering any questions or showing on the ground where events had taken place, and so, after a while, they had given up.

Another very unusual, but in this case happy, occasion now presented itself. *Woman's Own* magazine had for many years held an annual Children of Courage awards ceremony in Westminster Abbey. This year, the magazine's readers had voted for Josie to receive one of the awards, and we had received an invitation to attend the presentations. The Duchess of Kent would be presenting the awards, and I remembered her kind letter to me at the time of the murders. Josie was also asked to name her favourite celebrity, so that the magazine might try to arrange that person's presence at the lunch in the House of Lords after the event. Josie's favourite TV programme was *Animal Hospital* and so she chose Rolf Harris as her preferred star.

With a week to go until the ceremony, and lots of packing still to do, I arranged for a removal company to give us a quote and leave us more boxes. Josie and I were starting to attend various leaving dinners and parties in the evenings, as friends queued up to wish us goodbye and the best of luck for our future in North Wales. We had completed on the purchase of the cottage in Wales and the removers were due on 12 December to take our house contents up to Wales in time for Christmas.

Amid the hustle and bustle of these final few days in Kent, and with the increasing jollity as Christmas approached, something happened that brought my feet down to earth again with a bump, and put me rather than Josie back into the spotlight of the police enquiry. One evening, Ed and Pauline had arranged to take Josie off to her final Brownies meeting, while DCI Dave Stevens called by to have a chat with me. As we sat down in the lounge at Granary Cottage over a cup of tea, I sensed that Dave was not quite his usual friendly self. He seemed more cool and aloof and when he began to explain the reason for his visit I realized why. On the night of the murders I had started to phone around the local hospitals, starting with the District Hospital at Dover, at about half past nine. (I had got to know that hospital quite well over the last couple of weeks, as the wife of a close neighbour who was overseas had been admitted to the hospital with stomach problems and I had been running her parents and young child to the hospital most evenings to visit her.)

Dave Stevens explained to me slowly, scrutinizing my face, that the telephone receptionist at the Dover hospital had made a sworn statement that she had taken a call enquiring about whether a Mrs Russell had been admitted to the hospital, *at about 6 pm in the early evening*. This was only about two hours after Lin and the girls had been attacked, and was two hours *before* I had said that I returned home from work and started wondering where they were. Dave Stevens's voice became stern and serious and his eyes fixed me with a look of steel. He asked me point-blank, 'Did you make that call?' I was unnerved both by the revelation of this 'new evidence', and by the implications of the question. Suddenly, it seemed, I was back in the frame again as a prime suspect for the murders. I tried at first to bluster my way out of the situation.

'Of course I didn't make the call,' I snorted. 'How could I have as I didn't get home from work until much later?'

'Are you sure you didn't start calling around the hospitals much earlier in the evening?' asked Dave.

'Absolutely not. The lady on the exchange must be mistaken,' I replied.

'We have interviewed her several times and her story is consistent,' he retorted. 'We have thoroughly questioned her about the call and her story remains the same.'

I was flabbergasted. 'Maybe if someone did call, they were enquiring after another Mrs Russell?' I ventured.

'There were no other Mrs Russells at any of the East Kent hospitals that night, and none admitted over the next two days.'

'But the telephonist has to be mistaken,' I said. 'What about the phone records?'

'The records are inadequate for the telephone company to be able to independently confirm the origin of the calls to Dover Hospital that evening.'

'But what about my call at around half-past nine?' I asked.

'The exchange operators changed shift at six, and the later telephonist remembers your nine-thirty call,' said Dave, 'but that still leaves the earlier call to be explained.'

'If it really was the murderer,' I said weakly, 'how did he know to ask for Mrs Russell by name?'

'Exactly. Now I want to ask you again, was it you who made that call?'

My mind was racing but I was overcoming my initial jitteriness in the face of Dave Stevens's line of questioning. I started to rationalize the situation. 'The chances of the murderer exposing himself by phoning to check whether or not his victim had been admitted to hospital seem to me so slim as to be untenable,' I said. 'In my experience as a biologist and a lifelong observer of fallible human behaviour, it is far more likely that the telephonist has deluded and convinced herself into believing that she received that call. She has been reading about the case and finds herself the centre of police attention regarding a possible vital clue to the murder. Weeks after the event she is asked to remember the exact timing of one telephone call among dozens of others she received that evening. She has discussed the affair over and over with her colleagues, including the one who did take my call later in the evening. All of this has doubly reinforced in her mind a sequence of events that may never have taken place.'

Dave looked sceptical. I could see him thinking: Is he trying to put one over on me? The conversation eased off into other matters, but it was not long before Dave found an excuse to take his leave. It was obvious that a lot of effort had gone into pursuing this line of enquiry, culminating in this 'putting Shaun on the spot' session where the outcome would be decided by good old police intuition and the minute observation of my behaviour. As it was, I never heard another thing about the telephonist's statement, and as far as I know it has never been satisfactorily explained.

The next day the removers came for our goods, and the day after Josie and I drove up to Wales with the car full to the gunnels. We started unpacking the first load into the house and into two caravans in the garden that we were going to use for storage until we could get settled in properly. On 15 December we travelled back to Sutton Coldfield to stay overnight with Peter and Irene, and then on to Canterbury early the next day.

On the Tuesday, Ed, Pauline, Josie and I travelled up to London to attend the *Woman's Own* Children of Courage awards. Ed and Pauline dropped us off in Mayfair, where Albert Roux's partner Fay had invited us back for tea at her flat next to Le Gavroche. We moved on to stay the night at the St Ermin's Hotel where we met some of the other Children of Courage award recipients. The next day we breakfasted and attended a photo session, and Josie played with friends she had made among the families of the other participants. She got on particularly well with Philippa, the sister of twelve-year-old Joe Davitt who was receiving an award for coolly taking the controls and flying a light plane when his father had to attend to an emergency in the rear of the aircraft. Philippa and her family came to stay with us the following year when on holiday in Wales; but this family too was to be struck by tragedy, when Philippa's father and grandfather died in an air accident in Yorkshire the following year.

I heard of another potential disaster on the news as we drove to the Children of Courage awards. Our friend John Illman, the British Ambassador in Peru, had been precipitated into an emergency situation when a member of his staff was taken hostage during the Japanese Embassy crisis that was developing in Lima.

The Children of Courage awards ceremony in Westminster Abbey was charged with emotion and the details of every story were deeply moving. My handkerchiefs were in full-time use during the ceremony, and I was overcome as the details of Josie's experience were read out by the actor Anthony Andrews. The Duchess of Kent presented the awards and the atmosphere cheered up as the children played together in an anteroom before another photo call. Then it was over to the imposing House of Lords for a marvellous lunch at the invitation of Lord Selsdon. We were met by Dr David Grant, the chief vet of the RSPCA's Harmondsworth Hospital, who 'starred' in the *Animal Hospital* programme and was standing in for Rolf Harris who was unable to attend due to other commitments. But Rolf had sent along with David Grant a couple of his books and records and several large signed cartoons drawn by his own hand. David Grant sat next to Josie at lunch, and she quizzed him as best she could about how she could be an RSPCA inspector when she grew up. I was flanked by a hero of my youth, Tony Hart, the TV artist. I had grown up watching his art programmes on the television, and he had influenced me in my decision to take art right through school to 'A' level. Other celebrities present at the awards included Gaby Roslin and Mystic Meg, the pop-star Gary Barlow and the footballer Ian Wright. Josie appeared on the front pages of many of the national newspapers the next day, and once again I felt slightly ashamed that her celebrity had pushed the other children's stories into the background.

Now there were only two days remaining for us in Kent. We rushed around saying goodbye to friends and colleagues, and finishing off our packing. On the evening of 19 December, Dave Stevens called to say that they had arrested a man in connection with the enquiry. He did not seem overly excited however, and I realized why this was as soon as he identified the man in question. He lived close to the school, and was well known in Goodnestone village. He had often spoken to the girls when they walked past on their way home with Lin, and they were familiar with him. This could not be the murderer, then, as Josie was adamant that she did not know the man who attacked her.

Apparently, although he was potentially an important witness the Goodnestone man had refused to cooperate with the police in the enquiry and had become violently obstructive, which accounted for his arrest. On Josie's last day at Goodnestone School, we called briefly into the village post office to pick up the newspapers with their stories of the arrest. As we entered the shop we were taken aback by a woman ranting and raving to the postmaster. When she saw us she stopped abruptly and scurried out of the shop. I realized immediately that this must be the sister of the arrested man, and when I saw the papers I could see why she was agitated. There were stories in all the papers about the arrest, naming the man and even showing photos of his house and car. The fever for news of the case had led to articles that all but accused this poor man of being the murderer. No wonder his sister had been so upset.

On Saturday 21 December, we crammed our four-wheel-drive estate car to the limit inside, including our cats squeezed in wherever they could fit, and then we piled yet more baggage onto the roof rack. We were now going to ask our doughty vehicle to perform its most arduous journey to date, for we still had to hitch up the pony trailer! Josie and I loaded the ponies as our final act in Kent, and pulled away in low range gear to save the car's clutch. We waved goodbye to the couple of friends who had come to see us off, and headed down the rural back roads towards the motorway. I was sad to be leaving our friends and colleagues in the southeast, especially as they had all been so close to us and supportive in our greatest hour of need. But once again I was glad to leave behind me the brooding sense of menace in those otherwise beautiful country lanes. I did not look back.

That night we stayed over with Peter and Irene again, and put the ponies out to graze at a nearby farm in the Sutton Coldfield greenbelt. The next day, we completed our journey to Wales and released the ponies temporarily into the yard behind the cottage until we could find more permanent grazing. Our arrival was slightly marred by finding two BBC cameramen awaiting us on the track outside the cottage. We could not imagine how they had found out about our return to Wales on this date and at this time. They looked a bit sheepish and moved some distance away so as not to interfere too obviously with our homecoming.

We entered the house expecting to find it cold and gloomy and in a complete mess as a result of our having simply dumped all our belongings there during the previous visit when the removers came. However, unbeknown to me, friends in North Wales already had access to the house courtesy of the previous owner, and they had cleaned and redecorated throughout in preparation for our arrival. The smell of fresh paint mingled with the aroma of log fires as we entered the house, and we found the cottage hung with decorations and 'Welcome Home Shaun and Josie' signs. Our friends had even put in shelves and cupboards for us, and a sink unit in the kitchen. We realized that we had been saved the impossible task of getting the house straight in the last two days before Christmas. How could we ever thank everybody for being so kind?

An overwhelming sense of gratitude overcame me. I felt palpable relief to be back at home once again in Wales, and I needed to show it somehow. I am not a religious person, but when our neighbours suggested that we attend the evening carol service in the local church, I jumped at the opportunity. And so as dusk fell in the Nantlle Valley on the eve of Christmas 1996, Josie and I accompanied friends to the little chapel across the valley in Talysarn, and sang our hearts out in thanks for the providence that had smoothed our path back to the calm and peace of this beautiful and remote corner of north-west Wales. There were no furtive sideways looks or whispers as we joined the local community in song, even if we did struggle with the pronunciation of the words of the venerable Welsh hymns. There were just open, warm smiles welcoming us back to this, our adopted home, and I felt that at long last Josie and I could start to find some sort of respite from the trials of our present lives, and contentment in the bosom of this ancient landscape.

There were signs that it would not be easy, not least of which were the two cameramen who hovered around the chapel door as we came and went from the service. But, we would try and forget for a time the horror of the past half-year, and lose ourselves in the fun and relaxation of a quiet Christmas at home, with a few close and caring friends at hand to share the celebration.

Learning to Live with Loss

A few close friends joined Josie and me to welcome in the 1997 New Year in a low-key way, with a special meal at home and a bottle of champagne. We wished of course for a happier year than the one that had gone before, and, as usual, I dared look no further ahead than a few days as I wished simply for Josie's successful return to her old school at Nantlle.

I had finally agreed to do a series of exclusive interviews with the *Daily Mail*, and I had signed a contract that forbade me from talking to other newspapers for a month after publication of the resultant articles. I was also precluded from revealing the financial aspects of the contract in public. Accordingly I started work with Lynda Lee Potter of the *Daily Mail* on New Year's Day. I was amazed at Lynda's commitment to her craft, as she worked from early in the morning to late at night assembling her story, hardly stopping to eat. It was a gruelling time for me, and by the end of the two days I felt wrung out in rather the same way as when I had been examined by military psychologists before my trip to Marion Island sixteen years earlier!

We also posed for photographs with the *Mail*'s then senior photographer Chris Barham, whose genial and friendly manner eventually won Josie over. She was already displaying the reticence in front of a camera that would grow over the next couple of years into anathema. She was particularly set against any photos being taken of herself in physical contact with me, and once again I agonized over whether this was due to a deep-seated psychological aversion or simply her growing antipathy to soppiness and sentimentality. At the same time I felt immense relief and consolation. It was as though, through talking in depth with Lynda Lee Potter about what had happened, I had cleansed my body of poisonous toxins that had been building up since the time of the murders. Early on I had declined formal counselling, expecting to find it uncomfortable and humiliating to reveal my innermost thoughts to a stranger. However, with the pace of life over the last six months since the murders, I had barely had time to think deeply about the events of July 1996. The newspaper interviews gave me a rare chance to pour my heart out to a sympathetic and yet 'detached' listener in a way that I had not been able to with friends and relatives. With them I tended to put on a brave face, so as not to make them feel too embarrassed or uncomfortable. How could they begin to understand or sympathize with someone who had lost most of their immediate family in such tragic circumstances? I would feel this myself more and more in the future, as the experience of shared tragedy brought me in closer contact with the families of other high-profile crime victims. So, because it was now my obligation to reveal my innermost thoughts, I did so with the writer from the *Daily Mail*, and it felt strangely comforting.

I knew that cooperating with the media would involve heartache, and so it proved. On 4 January, only a couple of days after Lynda Lee Potter had completed her interview and before her articles had appeared, a woman appeared on my doorstep offering her sympathy and enquiring about Josie's progress. She was Welsh-speaking and casually dressed, unlike the smartly attired journalists who normally doorstepped me, and there was no tape-recorder, camera or notebook in evidence. Several other people from the local community had knocked on my door to offer their greetings and best wishes over the Christmas–New Year period, and so initially I took her to be one of these. I told her that Josie was doing fine and thanked her for her kind enquiry. However, she then told me that she was a journalist working for a local Welsh language newspaper and that she would like to interview me in more detail. I explained that with regret I could not invite her in or say anything further, and I bid her a polite goodbye.

Josie and I went to visit a friend's farm that afternoon. On our return my neighbour came to tell me that immediately we had left, the woman journalist had returned and spent the next three-quarters of an hour hanging around the house, peering in through the windows and making copious notes as she did so. Two days later a two-page article appeared in a leading national newspaper. It purported to be an exclusive first interview with Josie and myself in our new home. It gave the impression that an interview had been carried out inside our house, as there were detailed descriptions of the interior, right down to the Christmas decorations. The article also stated that the interview had been conducted as Josie and I sat looking over old family photographs.

It seemed too coincidental to have happened by chance, and we were sure that someone must have forewarned the newspaper concerned that we were about to be published by the *Mail* (it later transpired that a colleague had unwittingly passed on this information to a media contact). But we were still astonished to fall foul of this classic 'spoiler' tactic at such an early stage of our relationship with the newspapers. In fact we laughed in disbelief at the way the story had been concocted out of old material, the journalist's peering through our windows and fabricated quotes that had been falsely attributed to me. Whether it was the newspaper's intention to make a story out of nothing, or whether it was the journalist trying to cover up for not getting the story she came for, I don't know. But it was exactly the same kind of situation that André Hanscombe had described in *Last Thursday in July*. I thought ruefully that if the stress I had endured during the *Mail* interviews and photos went for naught and I lost the contract payment, then it was only my just reward for taking the 'Fleet Street Shilling' in the first place. My guilt and reservations about talking to the press appeared to be justified; and when a letter arrived the next day from the *Daily Mail*'s legal department claiming that I appeared to be in breach of the agreement, my fears were realized.

Once I had written a five-page report for Mark Stephens and gone to great lengths to explain what had really happened on my doorstep at Tan-yr-Allt, the *Mail* relented and the remuneration from the contract was eventually paid. And it was lucky that it was, for soon my period of grace with the University of Kent would come to an end, and the extended contract that had paid me a salary for the past few months would finally be terminated. Although more than half of the income from the newspaper articles was lost in tax and fees, it still made all the difference to my ability to tide Josie and myself over until I could get re-established with part-time work.

It was clear that Josie was now regarded as public property and on Monday 6 January I prepared her for her first day back at Nantlle School with a mixture of pleasure and trepidation. My happiness was due to Josie's obvious delight at the thought of being back with her old schoolmates and teachers, and I felt a sense of satisfaction that we had reached this very important milestone in Josie's recovery and in our plan to support her reintegration into the mainstream schooling system. But my worries about press intrusion were well founded, as we discovered journalists and photographers awaiting us at the school gate. I was hard-pressed not to say anything that could be construed as a quote, and I felt hypocritical saying that we could not speak to them when I knew that the *Daily Mail* articles were in the pipeline. The photographers were, however, polite and did not crush around Josie. They got their photos from a distance with long lenses, and some rather lovely pictures appeared in our local North Wales paper, the *Daily Post*, the following day.

The degree to which Josie had become a celebrity was brought home to me still further later in the week, when another newspaper article appeared under the headline 'Now She's a Trendsetter'. It had a full-colour photograph of Josie's floral Dr Martens boots, which she had worn at the funeral and the Children of Courage awards. Mention was also made of Josie's hats, which, according to the article, were inspiring a trend among youngsters to wear similar headgear. I thought wryly of the tragic reason for Josie's inseparability from her hats (she wore them even in bed at night) – she did not want the short hair or scars on her head to be visible. They reminded her of her operation and her time in hospital. And yet her hat drew attention to her and made her instantly recognizable in public.

Another reminder of the painful reason for Josie's notoriety came with the police team's first visit to our home in Wales. Dave Stevens, Ed and Pauline came up on 9 January to meet with us and the local liaison officer from the North Wales police. The killer was still at large and Dave Stevens had been continuing to issue regular press bulletins on progress with the case. He was here to explain to us how the interviews with Josie would be proceeding and to oversee arrangements for our ongoing security. Ed and Pauline would continue to work with Josie at a North Wales Police interview suite and 'safe house' in Bangor, where their discussions could be taped on

Above left: King's College Hospital, London, August 1996.

Above right: Josie with baby gorilla Kwam, at Howletts Zoo near Canterbury, September 1996.

Below: Josie's second trip home to Granary Cottage on release from hospital, August 1996. Josie's teachers Jan and Lynda, her friend Jazzmin Kelly, and family friend Steve Stratton are also present.

Left: Shaun and Josie walk away from the grave after burying Lin and Megan at St Mary's, Garndolbenmaen, 5 October 1996.

Right: Pauline Smith with the model of the murder scene.

Below: Pauline Smith and Ed Tingley with Josie at Granary Cottage, 31 October 1996.

Left: Josie, happy to be at home in Wales again, riding her pony Tegid at Tan-yr-Allt, Christmas 1996.

Right: Josie abseiling during an Airborne Adventure weekend in South Wales.

Below: Josie with other recipients of the 1997 Sunshine Awards, including her teacher Lynda Roberts (back left) and George Medal winner Lisa Potts (back centre).

Left: Josie with Prime Minister Tony Blair at the Pride of Britain awards in London, April 2000.

Right: Josie receiving her RSPCA Certificate of Merit at Colwyn Bay, May 2000, for her part in an animal rescue.

Below: Josie with Victoria Beckham and Emma Bunton of the Spice Girls, at the first Pride of Britain awards in May 1999.

Above: Josie and Shaun outside the house at Innisfree, Josie's first home, July 2000.

Below: Josie and the BBC TV crew after filming in Shamwari Game Reserve, July 2000.

video. At home we would have another panic button installed in the house, and regular police patrols would call by as in Kent. Happily, it was not thought necessary to continue any longer with overnight stationing of a police car next to the house.

Lynda Lee Potter's articles about us appeared over three days in the *Daily Mail* during the second week of January. They were detailed and emotional to read, but caring and sympathetic in tone. Most important to me was the phone call from Lin's parents after they had read them. They approved of the articles and were moved by the writing. They were also pleased to see the more attractive and flattering pictures of the family that I had released to the *Mail* from our private photo collection. Earlier newspaper coverage had made repeated use of a few poor-quality images that I had got together hastily for the police on that first visit to Granary Cottage directly after the murders.

Meanwhile Josie was absorbed in settling into her old school. Josie was to have a special-needs teaching assistant in class with her, but since she was sensitive to being singled out as having something wrong with her, Gwynedd Education Authority had agreed to provide special training to the classroom assistant Josie already knew and trusted from her previous time at Nantlle School. This meant providing extra cover, at an extra cost, for the assistant's previous duties, and it showed that, as in Kent, the authorities were bending over backwards to give all the help possible to Josie at school. She was also visited by a highly trained speech therapist who worked with Josie and a small group of friends, once again to alleviate Josie's concerns about being singled out as somebody odd or abnormal.

Naturally, I wanted to help my daughter in any way possible, and I had been impressed by a TV programme about the successful use of computers by dyslexic children. Josie's speech and rudimentary writing were showing many of the characteristics of dyslexia, especially the transposition of letters and words. The children in the film used voice recognition computer software so that they could speak in sentences to the computer and see their words written down for them on the screen. Special Information Technology provision was being made for Josie at school, but I was still keen to augment this input at home. In yet another of the many acts of generosity we have experienced, the local Curry's manager offered to provide Josie with an appropriate computer free of charge. I was delighted and very grateful, not least because he did not want any publicity for the donation.

Now that we were settled at home in a more remote, quieter part of Wales, there were fewer stimuli for Josie's panic attacks, although she continued to suffer them at regular intervals. Now she would shrink back and cling to me if we were approached in a lonely place. Once, on the moors near Snowdon, Josie heard a farmer shouting aggressively at his sheepdog. As the farmer came towards us, Josie became terrified, and dragged me off in the opposite direction as fast as she could. It was heart-rending to witness my daughter's terror and sense her overwhelming panic at events she would barely have noticed just a few months before. I did not want to have to think about what she might be remembering at times like this. Josie also became frightened whenever the gales battered our little cottage. She was convinced that the house was going to blow down, and she often ended up running to my bed in the middle of the night. She would always wake up early, however, and return to her own room, as she was embarrassed for me to find her still in my bed in the morning. It was another example of her post-traumatic stress symptoms of increased fear of things unrelated to the actual murders.

Although Josie had always said that she did not have nightmares while she was in Kent, she now admitted to having the occasional 'bad dream'. I tried to probe gently to find the content of these dreams, and they seemed to revolve mostly around her being chased by monsters. I can remember having similar nightmares when I was her age, but when she told me that a 'little girl died' in one of her dreams, I was forced to concede that there was probably a darker significance to these imaginations. Although upset by her distress, in one way I was relieved that she was now displaying some of the 'normal' responses to her ordeal that the psychologists had told me to look out for, and that she could no longer be accused of displaying an 'inappropriate euphoria'. I was helped in these assessments by a victim support counsellor from Devon, Ruth Harrison, who was doing research on the responses and needs of family members of murder victims. She had visited several victims of high-profile crime and asked if she could interview me. She brought with her John Dickinson, whose daughter Caroline was murdered in her dormitory while on a school trip to France only a week after our own family tragedy. Although we were both reticent at first about sharing our experiences, John and I did sense a common bond in our grief. We found that we were able to talk more easily about the practical rather than the emotional difficulties of living in the aftermath of a violent family bereavement. We struck up a friendship and promised to stay in touch. John was later to holiday with us in Wales, in the company of his surviving daughter Jenny, and I visited him at home in Cornwall also.

Three days after John and Ruth's visit we suffered another bereavement. Jackie, our faithful old golden retriever who had been born in South Africa thirteen years before, slowly drifted away in mid-February. Josie showed concern and sympathy at Jackie's death, and put flowers on the grave that I dug for our old dog in the garden. Josie had seen me shed a tear over Jackie's passing, but she seemed quite matter-of-fact about it. I wondered whether it was because she had already come to terms with death, at her young age, or whether she was merely trying to spare my feelings by seeming unmoved.

Josie's birthday on Good Friday in March 1997, was a happy affair, as our friend from America was visiting the UK and briefed us about her wedding later in the year. It would be in Wales so that her British relatives could attend, and she asked Josie if she would be her bridesmaid. Josie had been waiting for our friend to get married for years, just for this reason, and she was over the moon with anticipation and the excitement of being able to choose a special dress for the big day. When the wedding eventually took place that summer, Josie revelled in the opportunity to wear the beautiful flowery dress we had chosen. She performed her duties flawlessly and beamed with pleasure throughout the event.

For Josie's birthday treat I did what Lin had always done, and took her with some friends for a day out at the Butlin's holiday camp and amusement park near Pwllheli. The girls worked themselves into a frenzy of excitement, swimming in the aquadrome, going on as many rides as possible and stuffing themselves with ice cream and candy floss. So much of it reminded me of the times that Lin and I had taken Josie and Megan to the same place in previous years, and whenever I saw a six-year-old with the same petite round face and short dark hair as Megan, I felt sharp pangs of sadness. Megan has remained firmly fixed in my mind at the age of six, and yet Josie often likes to think of her sister at the age she would have been if she had survived, two years younger than herself.

On 15 April 1997 Josie and I travelled to London as we had done for the Children of Courage awards. Readers of the *Sun* had voted for Josie to receive a Sunshine Award, given to children and adults who have shown bravery and steadfastness in the face of adversity. It was a happy occasion, and exciting to sit with celebrities like Bob Monkhouse and David Baddiel, who sparred continuously with their razor wits. Josie also made sure that she got around many of the other notables like Sharron Davies, Anthea Turner, Faith Brown, Heather Mills, Jilly Johnson, Mystic Meg and Paul McKenna. She was particularly pleased to meet Louise, as she had heard her friends at school talking about this talented young pop star. Josie was most intrigued of all by a joker on stilts who moved among the glittering crowd, and did some magic tricks especially for Josie. It fanned in her the flames of a fascination for magic that has stayed with her to the present day.

It was particularly pleasing to meet up again with Lynda Roberts, Josie's class teacher from Goodnestone School, who was receiving a Sunshine Award for the selfless work she had done in the aftermath of the murders. Lynda told us that Josie's old classmates from Kent would soon be coming for a school trip to a Mountain Centre in Snowdonia, and we agreed to meet up there the following week.

In the end we drove over to the Mountain Centre at Llanberis two evenings in a row when the children from Goodnestone arrived for their activity weekend. Josie instantly slipped back into her old circle, especially with her friends Lucy and Jazzmin. They talked and played together late into the evenings, and I sat and chatted about 'old times' with Lynda and the other teachers. During her final term at Goodnestone School, Josie had signed up for a school trip to France. The school had allowed us to keep this option open even though we were now in Wales, so that Josie would not lose links with her old friends, and to assist the healing process on both sides by allowing the children to see how they were all doing fine.

A week later in early May, I drove Josie down to Kent where she spent an afternoon in further interviews with Ed and Pauline, before going off to France with her old classmates. I stayed with a friend in Kent and tried not to worry about her. I knew she was in excellent hands but I could not quell a twinge of concern. This was partly due to the recent death of Caroline Dickinson on her school trip to France, but also because I had not been separated from Josie for this long (four days) since before the time of the murders. Josie, meanwhile, tackled an assault course, tried her hand at archery and shooting, visited a bakery and explored German fortifications from the Second World War.

And when she returned and I saw her beaming face at the bus window, I could see she'd had a whale of a time and couldn't wait to tell me about it. Lynda Roberts told me that Josie had shown no sign of anxiety or panic attacks during the whole time she had been away. I felt we'd reached another important milestone – Josie and I being able to let each other out of our sight for overnight stays away from home. Living back in Wales was helping us to relax and accept more normal living patterns once again.

Josie's interviews with Ed and Pauline had thrown up some more important clues to the events at the murder scene. And so, the two long-suffering police officers made another arduous trip to see us in Wales, soon after Josie's return from France. Josie was speaking in rudimentary but connected sentences of three or four words by now, and was suddenly able to express herself much more efficiently than when she was uttering single words and 'playing' with Pauline's model. Now the information was coming thick and fast, and she was filling in many of the gaps in the police evidence about the attack. Dave Stevens was willing to keep me apprised of the details that were emerging, but once again I did not press him on particulars. I knew that he would be releasing information gradually to the press to keep the case 'on the boil' in the media and in the public eye. I was still wary of compromising his freedom for manoeuvre by knowing too much and therefore risking giving it away. But most of all I could not bear to hear all of the hideous details of the last moments of my loved ones' lives.

All I knew then and now, and more than I want to know, is the following. At four o'clock in the afternoon of 9 July 1996 Josie and Megan returned on the school bus from their swimming gala in Canterbury. Lin and Lucy were waiting for them, and they started on their normal walk home across the rape field behind Goodnestone, through the 'Woodpecker Wood' and over the gate onto the by-road that led past the entrance to Cherry Garden Lane. They walked down the lane to where it curves to the right and heard a car coming along the lane behind them (a very rare occurrence as few people ever bother to drive along the lane). They stood aside from the car, and Josie waved to the driver as he passed. His face was grim and he did not acknowledge their greeting.

After he had passed they walked on around the corner to find his car parked broadside across the track. It was a few yards before the entrance to the Mount Ephraim house where Lin and the girls would have turned off the lane along the footpath to the Bruderhof Community's grounds. If the bus had been back from swimming three minutes earlier, they would have been off the lane and along the path before the murderer drove by. If, if, if . . .

The man got out of the car and reached in through the back window for a hammer off the rear shelf. He faced Lin and the girls and, according to Josie, he demanded money. Lin would not have been carrying any money with her on the school walk and she told him she had none. The murderer menaced them, and Lin asked him if he would come home with them and she would find him some money there. The man said, 'No'. I don't know if Lin urged Josie to run for her life at this point, or whether the man started beating Lin first. There is evidence to the effect that the man grabbed Megan and double looped his bootlace or drug tourniquet around her neck to hold her. Lin may have been rendered powerless by this 'hostage-taking'. Josie has said that she ran away 'when Lin was nearly dead', but this may mean that it all happened at once: Lin attempting to free Megan but receiving the first hammer blows; Josie seeing her mother injured and hearing Lin shouting for her to run away; Josie breaking away and running to the gate at Mount Ephraim; and the man running after her and dragging her back.

Forensic evidence and Josie's testimony point to the murderer then shepherding them all into the bushes and seating them on the ground. He methodically tore the damp towels from the girls' swimming bags into strips, and with these and their own shoelaces, he bound and gagged them. He tied Josie to a tree and asked her if the bindings were not too uncomfortable. He then walked around behind each victim in turn and rained down blows on their heads with his hammer until he felt that he had done enough. Josie remembers hearing Lin's dying cries. He meted out the same treatment to our dog Lucy, although

Josie does not remember at what stage of the murder our pet was killed. The whole encounter took about fifteen minutes.

The murderer gathered up the blood-stained towel strips and put them back into a swimming bag. He returned to his car and drove back out of Cherry Garden Lane and onto the by-road. He pulled out at a junction without looking, in front of a witness in another car who had to brake to avoid a collision. A short while later, a man was seen fairly near to the murder scene, hiding the swimming bag with the blood-stained towel strips in a hedge. Lin, Josie, Megan and Lucy lay where they fell for another eight hours before they were discovered by the police search team.

And that information has appeared in the newspapers over and over again since it was released. But my body and my mind cannot still come to terms with it. To write those five paragraphs in the summer of 2000, four years after the event, has required an immense effort of willpower. I have had to stare at my computer screen through a continuous stream of tears with my stomach churning and my heart pounding. My mind wants constantly to leap on beyond the bald facts of movements and actions, to how they must all have been feeling. The uncomprehending terror of my innocent and loving children at seeing and hearing their mother being beaten mercilessly and crying out in pain. Lin's horror and desperation in her last moments as, bound and gagged, injured and dying, her last hopes would have been for the survival of her children against the slaughter that was raining down upon them.

That is why I don't want to know any more. Isn't it enough? My mind baulks at pursuing these thoughts any further. I know better than any other how my wife and children acted and felt. Putting myself in their minds at the time of their death is like inviting death or madness upon myself. I could not save them; I must at least try to save myself.

Dave Stevens released much of this information to the media at the end of May 1997. I had come under great pressure to comment to the press on the revelations, and had given a couple of 'doorstep' interviews accordingly. However, the thirst for knowledge of Josie's progress was insatiable, and I let slip that Josie was worried about the second head operation that she would have to have before long (the necessity for the operation had been public knowledge since before we left Kent). A flood of articles ensued: 'Operation terror of hammer attack Josie'; 'Girl left for dead is terrified of head operation'; 'Surgery poses new horrors for victim of hammer attack'. The outburst thrust the question of Josie's operation back into my mind. I had been trying to ignore it as it was such a painful prospect for both of us. I remembered how Josie had flown at me in fury at the thought of yet another operation, kicking and screaming and then retreating to her room and locking the door behind her. I had put the idea out of my mind until after we moved to Wales, but now I knew I had to face up to the problem. I negotiated with the doctors at King's College Hospital that we should have the operation carried out at a hospital closer to home to avoid a return to London. Josie's file was transferred to Manchester Children's Hospital, and we agreed that Josie could have her check-ups in Manchester as well from now on. These preparations took several months and allowed me to 'put off the evil day' for a while longer.

In the meantime, Josie and I got on with our own peculiar version of normal. We spent Josie's half-term with family on the Isles of Scilly, staying on the way in a holiday cottage lent by one of our well-wishers. After the murders I had been inundated with letters from people inviting us to get away to their cottages and retreats around the country, and Margaret Bell's was the first we were able to accept. Margaret had suffered tragedy in her own life and now devoted herself to charity and overseas aid work. She took Josie and me to her heart and often sent supportive letters with gifts for us both.

The week was glorious, and we had a traditional 'normal', seaside family holiday, making sandcastles on the beach, catching boat trips over to some of the other islands, and browsing in the shops where Josie loved to fossick among all the trinkets and souvenirs. In the evenings Josie would delight her grandmother and great-aunt with her magic tricks, and they engrossed Josie in the fascination of card games. It was a truly relaxing and restoring time for us, and the picture on the back cover of this book of Josie and I on the beach at St Mary's speaks for itself of the distance we had already managed to put between ourselves and the events of the previous year.

Back at home, we got ready for another visit to our home by a journalist and photographer. We had agreed to do a second 'exclusive article', this time with *Hello!* magazine. We felt comfortable that we would receive a sympathetic hearing through this publication, and once again I could not quite believe that they were willing to offer a five-figure sum for access to us. When the article appeared, the pictures taken by the photographer Mike Lawn were wonderful, and he sent me copies of other photos he had taken but which were not used in the publication. The pictures show the pattern that was emerging in Josie's relationship with the press, and with photographers in particular. She is laughing happily when photographed in the company of friends of her own age, and she doesn't mind too much being photographed on her own, in fact she even begins to play to the camera and pose. Pictured with me she is more reticent and embarrassed, and if there is pressure to photograph her in a situation she doesn't like, then she shows her displeasure and grumpiness and will not cooperate with even the most skilled and sensitive photographer. Josie had fallen for Mike from the moment he revealed his skill at magic tricks, but he still could not get her to smile when she was with her pony Tegid. Josie likes to keep her relationship with Tegid private, and hates to be photographed with him by anyone except me.

It was during her photo sessions with first the *Mail* photographer and then *Hello!* that Josie really started to show how she was taking charge of her life again. As we had found with Ed and Pauline, Josie had to be left alone with the photographer before she would cooperate. If I was present she would take the opportunity to embarrass me as much as possible and treat me in a way I would not tolerate when we were alone. She knew that I felt I had to be polite and responsive to outsiders and would always try to avoid conflict and not create a scene by telling her off publicly. I was sneakingly proud of the strength that Josie was showing by not being dictated to by an adult outsider. But I was also troubled by Josie's irritability and rudeness. By exposing her to these two photo sessions, had I unwittingly triggered her bad behaviour? Was media-exposure already turning her into a celebrity brat? However, over the ensuing weeks I saw that the same behaviour would emerge in any kind of polite adult company. Whether it was a journalist, a work colleague, a well-wisher or an aged relative, Josie's strategy would be the same. Because people were always being nice to her, making allowances 'for what she must have been through', Josie seemed to revel in the opportunity to explore the limits of bad manners.

I was walking the same tightrope experienced by a million other parents. How far do you go in disciplining your child? Do you come down heavily when your child misbehaves in any situation, polite or otherwise? Or do you let them get away with it out of a mixture of sympathy and the sheer lack of time to waste on trivial conflict. I had, of course, to find the middle road. It was excruciating for me to tell Josie off or make her cry after all she had been through. But I had to steel myself to be ready to rebuke her, even in public, and even if others were shocked that I might 'treat this poor child so'. Backing off from taking Josie out into public so as to avoid conflict was not the way to treat the problem if Josie was going to grow up with a balanced ability to interact with the outside world. And the press were certainly not going to leave us alone; the fall-out from 'one of the vilest crimes in British history' made sure of that. We were just going to have to handle them the best we could, and so I decided to compromise. I impressed on Josie that in future she should be pleasant and polite if we were accosted by press or well-wishers in public. In return I promised to try to handle as many future interviews as possible on my own and away from home, and that any photography of her would have to be done by myself and not by a stranger.

My closest friends were often despairing of my softness with Josie and told me in no uncertain terms that Lin would never have put up with Josie's insolent behaviour. She would have thrown Josie into her room and told her to learn some manners before she came out. But then would Lin have allowed Josie to be exposed to the two photo sessions in the way that I had done? Probably not. She was never compliant with or appeasing to outsiders in the way that I was. However, some of her closest friends told me that she would have been even more concerned than I was to secure the family's financial future. They tried to reassure me that Lin would also have taken the newspapers' money if she found herself in the same dire financial situation, but I knew that she would have exerted more control over the process of interacting with the media.

With this in mind, I attended a meeting with the head of the BBC in North Wales, who had approached me with a request to make a documentary about us. The pressure had been mounting for television coverage of our situation for some time now, and I was looking for a way to deflect this constant nagging. The approach of the local television unit offered a way out, and I went into the meeting with firm ideas of what I would and would not allow. I explained to the BBC chief that I would appreciate the opportunity to say thanks on TV to the many well-wishers who had been so supportive of us over the preceding months. But I did not like the idea of a fly-on-the-wall documentary team following Josie and me around or disrupting our home life. I suggested instead that they might use a mixture of archive footage, interviews with me, and home video that I could shoot personally so as to minimize the need for anyone to come to our home. The BBC senior producer was sympathetic to all my concerns and she agreed to the plan with the proviso that I attend a three-day BBC video production course, so that my own filming was of a sufficient standard for broadcast. And so, after clearing the plan with the Kent Police, I was issued with a high-quality digital video camera, and began shooting home movie footage. This eventually appeared in the half-hour documentary film *Josie's Story* which was shown later in the year.

In early July, on the anniversary of the murders, the BBC ran another edition of the *Crimewatch* programme, in which a renewed plea was made for evidence and public cooperation on 'The Russell Murders'. As a result of the broadcast, a psychologist working in Kent phoned in the description of one of his patients to the Kent police. The patient bore some similarity to the e-fit picture of the driver seen leaving the area of the murder scene and who had not yet come forward. The patient also had a history of violence. After further investigations, Ed Tingley was sent to arrest him. The man's name was not released at the time, but it transpired that he had a string of crimes on his sheet. He was charged with robbery and burglary and was held to await trial. Over the next few months the Kent police interviewed him extensively in relation to Lin's and Megan's deaths and the attack on Josie.

Two days after the *Crimewatch* programme, I took Josie to Manchester for her first assessment by the neurosurgeon who would perform her second head operation. I had had a long and serious discussion with Josie over the dangers of leaving the injury to her skull unattended. There was a nine-square-inch area of bone missing from the left-hand side of her head, and only her hair, skin and the repaired membrane beneath the skin protected Josie's brain from possible injury if she were to receive a bump on the head there. The lack of bone also created a concave area that gave Josie's head a slightly misshapen profile.

I told Josie that this was just a preliminary examination and that we should go along to see what the doctors said. Ms Bannister the neurosurgeon was very gentle with Josie but determined to speak directly to her about the potential problems and reasons for the surgery. Josie was old enough now that she should make her own mind up about what was done to her body. The neurosurgeon explained about patients' rights to me, and described the intricacies of the operation to Josie. But Josie still had very little comprehension of normal spoken sentences, and most of the technical discussion was lost on her. I had to smile when Ms Bannister finally asked Josie if she was happy to go through with the operation and Josie just said, 'No'. We agreed to come back in a couple of months for further X-rays and scans, and I breathed another sigh of relief that we would not have to face the operation for some time to come after all.

That summer we received a flood of visitors at home. Friends and relatives descended on us in droves, sleeping in the house or in the holiday caravan behind the cottage. I was worked off my feet with cooking, cleaning and entertaining, but Josie loved it all. She packed in as much playtime as the daylight hours would allow, and enjoyed plenty of staying up late as 'special treats' because we had guests.

When the time came for our own holiday away, I was really ready for it. We spent a week in a friend's cottage on the Mull of Kintyre, walking the headlands and swimming off the beautiful beaches, where we saw dolphins several times. There were children for Josie to play with, and we went shopping and souvenir hunting and explored further afield to Machrihanish where my mother had been stationed in the WRNS in the war. We felt far away from the cares of life down south, although there was one poignant reminder of another tragedy. This was the memorial cairn that marked the site of the Chinook Helicopter crash on the Mull, which killed twenty-eight officials from Northern Ireland in 1994. The Cairn stood only a few yards from our remote cottage, and was another reminder that disaster can strike when least expected, and in the most beautiful and unlikely places.

Soon after Josie had returned to school in September 1997, we were called to Kent for the event that we had awaited in trepidation, the police identity parade. The suspect held by the police had been brought to the Medway ID suite and lined up with nine other men behind the one-way mirrors. I was on tenterhooks at the thought of entering the same building as the man who might possibly have murdered my wife and child. As we went in with Ed and Pauline, Josie put on a brave face; but I could see that she too was terrified. The tension was palpable among all the people present and this can only have added to Josie's fear. It was explained that I could walk with Josie through the gallery behind the mirror facing the assembled men, but I was not allowed to say anything to Josie, nor were Ed and Pauline allowed to be present. In the gloom of the ID gallery, Josie would be asked by a police officer she did not know, whether or not she had recognized anybody. I saw problems straight away; however, there was no time to hold back. The men in the line-up had been waiting a long time for the parade and were looking restless.

Josie and I were ushered into the dark gallery, and on our left we saw the line of ten men standing well back from the mirror against the wall on the far side of the glass. With her head down Josie fairly rushed through the gallery, barely looking to her left at all, as though terrified of facing the man who had attacked her. At the far end of the gallery, elevated behind a lectern, was a tall, male police officer whom we had not seen before. He asked Josie, 'Did you recognize anybody in the room?' Josie mumbled, 'No', and 'No' again when the question was put to her a second time. I could not help feeling frustrated with Josie's reluctance to examine their faces properly. Josie obviously had not looked properly at any of the men, and I longed to be able to plead with her to go back and take a long hard look at each person, several times if necessary. At least then we could all be sure that she had tried properly and that her answer, positive or negative, could be relied upon. But life isn't like that. Much as I felt we had been living as though in a movie, cut-and-dried Hollywood endings rarely happen in the real world. The ID parade had been videoed, and, as the tape was played back, it was plain to all present that the results could not be relied upon either to prove or disprove that anybody recognizable to Josie had been present in that room.

The whole event made me feel extremely creepy and I was enormously relieved to be out of that claustrophobic, slightly threatening environment. I did not envy the other witnesses who were being brought in to see the same line-up. It later transpired that the woman who had seen a man driving erratically away from the crime scene picked out 'number seven' as familiar. But she could not say with certainty that it was the same man she had briefly seen reflected in a wing mirror fourteen months before.

Josie did not show any sign of being disturbed by the day's events on the journey home. However, I could sense that it had been traumatic for her, as she seemed relieved and happy at home that evening.

More happily, in mid-September we were visited at home by Kent and Matt, two of my students from the University of Kent. They had been tirelessly campaigning to raise money for a tandem bicycle for Josie and me, as they knew that we often cycled to and from school together. They had raised enough to commission a beautiful hand-built tandem, and they now arrived in North Wales having piloted the machine across the country. Josie and I were overawed by this superb present, and we began to ride it to school at every opportunity. It wasn't long before we were spotted and photographed on the bike, and the pictures later appeared in national newspapers. However, by then the novelty was wearing off for Josie and she soon began to feel embarrassed at being seen on the same bike as her dad. She eventually refused to ride on it with me, and asked instead for her own trendy mountain bike. But Josie is still very proud of her tandem, and she will ride it perfectly happily with friends instead of me. And so I prepare myself grudgingly for the day when one of those friends will turn out to be a boy rather than a girl!

Another happy event intervened in October, when we travelled to London for the Teacher of the Year awards ceremony. Lynda Roberts, Josie's teacher at Goodnestone School, had won the top award. She had done so much dedicated and sensitive work with Josie, her classmates and their parents in the aftermath of the murders, and we were proud and happy for her. Behind the scenes at the awards we met up again with Josie's school chums and they surprised Lynda on stage as she received her award.

Bizarrely, while we were in London we, quite literally, 'bumped into' Craig Charles of *Red Dwarf* fame, who invited us to watch the filming of that year's Christmas special. I was a great fan, and Josie really enjoyed watching Ainsley Harriott, one of the guests. It was an extraordinary relief to visit the show later that year, after, possibly, Josie's most gruelling interviews to date – daily sessions with the police recalling her attacker in minute detail.

During this time I had begun lecturing again with the University of Wales at Aberystwyth, which relieved some of my financial worries (I had been on Income Support over the summer months since my contract at Kent expired, and while Lin's money was tied up in probate. And the 'media money' we had earned had either been ploughed into buying the Welsh cottage or was still in the pipeline.) However, the teaching meant that I had still more to contend with, and never a spare minute in the day to catch up with everything. It was certainly a good feeling to get back into lecturing again, but the preparation and marking added to the stresses of daily life. I was beginning to feel the full weight of the working single parent's burden, compounded by all the police and media 'business' that continued to whirl around us.

And so it was with some relief that Josie and I escaped for some welcome rest and recreation during the half-term holiday at the end of October. For her Sunshine Award Josie had been given four plane tickets to Florida, courtesy of the *Sun* and Virgin Holidays. We travelled to Gatwick with two of Josie's friends and before flying had a nasty experience when the airport monorail broke down. We were stranded high above the ground for more than half an hour, while the closed glass cabin heated up to a sweltering temperature. We joked our way through the ordeal, and I can remember being impressed by how little concern Josie showed in the stressful situation.

In Orlando we spent a few days enjoying ourselves in the amusement parks, before moving on to stay with friends who owned a cabin in the Florida swamps. The time spent relaxing and observing the sub-tropical wildlife as we canoed in the Everglades, was a perfect antidote to the hurly-burly of the theme parks, and we returned to the UK refreshed and ready to face the pressures of daily life once again.

And we returned to unusually high pressure. While we were away, the murder suspect had been charged, and the police enquiry had gone up a gear in order to consolidate evidence for the forthcoming trial. The Public Prosecution Service was convinced that there was sufficient evidence to justify a trial, but many details remained to be filled in. Josie began another series of police interviews at the Bangor safe house, while I busied myself with funding proposals to win myself a more secure contract at Aberystwyth. I had also agreed to help with the production of a victim support training video that was being prepared for police and counselling agencies. In mid-November, therefore, I subjected myself to several more hours of harrowing televised interviews to assist with that project.

At the end of November we travelled again to Manchester for a meeting with the doctors about Josie's next head operation. This time Josie was due for a scan and she was extremely reticent about going through with it. It was eventually only the no-nonsense attitude of a brusque Mancunian staff nurse that secured Josie's compliance with the scanning procedure. She was as unwilling as before to submit to the doctors' pleas for her to undergo the surgery. With Josie present it was not possible for me to get the answers to the technical questions I wanted to ask, as Josie bridled at her 'problems' being discussed in my presence. I needed to be able to put our minds at rest regarding the safety of the procedure. Was it really necessary to have this operation, or would the bone grow back in time? What would be the risks if we left it, compared to the risks if we went ahead? How big would the plate be and could it be seen or felt under the surface of the skin? How much of Josie's hair would have to be removed during the operation? When would the operation be, and how long would it take? Was Josie's skull still growing and would she need a new plate at some point in the future? These and many more questions I set out in a letter to the doctors, and soon I received a detailed reply.

The upshot was that Josie's skull defect was too large to leave unattended. The operation was routine and safe, and once it was over Josie would be unlikely to have to return to hospital again. Best of all, the doctors were willing to try to use her existing operation scar for the incision, so she would not need any hair removed at all. We still had some more visits to Manchester for additional scans and examinations before the operation could go ahead; an autumn 1998 date was suggested for the procedure. At least I was now armed with the necessary information to argue the case with Josie over the coming months before she had to go into hospital again.

It was around this time that Josie began to worry less about wearing her hat at all times. The breakthrough began in Florida, where it was hot and where Josie felt that people did not recognize her. Now, her hair had grown long and was dark and glossy and very pretty. Telling her this enough times helped her come round to the idea that perhaps wearing a hat all the time was not such a cool thing to do. She was becoming more self- and fashion-conscious and so she began to leave her hat off more frequently when we went out. The word soon got out, and with Christmas approaching I came under increasing pressure to allow another newspaper 'photo shoot'.

I was in a stronger position to resist now that the murder suspect was awaiting trial and any public discussion of the case could be deemed *sub judice*. However, the *Sun* came up with an offer that was difficult to refuse. I already felt indebted to them for putting up the original reward for information leading to the arrest of the suspect, and we had only recently returned from the Sunshine Award trip to America. When the newspaper then offered Josie the chance to skate with Torvill and Dean during rehearsals for their ice show at the Birmingham National Arena in return for a couple of Christmas photos, she was so excited at the prospect that I did not feel I could refuse. Josie had loved the couple of times that she went skating in Kent, and when she heard that she would be able to choose a new pair of skating boots and a dress too, there were no more arguments. The *Sun* was offering once more to pay a fee for access, and my solicitors were still pessimistic about Josie receiving any criminal injuries compensation for another year or more. And so I agreed to this third and final photo shoot of the year.

The time we spent with Torvill and Dean was magical. We had never seen an ice show up close, and the spectacle presented by the champion skaters and their supporting cast was awe-inspiring. Josie was reticent at first to go out on the ice during the rehearsals, but slowly warmed to the attention of the dancers. Eventually she took a couple of turns around the rink with Jayne Torvill and seemed particularly pleased that her new boots and skating dress made her look good even in this elevated company. Although a little overawed by it all, Josie must have enjoyed it, because afterwards she begged me to take her and her friends to our nearest ice rink in North Wales for her Christmas treat.

The *Sun*'s pictures of Josie without her hat on made her look very pretty, although the Christmas shots of her draped in tinsel were fairly 'cheesy'. The amount of interest generated was such that several other papers published the hatless photos and I received a fresh deluge of kindly and admiring letters, commenting on Josie's 'miraculous' progress and complimenting me on the efforts that I was making to bring Josie through her ordeal. However, it was the one discordant letter that had the most impact on me:

> I cannot be the only person who feels an increasing sense of unease at seeing Josie once more in the limelight. The child has been through a dreadful ordeal from which she may never recover, mentally or physically. The healing process can begin only when she is allowed to go back to some kind of normal childhood. Asking her to pose smiling bravely yet again is unfair on the child and is certainly more information than the public needs, or has the right to be given. Please, Mr Russell, stop seeming to exploit your little girl and let her slip back into anonymity while she is growing up – it's the best she deserves.

I was deeply stung by this letter, which was published in one of the papers that had done most to publicize Josie's story. It touched the nerve I had about accepting money from the newspapers and being thought of as 'cashing in' on my family's tragedy. It fuelled my misgivings about our relationship with the press; and yet the spectre of what had happened to André Hanscombe still haunted me and I continued to fear the harassment we might have to endure if I tried to cut ourselves off entirely from public scrutiny.

The last couple of weeks of the year gave us some blessed relief as everyone else seemed too caught up in their Christmas preparations to worry about us. Josie took part in the school nativity play and the Christmas service which was held in the chapel in Nantlle, before we drove south to spend time with my mother and then Lin's parents in Sutton Coldfield. We spent Christmas itself at home, in the peace and quiet of our little Welsh miner's cottage. Our closest friends joined us as they had the year before, but this time there seemed to be less hidden pain and a more relaxed atmosphere as we remembered Lin and Megan, and made a toast to happiness in the future such as we had shared with them in the past. We had survived the first eighteen months of 'the aftermath', and although there were still many worries and uncertainties in our future, we were sufficiently settled now to face these tribulations with a degree of confidence born of the knowledge that we had weathered the worst of the storm.

In January 1998, the *Sun* ran a series of articles on our lives, based on the interviews that we had given Sue Evison, the chief feature writer, at the time of the Christmas photo shoot. I was quite surprised to see the detail of her inner thoughts that Josie had revealed to Sue when they had been alone together in Josie's bedroom. Josie would not talk about the tragedy, but she was at ease when remembering Lin and Megan in happier times. Sue was obviously on Josie's wavelength, as she had got her to open up about all the day-to-day things that interest a ten-year-old girl. Josie talked about growing her hair long, achieving a longer distance swimming badge, her favourite TV shows (*Clothes Show, Casualty, Gladiators, Chucklevision, Get Your Own Back, Blue Peter*, etc.), favourite lessons at school (Art and Technology), games she liked to play (lost dogs, nurses), favourite pop music (Aqua), favourite video (*101 Dalmatians*), being a bridesmaid at our friend's wedding, wanting to go up to secondary school, wanting to be a vet when she grew up, and things like that. It was a good sign that Josie was feeling more at ease with adults outside our immediate circle, and that she could communicate in a more easy and assured manner.

In April I was asked by my employers to complete a two-week environmental training consultancy in Kenya. At first I was reticent as I had not been away from Josie for so long since the time of the tragedy. But as Josie's confidence had grown, and as she herself seemed to savour the chance of staying with friends while I was away, I agreed to carry out the mission. The day after I left, another 'Josie story' hit the headlines. A month before, we had received the first notification of an interim payment of £18,500 to Josie from the Criminal Injuries Compensation Authority for 'loss of mother's services'. I was quoted as saying that this was like a 'slap in the face'. I *had* told a friend that valuing Lin's worth to Josie in this way was like a slap in the face but I also understood the limitations of the government compensation scheme, and that in any case this was only an initial offer. Larger amounts were likely to be awarded in respect of other areas of the claim, such as Josie's personal injury and my loss of earnings. But this did not come across in the stories that were printed. The Prime Minister's office and the Home Secretary Jack Straw were said to have commented on the case and urged me to appeal the decision.

The news reached me in Kenya and I shuddered at the thought of having to face the press again when I returned. I worried that my 'slap in the face' quote might annoy the people at CICA who would be adjudicating on our other claims. But I also worried that if I were to resign myself to a low payout then that would not be showing solidarity with my supremely hard-working lawyer who was pressurizing the authority for a better award. I had always been uneasy about applying for a government handout, as Lin and I had lived most of our working life overseas and had not been long-term British tax-payers. It was partly because I did not want us to have to rely on a CICA handout that I had 'sold our story' to the press in the first place, and yet now the newspapers were leading the clamour for a better payout for us. It was very touching to read the outraged letters that flooded into the papers calling upon CICA to relent on Josie's award. But I also felt a twinge of embarrassment for the head of the authority who was pilloried for doing no more than presiding over a scheme that was tightly limited by statute and treasury grant.

In Kenya I phoned home almost every night, notwithstanding the cost, as I felt very remote and helpless in case anything should happen while I was away. I had never felt as worried when travelling overseas before, but now Josie was so much more central to my life, I had a continual sense of unease while I was away from her. My friends at home who were looking after Josie were insistent that she was fine and that I should not worry. But I found myself counting the days until my return, in a way that I had never done in the past.

Two days before I was due to return to the UK, my hotel bedroom in Nairobi was raided by thieves and my camera, money and passport stolen. The British Council and the Consulate at the High Commission rose to the challenge, and organized me with emergency travel documents in the space of a single day. On my return to Britain I found that the furore over the compensation had died down and that Josie had actually missed me while I was away! Though she never would have admitted it, I could tell by her behaviour that she was pleased to have me home again. I had grown accustomed to her lack of overt affection towards me and so it was heart-warming to receive a big Welcome Home card and find that she wanted to be close by me for a change.

Soon after, I had to attend a meeting at the local education authority headquarters to decide on Josie's schooling and special needs for the next year. She was now eleven and under normal circumstances she would have been due to move up to the local comprehensive school this year. Since she had been back at Nantlle Josie had been making steady progress with the help of her teacher Susan Owen, and classroom assistant Catherine Williams. She was doing fine in art and numeracy, but still struggling with the written word, as the capability of the damaged speech and language centre on the left side of her brain was only slowly re-establishing itself on the right side.

We all agreed that, rather than upsetting Josie's routine at this critical time and throwing her in at the deep end in a large and unfamiliar secondary school, we should instead 'hold her back' for an extra year at primary school to build on the good progress she was making there. I knew this would mean more fights with Josie as she expected to move up at the same time as her friends to the big school; she certainly did not want to 'stay down with the babies'. However, because the classes at the 'little school' were integrated over more than a year's age-range, and a couple of Josie's other classmates would also be staying on for an extra year, I didn't feel too bad about forcing the issue.

In May 1998 we received a visit from Nick Baldock, a well-wisher who lived in Hertfordshire. Nick visited us with his ten-year-old daughter Lauren who immediately struck up a friendship with Josie. He had asked if he might make a donation to Josie's Trust Fund which my solicitors had set up to hold Josie's criminal injuries compensation money and her inheritance from Lin's estate. Nick had been one of the many people who were dismayed by the level of Josie's initial payout from CICA, and he wanted to do something to improve the financial provision for her. I explained that it was likely that Josie would receive more from the authority in due course, but he was still keen to do something to help. Nick was a management training consultant and had been an ultra-marathon runner in his earlier career. He had run for charity on several previous occasions, including a long-distance run from John o' Groats to Lands End. But what Nick was now planning to do to raise money for Josie was altogether more ambitious and daunting. He was proposing to run 3000 miles across America!

Nick had always dreamed of doing the cross-America run, and he had already conferred with the famous British transcontinental runner of the 1960s, Bruce Tulloh, about planning for the attempt. He had been deeply moved by Josie's story and was desperate to do something to help, and so I agreed that he could use Josie's Trust Fund as the focus for his latest charitable project. Nick at once started work on raising the additional money he needed to finance the run itself, and he soon attracted a group of similarly motivated young volunteer helpers to assist with publicity and planning for the project, and to act as his support team during the run itself, which was planned to start in May 1999.

Two months later Josie received a revised offer of £79,000 from CICA. This was a great relief to me as it meant that Josie could now look forward to receiving a valuable nest-egg when she came of age, and it lessened the pressure on me to build a large provision for Josie when she grew up. It meant I could be more at ease over my decision to work only half-time so that I could be at home with Josie, and it reduced the need for me to take on the well-paid overseas consultancy work that had previously taken up so much time and kept me away from the family.

During the summer term of 1998 I continued to build up a library of home movie material for the BBC documentary, and Josie helped by filming some of her daily activities. I joined several other camcorder-wielding parents to record the school play and sports day, while Josie filmed her friends and her pets. The BBC production team were sensitive to our needs for privacy and kept out of the way for most of the time. I did allow them to film mocked-up re-enactments of my meetings with the education authority to decide on Josie's future schooling provision, and with the doctors to discuss Josie's forthcoming operation. But I was thankful that the team never put any pressure on me to do 'real-time' fly-on-the-wall filming in such sensitive situations.

Josie's primary school was off-limits to all the media, as her teachers and I were keen to have at least one place where Josie felt she would never be accosted by photographers. This was not possible at home, as we lived on a publicly accessible track and could be doorstepped or photographed without warning. There seemed to be such a craving for information about Josie that comments made by me, my friends or relatives would be passed on and reach the newspapers through the most circuitous of routes. And so we had to accept the regular appearance of shiny hire cars on our dead-end track, with sheepish-looking journalists requesting quotes and photos whenever anything relating to our case appeared on the newswires. With the court case of the man charged with the murders rapidly approaching, I was under instructions not even to say 'Hello' to these visitors, as I could then be quoted as having 'spoken to the press'. Mark Stephens would call regularly with the refrain: 'Hi Shaun, have you been keeping that big gob of yours shut? How many times have you stuck your foot in it this week!'

The triggers for the media to appear at our home were diverse. Another revelation in the police investigation, the tandem bicycle, news of Josie's compensation claim or her operation, stories about Josie's old school and teachers in Kent, the run across America, the Home Secretary's rethinking of victim's payouts, all were enough to precipitate visits of the press to the Nantlle valley. I began to feel sorry for one journalist who regularly made the long trip from Manchester on the offchance that he might obtain a quote. He was sent away so many times with nothing to show for his journey, that he became quite familiar with the traditional red phonebox at the bottom of our track, from where he used to call his newsroom to tell them of his wasted journey. He must have got into a conversation with the operator from the phonebox one day, because the next day a quirky and amusing article appeared in his national daily, concerning 'Britain's Loneliest Phonebox'. It appeared that the little red kiosk at the bottom of our track was the 'least-used payphone in the country'.

The article precipitated a spate of copycat stories in other newspapers and our local phone box suddenly became the focus of national attention. Several times when passing the kiosk on the way to school, Josie and I found camera teams doing items about it for the various channels. One newspaper even quoted the box's telephone number and hundreds of people from all over Britain started to ring into the phone in the hope of catching someone there to talk to. For weeks we could not pass the phone without hearing it ring, and on the one or two occasions that we picked up the phone, it was always someone saying, 'Is that Britain's loneliest phonebox?' Kids living in the houses near to the box would spend hours answering the phone, until eventually BT sent these households free phone vouchers for their trouble – as long as the calls were answered, BT was suddenly making far more money out of this phone than they ever could have hoped to make without the kids' assistance!

The early part of the summer holiday was spent entertaining a stream of friends and relatives at home as usual, and at one point we had three families staying with us at the same time in our little two-bedroomed miner's cottage. By mid-August however, the visits had to stop, as Josie was due for an unavoidable appointment. The time had come for her head operation.

I had been preparing the ground for weeks in advance. On the rare occasions that we had any quiet time alone, I would try to bring the conversation around to the topic of the forthcoming operation. I worked away at lessening Josie's fears and passing the whole thing off as a necessary but painless procedure that hundreds of other kids who had had accidents went through every week in Britain. But from the moment we left in the car for Manchester Children's Hospital, I could tell that it was going to be an almighty battle. Josie was tearful and afraid. But more than this she was obstinate and determined that she would try any way of getting out of the ordeal.

We arrived at the hospital and were installed in a cubicle room on a convalescence ward where we had to sleep overnight before the operation. We spent the intervening hours being visited by a series of surgeons, anaesthetists and nurses, trying to explain to Josie what was in store for her and why she shouldn't worry, and asking for her agreement to go through with the procedure. This worked Josie up into a frenzy of fear and she kept on insisting that she had been told that she didn't have to do it if she didn't want to, and that she just wanted to go home.

Next day the time for the operation was approaching rapidly, and Josie had to be 'prepped' with a sedative in advance of the anaesthesia for the operation. She was told she could take a pill or breathe gas through a mask, but she resolutely refused to cooperate. At one point a jolly young male anaesthetist we hadn't met before, who was being kept waiting by Josie's intransigence, breezed into the room and plonked himself down in the same chair that Josie was cowering in. Josie just about went through the roof, and we hastily took the young man aside and explained Josie's phobia about close physical contact with adult males.

The hour for our operation slot passed, and I had reached the end of my tether. We had been battling with Josie for twenty-four hours and I felt totally drained and wrung out by the tension of the situation, and having to watch Josie's suffering. When she screamed at me that Lin would not have made her do this, I finally broke down and had to leave the room to be comforted by the nurses. Minutes later I was amazed to see Josie walking from the room with an entourage of nurses at her side, heading for the operating theatre. 'She doesn't want the prep or the trolley,' I was told, 'she is going straight into the operation without it.' We hurried along to the theatre where the surgeons had remained on standby. Josie climbed straight onto the trolley in the anteroom and reached for the gas mask, which she had been shown how to use the previous day. Within seconds she was out for the count and I watched through tearful eyes as she was wheeled through into the operating theatre.

Several hours later I crept into the same anteroom where I had left her, to see Josie's sleepy face smiling up at me. Her face and hair were covered in sticky brown disinfectant, but not a hair had been removed from her head. The surgeons had gone to extra lengths to insert the titanium plate through an incision along Josie's previous operation scar. Her hair was so dense that it was almost impossible to avoid a few tiny hairs being stitched back in along the incision, and the worry was that this would introduce a source of infection into the wound. This was why such copious quantities of antiseptic had been used during the operation, and why Josie now had to undergo a heavy course of antibiotics following the operation. The nurses spent some time carefully washing Josie's hair before we wheeled her back to the ward. As soon as she arrived Josie started groggily packing her things ready to leave. When we told her she should rest for a while, she reminded me crossly that I had told her that she could go home after the operation. There followed another round of arguments before Josie settled down for the afternoon. The nurses discovered that she had a temperature and would have to stay in overnight for observation. However, by now I was so relieved to have put the operation behind us, that I was less keyed up and vulnerable to Josie's testiness. Pretty soon she realized that we were not going to budge and that she would have to put up with another night in hospital. Next day the arguments about leaving to go home continued, but the nurses insisted on keeping Josie in for yet another night because of her temperature. I eventually stooped to bribery and offered to let Josie have her choice of anything out of the Argos store catalogue if she would just agree to let the doctors say when we could go home!

Two days after the operation, we drove home to North Wales via Bangor, where we stopped for Josie's visit to Argos. Her hair was still matted and stuck out like a clown's wig, but this didn't stop Josie from dashing through the streets to get to the shop as fast as possible. At the Argos shop she chose a miniature press for printing sticky labels, and then she chose a bicycle speedometer for my birthday the next day – she'd been wanting to get me this present for a long time.

We celebrated my birthday with Lin's parents at their caravan in mid-Wales. Josie and her friend Christina made me a cake after we arrived, and we spent the next three days relaxing in the countryside around Llangadfan and Lake Vyrnwy. Josie walked, cycled and canoed as though nothing had happened, and seemed oblivious to the fact that she had a new nine-inch metal plate screwed into her skull under a long line of stitches. I took some home video of Josie and Christina playing in the canoe in the river near Llangadfan, and this later appeared in the documentary *Josie's Story*. Looking at the footage, there is no indication that Josie had just undergone a three-hour skull operation.

The day after we returned from the caravan, we drove again to the hospital for Josie to have her stitches out. This time everything was sweetness and light, and Josie made no fuss at all over the soreness of having the stitches removed. It was as though all the worry and fear of the previous weeks had fallen away from her; she felt no pain, she did not look any different, she could now get on with her life without the spectre of a return to hospital hanging over her.

At the beginning of September, I braced myself for the task of starting Josie back at Ysgol Baladeulyn for her extra year. Josie went off to school happily enough in the morning of the first day, perhaps she had forgotten the full significance of this step. However, that afternoon on the way home in the car she broke down in tears. Once in school she had realized that some of her friends had gone on to secondary school, and that she was being 'left behind'. My heart was rent by her words as she sobbed plaintively, 'I just want to be normal'. One of the most important things in a child's life, it seems, is to fit in completely with her peers and not to be thought of as being out of the ordinary in any way. Having to face the younger children who had moved up into her class, and imagining that the older ones would be thinking she was not clever enough to move up to big school, must have been excruciating for Josie. It would have reminded her of the thing that she least wanted to acknowledge, that she had a disability, and it would have brought back thoughts of the reasons for her 'abnormality'.

We had already had to be cruel to be kind the previous term when warning Josie of her extra year at primary school. The visiting speech therapist and the educational psychologist had soon picked up the fact that Josie refused to believe there was anything wrong with her, and that she had become masterful at masking her difficulty with comprehension. We had set such store by boosting her confidence and never knocking her, that it was hard when I finally had to have it out with Josie that she did have a major problem with her speech and language capability and therefore a severe learning disability. But this made it no easier to cope with Josie's anguish when it was brought home to her in practical terms on that first day of her last year at primary school, that she was now a special-needs child who would have to have a classroom assistant to help her, a speech therapist coming to call and extra lessons that the other kids did not have to attend.

The teachers were aware of this, of course, and made special efforts to soften the blow for Josie. She was able to work in small groups with other children, some of whom also had learning difficulties, but often attended by other 'normal' kids who liked to join in with the special games and tasks that were set for Josie. The special-needs assistant and the speech therapist never singled Josie out but always included her in group activity that prevented her getting a complex about her impairment. The headteacher Mrs Owen was particularly understanding of Josie's needs and always mindful of her sensitivities. Yet at the same time she began to give Josie more responsibility as the oldest child in the school, so that over the ensuing weeks Josie rose to the challenge of her extra tasks and became more self-assured and confident as a result.

By late September 1998 I felt secure enough in the routine that we had established for Josie, that I could spend five days away in my old workplace of Windhoek, Namibia. I was invited to present a keynote address at a science education conference there, and while I was away I spent a fortune on phone calls home just as I had from Kenya. I arrived back home to find Josie as pleased to see me as when I had returned from my earlier trip. It really did seem as though absence made the heart grow fonder as far as she was concerned.

A week after my return from Namibia, the jury was sworn in at Maidstone Crown Court for the trial of the man who had been charged with murdering Lin and Megan. Luckily, neither Josie nor I was required to be present at the court, as our evidence was presented in written or videotaped form. Ed and Pauline took turns to spend time with us in Wales during the course of the trial, keeping us in touch with the events in Maidstone and helping us to understand the complexities of the proceedings. Suddenly Josie's face seemed to be back on the front pages of all the national newspapers and the detailed events of the day of the murder were made public. Josie's videotaped evidence was played to the court and by all accounts elicited much concern and sympathy from those present in the courtroom.

Meanwhile I did some more lecturing at Aberystwyth to try to keep my mind off the trial. I certainly did not want to be present myself during the proceedings as I could not bear having to face the person who possibly had been the cause of my family's misfortune. I knew that if he appeared insolent or dismissive of our trauma then it would make my ability to cope with the tragedy all the more difficult. The man continued to protest his innocence throughout the proceedings, and this did little for my need to know how and why this tragedy happened, or to see someone showing true remorse for what they had done.

The trial carried on for over two weeks and probably the most distressing point for me was to hear my departed wife and child referred to as 'slags and whores' by some of the criminals giving evidence in court. The police and prosecutors were despairing as the judge ruled that large amounts of what they considered to be pertinent and solid evidence could not be brought forward as it might unfairly prejudice the minds of the jury members against the accused. However, Dave Stevens was philosophical and explained that the judge was doing his utmost in this high-profile case to guard against any suggestion of unfairness and to reduce the likelihood of technicalities proving substantive at a possible later appeal.

Josie was only vaguely aware of the trial going on, and she was not particularly interested in the newspapers or TV reports of the trial. She carried on as normal at school and then was at home for half-term having fun with her friends as the trial drew to a close. I stood by to travel to Kent for the end of the trial, as I was expected to give a press conference once the verdict was known. I mithered over what to say if the man was found innocent, or if he was found guilty, and how I could avoid causing offence to either side depending on the outcome.

When the jury were sent out to consider their verdict, I drove down to Kent and stayed at a friend's house to await their return.

As well as doing a video diary over this period, I was also taping an audio diary for a Radio 4 programme to go out after the trial – *Life with Josie* won a Sony Radio Award some months later. The following is a transcript of what I said in the audio diary at the time of the trial:

Thursday 22 October, 1998

It's Wednesday October 22nd – no, it's Thursday October 22nd – I've lost track of time. It's half past 11 in the morning and I'm at a friend's house in Kent, near to the scene of the court case in Maidstone. The jury have been out since yesterday afternoon considering their verdict, and I'm awaiting the call to police headquarters where I'll join the Detective Chief Inspector who's in charge of the case, for a press conference after the verdict is known . . .

I'm trembling all the time in anticipation, not knowing what to expect. I've just called home and learnt that Josie by chance watched the news last night and has picked up that there was the possibility that the man who's been accused may be found not guilty, and she seemed quite worried about it. She's tried to put it as far into the background as she can and just get on with her normal life. I can't do that, I've become sort of consumed by the whole thing.

Friday 23 October, 1998

It's quarter past eleven on the morning of Friday in the final week of the court case. The jury have been out for nearly two days. It's terrible waiting. It's just a continuous stream of adrenaline going into your system, keeping you trembling and on tenterhooks the whole time, waiting for that phone call to come through to tell you what the verdict is going to be – never mind the added worry of having to face the media at the press conference after the verdict comes out. There's nothing more to do other than wait . . .
I've been trying to relax in the evenings with friends who are kindly putting me up in Kent. We've been out for a restaurant meal

one night and out to see a film, *The Truman Show* with Jim Carrey, which is all about one's life being watched by the media all the time. There were quite a few parallels one could read into my situation . . . I had a swim in the local pool this morning before running back to wait by the phone again. I'll continue to fidget and pace up and down through the day to see what happens.

Pauline was with me when the guilty verdict finally came through. There was an immediate sense of elation and we hugged and congratulated each other. But I retired to the bedroom almost immediately and broke down in tears as the tension ebbed out of me. I drove over to Maidstone for the press conference, hardly able to see as my emotions kept welling up and my eyes kept filling.

The following day, many of the newspapers quoted verbatim my comments at the press conference:

I have been so keyed up that I am still shaking after what the week has been like. My first reaction to the verdict was one of elation and pleasure for all those around me who had put so much into the case. The initial elation has been slowly draining away as I have driven over here to the press conference. I feel relief that it is all over at last and that the verdict is what I consider a good one. I phoned Josie at home in Wales and told her that the 'bad man' had been found guilty. She just said, 'Good' with a firm emphasis in her voice, and then went on to tell me about how she had gone out to the movies last night with her friend and her friend's parents.

Her reaction was just 'Good' and that is my reaction. If you ask me what I feel about the convicted man, I honestly can't say that I feel emotions like hatred or anything. If anything I feel pity for him. I have heard about his terrible childhood and his problems. I certainly feel sympathy for his mother and sister who have had to endure an awful lot in the last weeks. But mainly I feel sadness at what we have all lost and the fact that we can never regain what we have lost.

I rang my late wife's parents and the sense of desolation and loss in their voices was something that reminded me that they have lost their only daughter. I have lost my wife and daughter. Josie has lost her mother and sister. They will never come back again. I have had to endure hearing dreadful things during the time of the trial. It is not very nice to hear your loved ones referred to in the way that some people described them. Another thing I can never forgive the murderer for, is that whenever I think of my wife and daughter, the terrible image of them lying side by side on a mortuary slab so often comes back to me. And so I do feel anger too.

I want to thank the police especially for the tremendous effort that has gone into this case. I also want to thank the Crown Prosecution Service for being firm in their belief in the case. I want to thank all the witnesses who have gone through such a lot and all the people in general who have supported Josie and I over the last two years. I also want to thank the jury. They have had the hardest job of all. I tried to put myself in their position but I just can't believe how difficult it must have been for them to come to a verdict.

Responding to questions about my feelings if the accused man had been acquitted I said:

I would have been shattered. I would have dreaded going back to Josie to tell her, and that we had to go back into a kind of limbo still not knowing who had really done it.

And in response to questions about how I was coping I said:

Josie is the one who keeps me on track. She is a handful enough for any parent but my mother helps me with advice and I have other close friends who are helping me too. Josie is very happy with the life we lead in North Wales. It was really essential to keep her away from the court case as much as possible. She just wants to get on with her life as a little girl of her age normally does. Josie is still struggling with her reading, writing and speech, but from the beginning my main thought has been Josie's future and trying to ensure that in future she has as normal a life as possible. Josie has no hang-ups about talking about her mother and sister and she constantly badgers me for a new dog to replace our pet Lucy who she lost in the attack. Josie knows she will never get her mum and sister back, but she might get a dog back.

At this point I broke down and Dave Stevens moved quickly to close the conference. I experienced again the typical ending of an emotional press conference, where there is a flurry of photoflashes as the photographers try to catch the last, most fraught moment of the proceedings. But then they quickly turn away their cameras in a mixture of sympathy at the subject's grief, and embarrassment in case others present might see them feeding just a little too long on the spectacle.

During the last months of 1998, Josie and I were left alone to get on with as normal a life as we could manage. I developed more project proposals for my institute at Aberystwyth, and Sarah Harman was nominated for Lawyer of the Year by *The Times* newspaper, for her crusading work on the compensation claims of women who had received misdiagnoses of their cervical smear tests at the Canterbury Hospital.

Josie's interests were taking new directions, and we attended the Clothes Show Live in Birmingham at the beginning of December. Josie was now a fashion-conscious eleven-year-old, and she had received several trendy outfits among the gifts sent to her by well-wishers. I could tell by her new concern with personal appearance that she was starting to become a young woman, and that childlike pastimes would soon, indeed, be 'passed times'. Josie's tastes in music and television programmes were also changing, and the previously uninteresting topic of 'boys' began to crop up more frequently. Adolescence was looming and would present us with a whole new set of challenges.

Just before Christmas I travelled to Tanzania with a colleague from the University of Bradford, in order to present a training course in environmental impact assessment at the College of African Wildlife Management. I had managed to complete the visit within my pledge of spending no more than a maximum of four weeks overseas within the year, and I returned laden with African souvenirs for Christmas presents. It seemed inconceivable that this was now the third Christmas since Lin and Megan had died. Everything that had gone before seemed so fresh in my mind, as though it had only happened yesterday. Where had the time gone? Life had been so full and so much of a rush, that all our experiences seemed to have been compressed into a narrow 'aftermath zone'. The observation that I had still not had time to grieve properly still held true. Certainly Josie and I were no nearer being able to discuss the tragedy openly with each other. Would we ever be able to? Would we ever want to?

On Boxing Day Josie and I went for dinner with friends at the hotel in the famous Italianate village of Portmeirion a few miles from where we lived. One of the staff was the son of Josie's headteacher and we received special treatment as we partook of a wonderful meal in relaxed and elegant surroundings. It is true that the spectre of the legal appeal continued to haunt me, and we still had to face the hurdle of Josie's move up to secondary school. There was also my own battle to find a more secure source of income to allow me to continue working and supporting Josie at home. In the meantime, however, we could enjoy the Christmas festivities. Looking around the cheerful faces I tried to believe that the coming year might bring us closer to 'normality' again, and that tragic memories might begin to be banished below the pain threshold.

On New Year's Day 1999 the *Sun* newspaper carried a centre spread on its Woman and Man of the Year awards for 1998. While I had been in Tanzania before Christmas I had been nominated without my knowledge as a contender for the Man of the Year Award, along with personalities such as pop singer Robbie Williams and politicians David Trimble and Tony Blair. To my astonishment, I got by far the largest number of votes, and out of the blue I received a phone call asking me to attend a photo session where I was presented with a plaque by one of the kind readers who had voted for me. This all created much amusement at home, of course, and plenty of talk about widening the door jambs so that my expanded head would be able to get through. I certainly felt unworthy in the company of sports presenter Helen Rollason who had won the Woman of the Year award and who was sadly to lose her long and courageous battle against cancer later in the year.

The *Sun* readers' recognition of my role as Josie's Dad did give me a boost, however, and Josie and I sent a Thank You card to the newspaper. Josie sent a coloured picture that she had drawn of our old house in the Nantlle Valley, with a happy sun shining over the hills, ripe apples on the trees, cats and dogs running around and herself riding past on Tegid. Although I was not normally given to placing much credence on interpretations of such drawings by psychologists, I had to agree in this case that it did not seem to be the sort of drawing that an anxious or troubled child would make.

Later in the month we had another even more practical occurrence to cheer us up. Our ten-year-old Subaru estate car had done over

100,000 miles, and as I was now doing over 20,000 miles a year running Josie around and buzzing back and forth to my bits and pieces of self-employed work around the country, it was clearly time for something newer. Josie and I had been to look at second-hand cars at the nearest dealer and the helpful sales representative said that he might be able to make us a 'special offer'. Soon Subaru UK offered us a brand new Legacy Outback estate for the same price that we would have paid for a three-year-old model. This was supremely generous. We had never had a completely new car before, and although I felt a bit embarrassed in our shiny new chariot, Josie and our friends could tell how pleased I was. They humoured me in my childlike glee and told me that I deserved a 'little present'!

In March I travelled overseas again for another consultancy in Tanzania. This time I had to have meetings with the heads of Wildlife and National Parks Departments in nine African countries, and it was a nightmare trying to squeeze the schedule into the fortnight limit that I set for being away from Josie. Starting from Tanzania, I travelled to Kenya, Uganda, South Africa, Mozambique, Zimbabwe, Botswana, Zambia and Malawi, before returning to Tanzania again. While meeting with staff at the Uganda Wildlife Authority in Kampala, news came in of the massacre of gorilla-viewing tourists and parks staff at the Bwindi Impenetrable Forest National Park. My meetings were cut short as headquarters personnel busied themselves with preparations to receive the bodies of their colleagues who had been killed at Bwindi. It was ironic that they commented to me unknowingly that life must be much more secure and uneventful for me in the 'safe' environment of the UK. While staying at my hotel in Kampala I was recognized by an English tourist from Canterbury, and also by several of the British journalists who flew out to cover the crisis. To their credit they did not try to collar me for an interview, although they were certainly intrigued as to what I was doing there.

While I was away, the *Sun* was doing yet more to help Josie. They arranged a phone-in auction of celebrity clothing to raise money for Josie's Trust Fund and to assist Nick Baldock with the financing of his 'Run for Josie' across America. When I returned to the UK I was amazed to find that £13,000 had been raised through generous donations of clothing from a glittering array of public figures and personalities: the Duchess of York, Cherie Blair, Mo Mowlam, Ross

Kemp, Kelly Brook, Prince Nazeem, Nick Berry, Sheryl Gascoigne, Noel Gallagher, Ffion and William Hague, Louise Nurding, Eamonn Holmes, Nasser Hussein, Greg Rusedski, Damon Albarn, Brian Conley, Emma Noble, Jamie Redknapp, Meg Matthews, Robbie Williams and David Beckham.

I was overwhelmed by people's generosity, even though I kept explaining that Josie's future was now financially secure. In the same month I accepted the latest offer from the Criminal Injuries Compensation Authority; the final disbursement was as follows:

£	
72,146.52	To Josie Russell re. loss of mother's services
146,304.00	To Josie Russell re. personal injury claim
12,150.00	To Josie Russell for special educational needs
5000.00	To Shaun Russell re. loss of wife
10,000.00	To Shaun Russell re. loss of daughter
2630.00	To Shaun Russell for funeral expenses
7500.00	To Shaun Russell re. post-traumatic stress
18,220.00	To Shaun Russell for loss of earnings
5000.00	To Peter Wilcox re. loss of daughter
5000.00	To Irene Wilcox re. loss of daughter

Sarah Harman was convinced that the improved offers we had received from CICA had a lot to do with the publicity that arose around our case, and with the newspapers' campaigning in our support. I knew that the main reason for our good fortune was the skilled and tireless work that she had put in for us over the preceding two and a half years. And still she would not bill us for an adequate amount to cover her unstinting efforts.

With Josie's inheritance from Lin's estate, even after legal fees had been paid, the generous payout allowed us to establish a Trust Fund which Josie will have access to when she comes of age. She will have a comfortable start in her adult life, and I have been relieved of much of the pressure to provide for Josie's future in financial terms. I explained all this to the cross-America runner Nick Baldock when he visited us again with his daughter Lauren at Easter 1999. I suggested that there were many more worthwhile causes for Nick to raise money for. But Nick was adamant that he wanted to contribute further to Josie's Fund. As a businessman he cautioned me that the nest-egg could easily lose value in real terms over the years ahead, and that tax and investment management fees would also eat away at the capital.

Mark Stephens had also been cautioning me about my own financial position, and wanted to see me with a more solid source of income than my part-time lecturing afforded. Josie and I were now comfortable, although we had still had to downshift somewhat as far as standard of living was concerned. However, the fact that we no longer had to run a five-bedroomed house with 15 acres of land was a blessing rather than a burden as far as I was concerned, even though Josie often looked longingly at our big old house next door, and especially the fields that we could no longer use for the ponies.

Mark Stephens (who was also one of Josie's Fund Trustees) was always on the look-out for ways to boost my income. He set up a meeting with one of his old college buddies – Maurice Melzak, an award-winning television programme producer. Maurice specialized in natural history documentaries, and my solicitor was sure that I could extend my career in environmental conservation by appearing on a couple of Maurice's nature programmes. The suggestion was that a first documentary might look at the way in which I had coped with the family tragedy in our lives, by working my way back into environmental conservation work. I met with Maurice, and we soon found that we had a lot in common. Maurice went away to seek a commissioning organization for a possible programme, and his ideas for the project developed gradually through 1999.

In May 1999 Josie and I, and two of Lin's oldest friends, journeyed to Sutton Coldfield for a lunch with Peter and Irene. It was their Golden Wedding Anniversary, and we were keen to make it a happy day for them. The weather was perfect, and after lunch we sat in the garden of the home where Lin had grown up. As usual Josie was bright and breezy and not willing to let us become bogged down in morbid or backwards-looking conversation. We played mini-golf and Josie did handstands on the lawn, and we all partook of celebratory tea and cake. Josie did magic tricks and rough and tumbled with Peter in a way that I had not seen her do with any man, myself included, since before the time of the murders. Irene laughed and joked, and we could not remember her appearing as happy as this for a very long time. I wished that we lived closer and could spend more time like this together. I knew that it would not be long before Josie's teenage interests would begin to pull her away from the older generation, but I wanted her to cherish this time with her grandparents. It had, after all, been the main reason that we had brought the children home to Britain.

Also in May the acclaimed television presenter Esther Rantzen wrote and asked if I would be willing to give a presentation at the 'Hearing Children's Voices' annual conference of the *Childline* organization. 1999 was to be a big year for this highly respected charity which ran telephone helplines for young people in distress across Britain. Cherie Booth QC and Hilary Clinton would both be speaking at the conference, and I was being asked particularly to relate our experiences during the time that Josie had to 'tell her story' for police evidence purposes. At the conference I met up again with Ed and Pauline and Dave Stevens, whom I hadn't seen for months. It was like a family reunion seeing these friendly faces again, and the police officers were eager to hear of Josie's progress. My talk went well, and afterwards I had the chance to speak with Cherie Booth who showed great sympathy and concern for the trials that Josie and I had been through. A week later we met again at the *Daily Mirror*'s first ever Pride of Britain awards ceremony. Josie had been asked if she would be willing to help present awards to the child recipients who were being honoured for acts of selflessness and bravery. The Prime Minister and Queen Noor of Jordan were present, along with a host of other public figures and luminaries.

The balance of power had been slowly shifting in our small family over the previous couple of years. Josie was no longer the biddable little girl that she had been before the murders. She had been hardened by the experience, and she was also old enough (now twelve) and her speech had improved sufficiently that she could argue her case when it came to family decisions. I told her about the invitation that had come from the *Daily Mirror*, and that it would involve having photos taken. I would be happy for her to decline if she so wished. However, I also had to tell Josie that her pop idol Ronan Keating of Boyzone and two of the Spice Girls were lined up to share a table with us at the Pride of Britain dinner if we agreed to go. Of course that did it for Josie. And so we travelled to London for the event, which caught the rest of the media by surprise. It was one of the biggest gatherings of stars and celebrities that had ever collected under one roof in the UK, and they were all enthralled by the tales of courage and devotion among 'ordinary' members of the public that were revealed at the ceremony. There was barely a dry eye in the house, and Josie was fascinated by the galaxy of stars from TV and the movies whom she recognized at the event. Josie only betrayed slight nervousness when she had to go up on stage with Posh and Baby Spice to present the awards. The two Spice Girls had been wonderful to Josie during the dinner and they went off to the toilets together to spruce themselves up and compare fashion tips. They put Josie completely at her ease, although she still betrayed some of her natural reticence in front of the cameras. Josie was no longer meekly willing to put on her flashing smile for the photographers, and instead they were treated to a somewhat cool and aloof look, as befits the self-conscious near-teenager.

I stayed in the background and was somewhat bemused by the recognition given to Josie by such famous figures as Tony Blair, Mo Mowlam, John Hume, Queen Noor, Sir Paul McCartney, Cilla Black, Richard Branson, Lennox Lewis, Chris Evans, David Ginola, Mick Hucknall, Zoë Ball, Sir Bobby Charlton, Clare King, Carol Vorderman – to name but a few! I still had not realized how well known Josie had become, even to these busy people. I could see that Josie was a little bemused, but her favourite moment was when she was photographed with footballer Michael Owen. (That caused a bit of a sensation among her schoolmates!) For me, as for most of the people there, the real stars of the day were the amazing people who were receiving awards, among them teachers, nurses and children who had fought crippling illness or raised money for charity. I was also particularly honoured to meet Doreen and Neville Lawrence, the parents of murdered London teenager Stephen Lawrence. Unlike me, they had responded tirelessly to pleas for their high-profile help with charitable work and crusades against discrimination and injustice. So too had the wonderful Lisa Potts, the George Medal winner who had defended her Wolverhampton schoolchildren during a machete attack, and whom we had also met at the Sunshine Awards. I felt small and inadequate in this awe-inspiring company.

In June 1999 Josie and I drove to South Wales for the weekend. I was helping the son of a friend to look for accommodation before he started as a student at the University in Cardiff. But Josie was going on an adventure. We had been approached by a small charity called Airborne Adventure, run voluntarily by members of the Parachute Regiment. They provided adventure weekends for young people who were suffering life-threatening illness and who came from some of Britain's largest children's hospitals. The director of the project had heard of Josie's difficulty relating to young men, and so he invited Josie to share in one of the adventure weekends. The charity wanted no publicity for its work, as its volunteer helpers were mainly dedicated young paratroopers who assisted the project in their spare time. The director felt sure that if Josie could be exposed to these attentive and caring young men, she might be helped to get over her fear of them. I was sceptical of Josie's interest in taking part in such an escapade, although I thought it would be good for her to learn to socialize and help out with the children with disabilities. Once again I put the offer to her, expecting a negative response. I was quite taken aback by the enthusiasm she showed for the idea. I really thought that the prospect of sharing a dormitory with strangers, getting up very early in the morning, eating army food, and getting cold, tired and muddy on an assault course would be her idea of hell. But it was the rock-climbing and abseiling, the quad-biking and off-road driving, the canoeing and the inshore rescue boat operations, the shooting and orienteering that really appealed to her. And when Airborne Adventure offered to let Josie take a friend along as well, the deal was clinched.

I was quite nervous about leaving Josie at the army camp. But meeting face to face with the people running the project soon put my mind at rest. There were nurses from the hospitals the children had come from, and wives and girlfriends and even pet dogs of the paratroopers themselves. And I realized how out of touch I was when I discovered young women soldiers there too! When I picked up Josie and her friend at the end of the weekend, they looked weather-beaten and flushed with excitement. They had had a marvellous time and been invited back on another project later in the year. Most of all, they crowed to me about being allowed to stay up late and dance the night away in the NAAFI with the handsome young paratroopers! Hello, I thought, what's all this then? Far from being put off by young men any longer, Josie was suddenly talking about what fun they were! Something had happened to change her opinions in this area. It was yet another sign that she was growing up and leaving childhood behind her.

In July I flew to Africa again, for my second two-week trip of the year while Josie stayed with close friends. Charlie, a colleague from Aberystwyth, and I were assisting with the development of a new Masters degree in Conservation Area Management at Moi University, Kenya. After our work in Kenya we travelled across the border to visit our other project partners in Tanzania. On our last day in the country we drove over to the Arusha National Park where I had carried out environmental impact assessment work with the college staff during a previous visit. Little did I know that I was about to experience another kind of 'environmental impact'

Charlie and I drove our hire car as far as we could go along the forested Ngurdoto Volcano Road, which looked hundreds of feet down into the broad depression of the crater. The area of marshland and savannah down below was like an African Eden, cut off from all human influence. The crater floor supported large herds of buffalo and many smaller species of wildlife including antelope, warthogs and baboons. Up above on the crater rim the forest rang with the calls of hornbills and turacos, and the chucking sounds of blue monkeys and black and white colobus. There were signs of elephants along the track, but we didn't see any of these majestic creatures. Sauntering slowly along a narrow forest track, I glanced down and commented to Charlie that there was an intriguingly fresh-looking cowpat on the track. All of a sudden I heard a crash and Charlie shouting a strangled expletive beside me. I glanced round to catch a fleeting glimpse of a large male buffalo, horns down, charging full tilt straight for me. I crashed down through the undergrowth over the edge of a cliff until I was suddenly pulled up short by a strangler vine liana around my ankle. I was left dangling upside down with no possibility of escape. I lay panting furiously with my heart beating nineteen to the dozen as I stared up through the tunnel that my body had smashed through the vegetation. If the animal had decided to follow me down I would have been at its mercy. After a couple of minutes I called tenuously to Charlie, 'Are you all right?' Charlie called back in an equally quavering voice and once we ascertained that we were each in one piece, we decided to work towards each other. I had to rotate myself around completely before my foot would come out of the vine trap, and we both listened intently to the sounds of the forest as we crawled back up the slope and peered over the edge into the clearing. The buffalo was nowhere to be seen. My picnic bag was where I'd dropped it in the middle of the clearing, and I carefully retrieved it before we tiptoed back along the path to the car. Every rustle and crack in the undergrowth made us jump out of our skins, and we were looking to the nearest scaleable tree trunks all the way back along the path in case we were attacked again.

Once back in the car we breathed easily again, and started laughing at our experience. I couldn't believe that after twenty years of working in African wildlife reserves, I could get caught out in this way. I had only ever seen buffalo at lower altitude and in more open habitats before, yet I had been looking straight at the signs of its presence only moments before the beast charged. Buffalos and hippos between them cause the largest number of human fatalities in Africa every year, and when we were back in Nairobi, Richard Leakey, Head of the Kenya Wildlife Service at the time, told us that one of his relatives had been gored and paralyzed by a buffalo that very same year. I shuddered at the thought of what might have happened and the impact on those at home who relied upon me if I had sustained injury or worse. I had been confident in my ability to gauge the risk in the work that I did, but now that confidence was shaken. The narrow escape made me more circumspect about the hazards involved in my job, and minded me to ensure even larger safety margins in my activities in the future.

Back at home Josie was completing her final term at Ysgol Baladeulyn. She competed in the sports day, somewhat unfairly I thought as she was now the oldest in the school. But I was touched to see that she showed some embarrassment at out-running or out-jumping some of the other children, and she broke off from competing on a couple of occasions rather than pressing home her advantage over her classmates.

Shortly before she finished at Ysgol Baladeulyn, Josie surprised everyone by mounting a theatrical presentation all of her own accord. Years before, I had made up a story one night when sending Josie and Megan off to sleep. It was about a lost puppy. Josie had remembered the gist of this story through all these years and she had rewritten it with her own slant on the tale. As she had moved from liking kids' television programmes to a fascination with the soaps and dramas (*Peak Practice* and *Casualty* were two favourites) so she had become more and more interested in acting. It was an extension of the fantasy games and role-plays she used to perform with Megan and other friends in earlier years. But now her dressing-up took on a more professional aspect as she planned miniature theatricals involving props, dialogue and rehearsals with her classmates. Towards the end of the summer term, Josie announced to me that she had written and rehearsed her play *The Lost Dog* with her friends, and that she was now producing it at the school and all the parents of her classmates were invited. Her teachers had colluded in this, although I was told that the costumes had all been made by the children themselves and that there had been absolutely no coaching from the staff at all. The play went ahead, directed by Josie, who was also the narrator and one of the principal actors. We videotaped the show and it is amazing to watch it now and relive the feeling of realization at what astounding progress Josie had made to bring herself to this point. She exudes confidence but without arrogance, and her performance was a testimony to the nurturing environment she had enjoyed at that wonderful little school.

The last week of term was an emotional time for me as Ysgol Baladeulyn had figured so importantly in my efforts to settle Josie and promote her recovery when we returned to Wales. And it had exceeded all my expectations. She had been protected and nourished in the warm and supportive atmosphere of that school, and it was impossible for me to convey the depth of my gratitude to the teachers there for what they had done for Josie. I tried in a faltering speech after the children's leaving ceremony at the end of term, which embarrassed Josie terribly. We gave presents to the teachers, and afterwards I set the ball in motion to secure an honour for the headteacher who was retiring at the end of the year. However, even with the enthusiastic support of my local MP, I soon learned from other quarters that this would only cause embarrassment to the lady concerned, as she did not regard anything that she had done as out of the ordinary or beyond the requirements of her calling. I knew better, of the deep emotional involvement that these outstanding teachers had developed with Josie, and the feelings of responsibility and commitment that they had to Lin's memory. However, I desisted from further attempts to have them recognized officially, out of deference to their reticence and sense of duty. And so, here, I want to place on record my heartfelt thanks and deep gratitude to the ladies of Ysgol Baladeulyn for the wonderful start in life that they have given to my daughter Josie.

During the early part of the summer holidays in 1999, Josie and I travelled to Dorset with my mother and sister and visited popular tourist spots in the Isle of Purbeck and wider region. The very hot weather took its toll on my mother who was now in her mid-seventies, and this was another sign that my wish to spend time with our older family members was starting to diverge from Josie's desire to hurl herself around and have maximum fun when on holiday, whether it was on the beach or in the shopping centre.

In the middle of the summer vacation, I took Josie and her friend Jessie from next door on a transatlantic flight to New York that had been donated to us by a police charity. We had been invited to stay with our American friends in upper New York State, and we spent the time exploring the woods and hills, swimming in the local ponds, going to movies and (inevitably) cruising the shopping malls. At the end of the trip we drove west to meet up with Nick Baldock and his support team. Nick had left San Francisco in May, and had reached the 2500-mile point of his 3000-mile run across the continent. We tracked him down in Ohio. He looked sleek and fit after his arduous journey, and tanned nut-brown by the sun since he had run through the desert states of Nevada and Utah in a heatwave. He had been suffering from the usual ailments of the long-distance runner, blisters and muscle problems, but his main problem was the sheer mental torture of running all day long, every day for months on end. I had been following his progress on his website and by phone and e-mail. It was a truly epic journey, and I feared for his health and safety all the way. Once again I felt humble in the company of this true enthusiast, and more so when I remembered that it was my daughter for whom he was doing all this.

Nick's back-up team on the road comprised volunteers Dave and Simon, who were driving the support truck, doing the cooking and cleaning, helping Nick with his physiotherapy every day and organizing publicity and collections along the way. They told me of the struggle that Nick was having mentally to keep going, but of how his cheerfulness and infectious zeal always shone through. This was in fine evidence when we met up with Nick. We went with them for a slap-up meal at a local restaurant, and our table rocked with merriment all evening as the jokes flew back and forth and Nick and Josie vied with each other, showing off their magic tricks. That night we stayed at a nearby motel and met up with Nick and the guys on the road again the following morning. We shared breakfast with them in their motor home and posed for a few photos before leaving Nick to jog purposefully off again on his heroic journey.

As soon as we arrived back in the UK Josie shot straight off with a friend for another Airborne Adventure weekend courtesy of the paratroopers. She arrived back home just as breathless and excited as before, having progressed further with her rock-climbing skills and stayed up even later in the NAAFI!

The last three days of the summer holiday were spent getting Josie ready for her start at secondary school. I had to make sure she had all the right bits and pieces, bags, stationery, school uniform . . . I was concerned that Josie might react badly to the strange new environment of the larger school, with hundreds of pupils and unfamiliar teachers. She had already been on a couple of familiarization visits the previous term, and had come back saying that she thought it was 'OK'. The best thing about the new school, she said, was the food in the canteen.

Everybody was doing their utmost to ensure that Josie's transition would be as smooth and painless as possible. Josie's reading age was still several years behind her chronological age, and her understanding of complex spoken sentences was still poor. The most important factors were that Josie would be moving up with three friends from her class at Ysgol Baladeulyn, and her best friend would be sitting beside her at the new school. Josie's support assistant Miss Williams was moving up with her too, although Josie resisted this at first, thinking that it would make her look 'odd' to her new circle of friends to have an adult accompanying her into the classroom.

I had met with the new headteacher at Ysgol Dyffryn Nantlle and agreed that the same ground rules be maintained as at the primary school: no journalists or photographers are ever to have access to Josie while at school. And so, with only a couple of days to go until Josie started at her new school, I felt that we had done all that was possible to prepare the ground for Josie's smooth transition to secondary education. I had reckoned without the media of course.

Did all the newspapers have Josie's start date at her new school noted in their diaries? Two days before the start of term I began to get a stream of requests for interviews, photographs, filming . . . At first I tried to fend them off and hide behind my undertaking to the headteacher that there would be no press exposure for Josie during her first day at school. The last thing I wanted to do was get off on the wrong foot with the man who was going to be overseeing my daughter's education for the next seven years. But the more I tried to brush off the pleading journalists, the more I began to detect the change in tone that I had always dreaded if ever I started to baulk at allowing media coverage of Josie. I soon got the message that, unless I cooperated, there would be a no-holds-barred media free-for-all at the school on Josie's first day. My solicitor advised that I take the middle road as I had done before, and so I agreed to provide some photos of Josie in her school uniform to our local paper and to allow interviews with a couple of the nationals, in the hope that this would take some of the sting out of the scrutiny that Josie would be exposed to on her first day.

It seemed to pay off, because there were only a couple of photographers and one film crew waiting on the morning that I took Josie into her new school for the first time. I made a half-hearted attempt to elude them by driving round the back way, but avoidance tactics just seemed to up the ante as far as the journalists were concerned. They responded by breaching the physical and psychological barrier of the school perimeter, and marching in to interview the headteacher himself. I retreated in acute embarrassment, wondering if I would ever be able to look him in the eye again.

When I saw the articles that appeared in the newspapers on and after Josie's first day, I felt conflicting emotions. The pictures were lovely and the stories were uplifting and inspirational. The next day, the *Sun*'s letter page carried eleven out of hundreds of letters that had been received, praising the newspaper for the coverage and congratulating Josie and myself in the most glowing and moving terms. Once again it was brought home to me that Josie had become a symbol of hope and inspiration to so many people. She was a revered public figure and I felt that we owed a duty of gratitude through openness to the wider public for all their support and kindness. And yet exposing Josie to public scrutiny went against all the virtues of reticence and modesty that I admired in others and seemed so incapable of practising myself! I should by now have become used to the fact that it would all be stale news by the next day, and that we would be forgotten about and left to carry on as normal until the next 'milestone' in Josie's career. And so it turned out. Josie's first day at school was a great success for her, as she had taken to the surroundings, the teachers, her new classmates and, of course, the new choice of school dinners! She came smiling home from school just as I remembered her returning from her first day at Ysgol Baladeulyn eight years before. As the days went by and this pattern continued, so my anxieties about Josie's school transition gradually receded. There were no upsets or repercussions, tribulations or traumas, and Josie began to widen her circle of friends to include, horror of horrors . . . boys!

In fact the autumn term seemed to fairly fly by. Nick Baldock arrived back from America having successfully completed his run. He now undertook to write a book about his experiences and donate the proceeds from its sale to Josie's Trust Fund. We attended Josie's last regular hospital appointment for a check-up on her head injury, and she was given the all clear not to have to come back to hospital again. We repeated our visit to the Clothes Show, with Josie even more absorbed and fascinated by the glitz and glamour of modern fashion.

Maurice Melzak the television producer came back to us after developing his ideas for a documentary about our lives. While trying to obtain interest from a broadcaster, he had received the clear message that everybody wanted a programme about Josie and not about me! During the same period I was also approached by other television producers wanting to do documentaries about Josie. My doubts about Josie's exposure surfaced again, especially as she seemed to have settled in so well at school and needed not to be disturbed. Josie herself was ambivalent about it, as she had developed a definite aversion to cameras, yet she had been pleased when the original BBC programme came out and she quite liked doing the home movie filming with our own camera.

Maurice had managed to interest the BBC in taking on this second filming project, and so we finally agreed to cooperate, but with the same contractual provisos that we contribute home movie footage ourselves, so as to minimize film crew intrusion at our home. The plan was also that we might film one of the overseas working trips that I did, and that Josie might join me for a holiday in one of these exotic destinations after I had completed my official work. Josie was always complaining that I left her behind when I went on these trips, and she wanted to know when she was going to get the chance to travel abroad as her parents had done before she was born. She had told me that it was her double ambition to be an RSPCA animal inspector when she grew up and to travel back to South Africa, the land of her birth where Lin and I had such an exciting life. Friends had also been urging me to take Josie back to South Africa for a holiday, when the opportunity arose for me to return to the Cape Province in the summer of 2000. I needed to visit one of my postgraduate research students who was working there, and so I arranged to take Josie with me and to let the BBC film crew accompany us for part of the trip.

1999 ended on a joyous note, as Josie's first end-of-term report from the secondary school reflected the settled and contented time that she had spent there since the summer. She had top grades for effort in all her subjects, and an A in her favourite subject, Art. In fact, she even won her year's Art prize in the school eisteddfod – for a drawing of our now-famous 'Loneliest Phone Box in the Land'!

However, Josie's scores for academic achievement were still well below average, as her speech and language impairments were holding her back in the considerably more demanding work she was experiencing at secondary school. Notwithstanding the extra input she was receiving at school, and the help I gave Josie with her homework, she obviously still had a long way to go to catch up with her peers. But there were years to go yet and the portents were good. Josie's enthusiasm was undimmed and she was trying as hard as she could. She had high self-esteem and she was completely relaxed and happy. What more could you want for your child? By Christmas 1999 we felt that we had made several important steps forwards as we put another year between us and the tragedy of 1996.

The millennium passed quietly for Josie and I as we watched the festivities on TV. The significant aspect of the celebrations for Josie was that the 'millennium colours' were purple and silver, her favourites, and so suddenly everything in the shops from clothes to pencil cases was just right for her. My New Year's Resolutions were to maintain my record of not travelling overseas away from Josie more than twice in the year, and to keep the lid on the demand from the media for access to Josie. She was becoming more self-assured and in charge of her own destiny, and although she enjoyed some of the trappings of celebrity (the presents, the invitations) she disliked the obligations that went with it ('Smile for the camera!'). Josie was a balanced and happy young girl at the moment; but how long would it be before her head was turned if we allowed our lives to carry on in this way?

My solicitor reminded me that there was one way that I could signal my desire for Josie and I to withdraw a little more from the limelight. He had for the last couple of years been trying to influence me to write a book about my life, including the time of the murders and the aftermath. He was convinced (as were several of my friends) that my need to grieve properly and expurgate some of my pent-up emotions, could be well served through the 'therapy and catharsis' of writing about our experiences. As we were collaborating on the television programme which would act as a watershed, then was it not also a good time to relate the whole story from our own perspective in the written word too?

It was coming up for four years since the time of the murders, the same point at which André Hanscombe had written *Last Thursday in July*. My wish to reimmerse myself in environmental conservation work meant that I must disentangle myself from what had gone before and move on. Here was a chance to tell the story in such a way that we might draw a line under our tragic experience, and finally put the past behind us. I agreed to 'write the book to accompany the film'.

Work on the television film progressed, and we were starting to do our own filming and receive occasional visits from a BBC film crew when out and about. We did some filming when Josie went with friends to the Deeside ice rink, and later when Josie was invited by Nick Baldock to share a day at a local zoo with his daughter and some other young children from Hertfordshire. And in April we accepted an invitation for the second time to the Pride of Britain Awards, where Josie met the Prime Minister Tony Blair and shared a dinner table with comedian Lee Evans and Natalie Appleton of the pop group All Saints. Josie helped Natalie present awards to the children recipients, and afterwards she received some stunning clothes and accessories from the All Saints fashion collection. Although Josie had wanted to go to the Pride of Britain awards and had loved the buzz when we got there, she had been less than happy about the posing for photos that was part and parcel of the day's activities; this helped to reassure me that I was right to keep planning our gradual withdrawal from high public profile.

In May 2000 an invitation came for us to attend a small ceremony at the local RSPCA animal hospital. Some months previously, Josie and a friend had spotted three sheep that seemed to be trapped on the cliffs where they had been grazing near the bottom of a disused slate quarry behind our house in North Wales. I had been to check on them with her but decided that when the sheep became hungry enough they would haul themselves out of the quarry somehow. Five days later, however, the sheep had not moved. They had eaten every blade of grass on their ledges, and one of them did not even seem to have enough space to lie down to sleep. Josie was becoming distraught with worry, just as her mother Lin would have done, and I eventually responded to her concerns by calling the RSPCA. When the inspectors arrived they realized that the animals were in danger and decided to trap them and hoist them out of the quarry. This required a specialist unit of five inspectors who were all trained in advanced rock-climbing techniques, and it took the team the best part of a day to perform the rescue in arduous and dangerous circumstances. Josie and her friend witnessed the latter part of the rescue when they returned home from school, and I videoed the events with my little home movie camera.

At the ceremony the rescue team were to receive medals for saving the animals' lives. Josie and her friend were also to receive certificates of merit for the part they had played in alerting the authorities to the plight of the sheep. Josie's reticence in front of the cameras at the Pride of Britain awards in the previous month prompted me to request that the RSPCA ceremony be publicised as little as possible, and the staff at the animal hospital did their best to keep the event quiet. However, the word leaked out somehow, and as we drove into the centre at Colwyn Bay, we were astonished to find banks of photographers lined up to greet us, with film camera teams and satellite outside broadcast units. The RSPCA press officer was apologetic, and he rushed us into the building to avoid the throng. During the award ceremony itself, Josie did her best to avoid the cameras and wore dark glasses to hide her face. The journalists pleaded with me to wheel Josie on for them, but I explained that she was now a teenager (she had turned thirteen only a few weeks before) and that she was not going to to be 'wheeled on' by or for anybody! It seemed that we had reached a bit of a turning point. Josie was now deciding for herself what she would and would not do in relation to the media, and I was no longer in a position to influence her, even if I had wanted to.

At the beginning of June I attended the annual review meeting for Josie's special-needs provision at her secondary school. It was a sombre meeting, as we had received the results of tests of Josie's language functioning, expressive language skills and reception of grammar. The good news was that Josie had caught up by the equivalent of two years in language skills over the last year. This showed that she was making some progress. The bad news was that she was still seven years behind her chronological age in reading, writing, comprehension and expressive capability. Josie's capacity to mask her difficulties was commented on again, and the importance of maintaining the presence of her classroom support assistant was emphasized. As had happened previously when I had seen Josie's 'severe impairment' baldly stated in test results, I broke down in tears. I had to remind myself again that her physical and mental well-being were more important issues that were being admirably catered for at the school, and that there were still years to go for Josie to catch up with her speech and language skills.

By now, however, Josie was starting to get excited about our rapidly approaching summer holiday trip to South Africa. She had always dreamed of going back to see the place where she was born, and discovering the fascinating and varied animal life of Africa. She had heard me talk about it all but had never seen it for herself. I could tell that she was also curious to explore the places that she knew her mother had loved so much, and intrigued to meet again the woman who had acted as her nanny for the first few months of her life. For me the journey would be bittersweet in the extreme. I too was eager to share with Josie the fascination and excitement of the beautiful places where Lin and I had shared so many happy years. But I was also anxious as to how the return to these places might affect me, and how I might cope with the disinterment of so many poignant memories. However, I wanted it to be a happy and a memorable time for Josie, and so I told myself that I would try for Josie's sake not to let the sad aspects of the journey impinge on the enjoyment of our pilgrimage 'back to Africa'.

Healing: Africa Pilgrimage

On Tuesday 25 July 2000, Josie and I left home in Wales to drive to London Heathrow airport for the Virgin Atlantic overnight flight to Johannesburg, South Africa. At the airport we met up with the four-person BBC TV film crew who were accompanying us for part of our South African holiday. After years' experience of uncomfortable long-haul flights, I was not looking forward to the journey, but Josie was as keen as mustard to get aboard the big A-340 Airbus and explore the facilities. Although we were quite happy to travel in economy class, we had a great surprise in store. Josie and I had been upgraded to first class, which neither of us had ever experienced before.

The flight was superb. We were treated like royalty and I was able to sleep soundly in my fully reclining seat for much of the night. Josie wasted little of this precious time sleeping and instead ordered meals whenever she felt like eating, played games and watched movies, and then had a professional hand massage and manicure in the middle of the night! Josie commented to me that this was her idea of heaven and that she would like to live full-time in Virgin Atlantic's Upper Class cabin!

Next day we arrived in Johannesburg and caught a domestic flight to Port Elizabeth in the Eastern Cape, before transferring to our hotel on the beachfront there. I had planned the holiday so that I would be able to indulge my nostalgic yearnings to explore my and Lin's old haunts, and for Josie to get close to African wildlife, as she had always wanted to. However, I was not so naïve as to forget Josie's teenage interests, and so to 'soften' the sudden change to a new environment and culture, I took her shopping in the town centre of Port Elizabeth during our first afternoon there. The central part of town had become run-down compared to how I remembered it and we were frequently accosted by beggars. Josie became frightened. This was Josie's first experience of truly poor people and she was torn between wanting to give all her money to them and running in fear from their aggressive attentions. I was painfully reminded of the panic attacks that Josie suffered in busy urban situations a couple of years earlier. And so we cut short our shopping expedition and headed back to the hotel.

The following day we were up bright and early for a trip to the Oceanarium at Port Elizabeth's famous 'Bay World' complex. Josie was fascinated by the antics of the dolphins and seals there, and we went behind the scenes to see how the staff were coping with the rehabilitation of many penguins that had been caught in a recent oil spill off the Cape coast. We also enjoyed visiting the reptile section of the complex, where we were allowed into an enclosure with giant African pythons, and held a beautiful and very friendly constrictor from Madagascar.

A day later we drove out of town and headed 100 miles inland, to the Mountain Zebra National Park near the town of Cradock on the fringe of the Karoo semi-desert. I was filled with nostalgia as endless vistas opened up before us of the pastel mountains and scrub-covered plains of the interior, and by evening we were ensconced in comfortable chalets with roaring log fires against the chill of the mid-winter mountain air. The National Park was established to conserve the last few remaining Cape Mountain zebras, a species distinct from the common plains zebra which occurs further north in Africa. Owing to lack of staff, the Park has not been able to accommodate pony trekking in recent years. However, when the park manager, Paddy Gordon, discovered Josie's love of riding, he offered two of the working horses used by his rangers for us to ride. The following day, therefore, Josie and I were able to combine our interests of horse-riding and wildlife-viewing in the unique experience of pony trekking through this wild and beautiful national park. The horses allowed us to get close not only to the zebra for which the park is famous, but also to view at close quarters many of the other striking species in the park, such as black wildebeest, hartebeest, blesbok and springbok.

That evening Josie danced to Shania Twain songs on her portable CD player as I gazed up at the immensity of the crystal-clear desert sky, filled with a billion stars. Eventually my cries at the spectacle of meteors slicing across the night sky enticed Josie to sit by my side, and she too gasped, 'Oh wow!', as she saw her first ever shooting star. I spent the remainder of the evening trying to field the same questions on the nature of the universe that must be asked of a thousand parents: where does it begin and where does it end? How did it start and is there life among the stars? My concerns about Josie being bored and disinterested by spending time with me alone and away from home were dissipating. I felt already that the trip was helping us to reaffirm the bond between us that was all too easily neglected in the hurly-burly of daily life back home in Wales.

Next day we headed eastwards along the foot of the escarpment that forms the southern outlier of the Drakensberg Mountains, towards our old home of Alice. Josie knew that her middle name commemorated this little Eastern Cape town, and I showed her where Lin and I had first arrived at the railway station 25 years before as naïve and excited young students. The buildings were all boarded up and dilapidated as the train no longer stops there, and so we moved on to the first house that Lin and I ever owned. We bought the house in Stocks Street in 1976, and so began our career of buying and 'fixing up' old houses. Josie was keen to look around and so we asked the present owners if we could wander about the garden and compare the house now with old pictures that I had brought along specially. The lady of the house and her young sons clustered around us as I pointed out parts of the house that Lin and I had built and renovated. Josie was as interested to hear the fascinating language of the house-owner and her family, as she was in the house itself. The local people in the Eastern Cape area speak in the Xhosa tongue, which includes many different 'click' sounds that are perplexing to the foreigner's ear.

I next drove Josie to the site of the old municipal stock pens where Lin and I trained and stabled our first horse – Trixie. The stables had since burnt down and there was only wasteground where we had had so much fun with the horses in the mid-1970s. However, as we drove past I recognized an old man walking his dog along the road and he recognized me too. He had been the municipal engineer's assistant in the days when Lin and I lived in Alice, and we briefly reminisced about the old times. 'I remember your wife', he said. 'You had those big yellow dogs' (golden retrievers). In fact this venerable gentleman had buried our first dog, Jackie, after she had been tragically run over on the main road near to our Stocks Street house in the mid-1980s.

We pressed on to drive around the campus of Fort Hare University where Lin and I had our first lecturing jobs. As it was a Saturday there were few people about, but I was able to show Josie the central quadrangle of the College – 'Freedom Square' – which had witnessed such momentous gatherings through the years of 'the Struggle' in South Africa. Josie and I then drove north through the densely populated Tyumie Valley, once part of the impoverished 'Ciskei' homeland area of South Africa, but which was now showing the results of government initiatives to provide the region with better water supplies, electricity and schools. As dusk fell, we followed the tortuous mountain pass that climbs through dense afromontane forest to the village of Hogsback at 4000 feet above sea level. Here we checked into the comfy Kings Lodge Hotel, where I was welcomed by the owners Clive and Vivienne Lodge, who remembered me from when Lin and I used to meet with friends in the bar there.

The weather had been perfect for the whole of our trip so far, and it dawned bright and sunny again in the crisp, cool mountain air the following day. Josie and I drove up the hill from the centre of the Hogsback village, and pulled into the drive of our old house at Innisfree. This was where Lin and I had moved to in 1982, and where we had spent seven happy years renovating the house and developing the garden. This was the home to which we had brought Josie on the day that she was born, and the place we had found so hard to leave when we moved to Namibia in 1989. The present owner was kindly allowing Josie and I to look around the house and garden during our fleeting visit, and my heart was in my mouth as I approached the front door. I had to suppress my emotion as I entered and moved around the house with Josie exploring before me. Josie's interest was heightened by the knowledge that she had spent the first two years of her life here, and I could sense that she was mildly engaged by my ramblings about the building work and fittings that had absorbed so much of my and Lin's energies in years gone by. But we had moved away from Hogsback when Josie was only two, and so she only knew of this place through photos and the stories of her parents.

For me, however, I had continually to suppress the flood of emotions that threatened to engulf me. The person who had bought the house from Lin and me had retained almost identical furniture in exactly the same arrangement as when we had lived here. There was therefore an intense feeling of *déjà vu* for me; a mixture of fascination at the familiar detail and the 'frozen in time' aspect of the house, and a sense that Lin was still there, even walking beside me as we moved through the rooms. Josie was taking everything in, but showing little emotion. I did not want to embarrass her by letting my feelings show. Instead I consoled myself with the thought that Josie might look back on this visit with greater appreciation when she was older, and that it was at least helping me to satisfy my need for community with Lin's spirit, and so hopefully moving my grieving on a step further.

The fact that the house was now only used occasionally as a holiday home was saddening, and the sombre, unlived-in feeling began to become oppressive – after a while I was pleased to emerge into the sunlight outside, where Josie awaited me. She was impatient to explore the garden and so we rambled off along the overgrown paths that led steeply down into the dense indigenous forest below the house. Almost immediately we spotted the exotic, dark-green crested Loeries, with their bright scarlet wings, that were denizens of this endangered 'jungle' vegetation. I told Josie of the monkeys and parrots that also made 'our garden' their home, and I showed her the spot by a lovely waterfall deep in the forest where Lin and I used to sit with Josie when she was a toddler, to watch and listen to the sights and sounds of the ancient forest. Josie collected some enormous pine cones from the forest floor, and crept up on a couple of shy African cattle that had found their way into our old orchard, now densely overgrown with weeds and brambles.

After a while we returned to the house and wandered across to the little, round, stone-and-thatch chapel of St Patrick's at the end of the garden, where the Sunday service had just been held. As we stood in the cool, dark and peaceful interior of this unique place of worship, I explained to Josie that it was here that our friends from all over South Africa had gathered, to remember Lin and Megan in a special memorial service at around the same time as our own funeral for our lost loved ones. For a fleeting moment I saw the same quizzical look on Josie's face as she had shown when we stood over the open grave at St Mary's Church, Garndolbenmaen, almost four years previously. But then Josie moved on to question me about this large group of our South African friends, most of whom she had never met. I promised to introduce her to a few of them that very evening.

During the afternoon, however, I had determined to show Josie a little of the beautiful natural environment in the Hogsback Mountain area. And so we took a picnic lunch up to the 'Kettlespout' waterfall, which plunges 400 feet over a cliff to water the forested slopes above the Hogsback village itself. The breeze was blowing the falls back over the crest in a fine spray and we gazed out on the enormous vista of the Eastern Cape below us through a glistening rainbow as we ate our picnic lunch. Water voles rustled in the bushes and a swarm of bees drank from the stream, as birds of prey including a large black eagle circled overhead. Josie chose this idyllic moment to use some of the time that I had promised her on our mobile phone, to call her friend Hazel in the UK. I sat slightly bemused as Josie, the modern teenager clad in her street-fashion gear and with mobile clamped to her ear, chatted happily from a remote corner of the wilds of South Africa to a friend in a remote corner of the wilds of North Wales!

That evening Josie and I excused ourselves from the company of the BBC film crew who had been our ever-present but tactfully distant shadows during the trip so far, and spent a pleasant time relaxing with old friends over dinner late into the evening. Several friends who lived locally came over to join us that evening, and after the initial bittersweet reunions, we whiled away the evening with a mixture of personal nostalgia and exciting talk of 'the new South Africa'. Josie chatted with the teenage kids of some of our friends, helped with the preparation of the evening meal, and spent time playing with the dogs of the house. And then it was her turn to look on in slightly bemused fashion, as I slipped back into local dialect and began to display the uninhibited 'touchy-feely' traits of physical closeness that are so typical of our South African friends, but so rarely demonstrated by the reserved British race!

On the morning of the following day I was interviewed by the TV crew about the journey so far, and then Josie and I went for tea with a couple – Hillary and Diana Graham – who were very close to us during the time that we lived at Hogsback. They were both well-known artists and Diana had won several awards for her pioneering environmental art in South Africa. She showed us around her uplifting 'Eco-Shrine', perched on the edge of the Hogsback escarpment, with its wonderful views of the plains and mountains beyond. Diana explained how some of her inspiration had come from Lin's friendship and shared love of the environment, including her geological explanations of the make-up of the Earth and the origins of life. As usual Josie was most interested in the animate objects, and I could see that she coveted the dozens of goldfish and two enormous Koi carp that swam in the pool at the Eco-Shrine!

Back at the hotel, Josie watched in rapt fascination the antics on the front lawn of a flock of guinea fowl, and high up in the trees a troupe of Samango monkeys, while I prepared for our last important task before we left Hogsback the next day. I had been asking around locally and putting the word out on the 'Bush Telegraph' for news of Josie's old nanny, Victoria Magadla, who had worked for Lin and me during our last couple of years in South Africa. But I had been receiving conflicting messages about Victoria's current whereabouts, and as time was running out, I decided that we should spend the rest of our last day at Hogsback in the car, carrying some old photos of Victoria around the local neighbourhood, to see if we could find her.

When Lin and I had last returned to Hogsback for a short visit from Namibia in 1991, we had been worried about Victoria's situation. When we originally left South Africa we had found her a job with a neighbour. But this person had moved away and Victoria had been forced to move back with her three children to live with her parents in a very remote and poor rural area. This had, in turn, put stress on her marriage and she had separated from her husband Lennox. We had given her some money and bid her well, but her welfare had continued to concern us. Now that we found ourselves back at Hogsback again after nine years, there was an even stronger reason to track down Victoria. Josie had always hinted that part of the reason she wanted to return to her first home in South Africa was to see this legendary lady who had shared with Lin the task of caring for her during the first two years of her life. And now that we were here, Josie seemed to be unusually excited and impatient to meet her.

The search proved to be more difficult than I had imagined, and we travelled many miles in a wide circle through the hinterland of the Hogsback region that day, calling at remote farmsteads and scattered rural settlements before we heard that Victoria's husband Lennox was working on the new water supply pipeline scheme back where we had started in the Hogsback village. So much for the much-vaunted 'Bush Telegraph', I thought! Back at Hogsback we asked at the Forestry Station for news of the progress of the water pipeline and the whereabouts of the construction team, and we found an old lady employee there who was sure she knew where Lennox and Victoria were living. They were apparently back together again and living nearby in the village. She agreed to take us there and we drove back out onto the main village street to begin the search again. And who should we see walking towards us down the road, but Victoria and her two sons, Two-boy and Tembela!

We screeched to a halt and clambered out of the car as a beam of recognition spread across Victoria's face. She shook hands shyly with me and moved to embrace Josie without hesitation. The woman and the girl could hardly take their eyes off each other, and for a moment I thought that I could understand Josie's fascination to meet this figure from the furthest recesses of her childhood memory. Could it be that sustained and loving physical contact between a woman and baby builds up a subliminal bond between them, even when they are not mother and child? From the looks on their faces I could believe it at that moment.

The BBC TV crew had been with us up to this moment, but they then graciously retired to allow us some time alone together. We took Victoria and her two sons back to where they lived, a couple of miles from the centre of the village, and we pored over our old photos together. We showed the family where we were living in Wales, including the site of Lin and Megan's grave, and Victoria's face went ashen grey when she heard of what had happened to them. But news of Victoria's family was a happier affair. She and Lennox were both working, and their daughter Bulelwa, who as a toddler used to play with Josie, was living with her grandparents and attending a good school in King William's Town 40 miles away. The family looked well dressed and the boys spoke good English. The old lady who had helped me find Victoria had said to me that they were a 'good family', respected in the local community for their honesty and kindness.

As darkness fell we excused ourselves and Victoria's youngest son, twelve-year-old Tembela, shook Josie's hand politely. We left a couple of our photos and a gift of some money with Victoria, and we noted her address so that we could begin sending out some presents to help Bulelwa and the boys through school. Josie was strangely animated in the car on the way back to the hotel. She told me that she thought Tembela was really nice and she would like to begin corresponding with him as her African pen-friend!

I felt sad the next morning as we drove down the steep pass away from Hogsback. There had been so little time to see friends and explore old haunts on the mountain. The feeling stayed with me as we dashed through the town of Alice again, calling in briefly on our old friends the Tremeers who had run the butchery there for generations. We also stopped 50 miles further south at Grahamstown, to lunch with friends and colleagues at Rhodes University where I had worked for a couple of years in the 1980s and obtained my PhD.

By the end of the day we were 100 miles south of Hogsback, ensconced in luxury accommodation at the Shamwari Game Reserve. We had booked in for three nights at this exciting conservation area, which had not existed when Lin and I left South Africa 11 years earlier. Over three days we were treated to the nature experience of a lifetime, as our personal ranger Kevin drove us around this award-winning wildlife preserve in an open-topped Land Rover. At Shamwari one is able to approach 'the big five' wildlife species (elephant, rhino, buffalo, lion and leopard) at close quarters and the rangers pulled out all the stops to give us some extra special treats. Josie was able to stroke the nose of a semi-tame young rhino named Aussie, who was being readied for release into a more natural lifestyle within the reserve, and we got very close to a giraffe named Dizzy who tried to take a kick at our Land Rover just to show us who was boss!

We also came rather too close for comfort to a bull elephant who crept up behind us as we were concentrating on the majestic spectacle of the rest of his 40-strong herd in front of us. And Josie was able finally to meet 'in person' the leopard named Rikki whom she had 'adopted' through the Born Free Foundation. Born Free maintains a sanctuary at Shamwari for rescued big cats, and, in addition to Rikki, Josie was able to make the acquaintance of lions Aslan, Gilda, Raffi and Anthea, who had been translocated to comfortable retirement in South Africa from unsuitable conditions in captivity elsewhere in the world.

It was inevitable that the press caught up with us in South Africa, as the story of our tragedy had hit the headlines in this country too. A representative of the local newspaper in the Eastern Cape tracked us down at Shamwari Game Reserve and we (and the BBC team) had to pose for some photos on our penultimate day there. The story appeared on the front page of the *Eastern Province Herald* the next day, and when we travelled on, we experienced the peculiar sensation of being recognized in a foreign country as well.

At the end of our all-too-short stay at Shamwari, however, the BBC team left us and returned to the UK, and Josie and I were able to spend a few more days travelling on together along the 'Garden Route' of the southern Cape. We visited several resorts along this beautiful coast where indigenous forest sweeps down from tall mountains to the rocky shore-line. Our last two nights in South Africa were spent in a Swiss Family Robinson-style log cabin perched among the trees of the forest at Knysna, halfway between Port Elizabeth and Cape Town. We were guests of the family of one of my current postgraduate students, who is researching elephant conservation in South Africa, and after-dinner conversation turned again to the plight of wildlife species around the world whose futures are uncertain and insecure.

I was impressed by the way that Josie joined in the conversation on these occasions, and proud that she was already expressing firm opinions on the often complex and difficult questions of environmental conservation in the modern world. During our South African pilgrimage, Josie had also been exposed to a whole new variety of people and lifestyles, even diets (on our last evening in South Africa we ate Nepali food!) and she had taken it all in her stride like a seasoned traveller.

As Josie and I boarded the plane back to the UK for our second helping of luxury in Upper Class, I reflected on the significance of our journey together. I felt that we had achieved most of what I had hoped for during the trip. I had indulged my own nostalgia by revisiting the homes that Lin and I had shared during our 15 happy years in South Africa, and put 'flesh on the bones' of the picture that Josie had in her mind of where she was born and first lived. I had all too briefly made contact with many of the friends that Lin and I had in South Africa, and shown Josie what great people they were. I need not have worried about Josie's indifference to the country itself, as the physical beauty of the landscape and the fascination of the wildlife captured Josie's imagination with little need for prompting from me. When she asked me how long it would be before we could come back, and that she could happily come and live in South Africa, I could tell that Josie had been smitten by the same allure that had kept Lin and I in this vibrant and beautiful land for the major part of our working lives.

I felt that I had been able to pass on to Josie something of the principles and concerns that underpinned Lin's work, and mine, and I had exposed her to some of the realities of life beyond the familiar surroundings of our home in North Wales. Just being together on holiday for a couple of weeks had also given Josie and me the chance to forget about the petty issues that often bring parent and child into conflict at home, and to find a welcome closeness in the shared experience of mind-expanding travel. For me the best times of this whole holiday had been simply sitting alone together with Josie in a car or on an aeroplane, on a verandah or on the beach, just chatting about the experiences of the day, or with me trying to answer Josie's stream of progressively more coherent and mature questions. Josie was growing up and developing the skills that would enable her ultimately to move away from home, but our South African pilgrimage had reassured me that, notwithstanding her outward nonchalance, Josie and I were now developing a more adult rapport founded on mutual love and understanding. If I needed evidence that Josie had largely healed the scars of the tragedy and trauma through which she had lived, then the pilgrimage back to Africa had provided such evidence in good measure.

Postscript

At the time of writing this postscript in August of the year 2000, Josie is carrying on her normal summer holiday routine of spending time with her friends Fiona and Hazel, riding her ponies Tegid and Rosie, swimming at the local leisure centre, picnicking at the beach, and visiting our caravan in mid-Wales. She looks forward with pleasure to the start of the new term in her second year at high school, where she is happy and settled and progressing well with her studies.

Shadows still hang over us, of course. The bald statistic of Josie's six-year lag in language comprehension is a chilling reminder of the damage done to her brain that still hampers her development. We still cannot be sure that she will ever be totally free of the speech and language impairments that frustrate her efforts, particularly in reading and writing. And then there is the legal appeal of the man convicted of attacking Josie and killing Lin and Megan. Once again we face the uncertainty of the outcome, and have no doubt that the media spotlight will focus on us again at the time of the hearing. We will accept the results of the legal process and can only hope that it will clarify the questions that arose following the original trial, for the sake of the convicted man and for our peace of mind as well.

A clear outcome at the time of the legal appeal will go some way towards helping Josie and me to draw a line under the whole tragic episode of the last four years. I am hoping by telling the story of Josie's Journey through this book and the BBC film, that this will also satisfy the public's desire for news of Josie's progress and recovery, and allow us to move ahead with our lives in a quieter and perhaps less public manner in future. Josie is now aware of the power that she has to do good through her notoriety, and she has voiced an interest in helping with charitable causes where her profile can be of benefit. She has already put this to good use in respect of appearances for NCH Action for Children and the Parachute Regiment's Airborne Adventure projects. She has also raised money for the RSPCA and the Born Free Foundation. However, a delicate balance has to be maintained in respect of the conflicting pressures on Josie's development. We feel undeniably a sense of duty to those who have shown concern and supported us in the past (not least, newspapers such as the *Mail* and the *Sun* who have helped us financially and have always printed sympathetic and uplifting stories about us). But Josie also needs the normalizing experience of relative anonymity as she passes through her impressionable teenage years. And so I hope that we can strike the right balance in future, between the public's 'need to know' about Josie's recovery and well-being, and the quiet home life that will provide the best background for her continuing physical and mental development and her positive academic progress at school.

People do hold Josie up as a shining example of courage and hope, although she herself has asked me to state here that she does not regard herself as the 'bravest girl in Britain', and that there are many other people who are far more courageous and worthy of acclaim. However, I am often asked to try and explain from whence comes Josie's strength. I am not normally given to placing much credence on such things as astrology, but I recently read a fascinating description of the characteristics of those born, as Josie and her mother Lin were, under the star sign of Aries. Arians are said to be rebellious and self-assertive, enthusiastic and rash, with boundless physical energy and a need to overcome all obstacles. They have a desire to conquer in sports and romance and they are full of ideas for projects with themselves at the helm. They get bored quickly and are easily enraged over minor issues, emotional sensitivity is difficult for them, and they are argumentative and not accommodating to other people. [Paraphrased from Rhoda Urman (1982), *The Astrological Birthday Book*, with permission of the publishers, Harry N. Abrams Inc, New York.]

Much of this could be the perfect description of just about any modern teenager of course! However, in many respects Josie fits the Arian picture very closely, and if the headstrong qualities of 'the Ram' have helped her to survive the worst of her traumas and come through her ordeal relatively unscathed, then I could just start to believe in astrology after all!

These same characteristics might make life with Josie difficult for me as her father on a day-to-day basis, but I have no complaints. In Josie's strength and beauty I am constantly reminded of why I loved and admired her mother so, and why I need not worry unduly about Josie's future. She is a survivor and will make the best of any situation that may befall her in her life to come, and through *her* strength, I know that I too will survive and be always proud and happy of her every achievement, no matter how large or small.

Josie has shown not only me, but thousands of others, that a child's purity of vision and innocent vitality can prevail in incredible adversity, and that the flame of the human spirit can light a path safely through the darkest and most desperate events in our lives. Wherever her journey may take her in future Josie's light will always sustain her, but I pray that she will never be tested so again.